TH_ DESPERATE MAN

MW00654055

LÉON BLOY (1846-1917) was a French writer and journalist who was the author of essays, novels, short stories, as well as a diary in eight volumes. In 1867 he made the acquaintance of Jules-Amadée Barbey d'Aurevilly, who not only stoked up his literary ambitions but was also responsible for his conversion to ardent Catholicism. Although primarily remembered today for his journals and essays, his volume of short stories *Histoires désobligeantes* is a work of great importance, as is his novel *Le Désespéré*.

RICHARD ROBINSON has done numerous translations over the years, both to and from English, including Georges Bataille's *The Trial of Gilles de Rais* (Amok Books, 1990), and Théodore Hannon's *Drinkers of Phosphorous and other Songs of Joy* (Snuggly Books, 2020). He holds a bachelor's degree from the California State University.

DANIEL CORRICK is an editor, philosopher and writer. From 2010 to 2014 he ran Hieroglyphic Press and edited the journal *Sacrum Regnum*. He has published essays on various nineteenth-century figures including Hugo von Hofmannsthal, Gabriele d'Annunzio and Arthur Machen, as well as contributing articles on philosophy of religion topics to the Ontological Investigations blog. He co-edited *Drowning in Beauty: The Neo-Decadent Anthology* (Snuggly Books, 2018).

SNUGGLY BOOKS

LÉON BLOY

THE DESPERATE MAN

TRANSLATED BY
RICHARD ROBINSON

AND WITH AN INTRODUCTION BY
DANIEL CORRICK

THIS IS A SNUGGLY BOOK

ISBN: 978-1-64525-031-9

CONTENTS

INTRODUCTION

One would struggle to find another Catholic in late nineteenth-century French literature who so excelled in infamy as Léon Bloy. Throughout his life Bloy tried his hand at the novel, the short story, the biography and mystical tract, yet it was clear his natural form of expression was the polemic. From his conversion to Catholicism in the late 1860s, Bloy produced a fiery torrent of articles attacking Naturalist writers, Prussians, the *nouveau riche*, critics of the Church, Catholics whom he believed hypocritical in their bourgeois comfort, not to mention sometimes anyone who offended him or transgressed his complicated ethics. Bloy's prose consistently maintains a level of apoplectic fury that most writers reach only at their highest pitch. The intensity of expression, from beginning to end, in *The Desperate Man* is seldom encountered in modern literature. "Notes From the Underground," by Russian novelist Fyodor Dostoevsky, is the closest work that comes to mind in comparative intensity, rage, suffering and pathos. Not until Céline would the French language again know such obscene violence. From all reports Bloy was as fiery and disagreeable in his personal life as he was with his pen: after spending years in great poverty he came to depend upon monetary donations from friends, admirers and other literary celebrities, often sending financial demands to people he'd never met with the implicit threat of literary scarification were they not to display the requisite minimum of charity. This bullying method of supporting himself earned him the title "the Ungrateful Beggar," along with other less tender epithets.

Bloy was born in 1846, the son of a civil servant and a devoutly Catholic mother of Spanish decent. His father was a Voltarian who upheld a rigid disciplinary regime throughout the household, conditions which inspired the distrust of father figures apparent in Bloy's fiction. After a sullen and lonely childhood, paternal auspices steered the adolescent Bloy into various administrative jobs, none of which lasted very long. It was whilst working in Paris that he first tried his hand at journalism and began to frequent literary circles. One evening, late in 1868, as a matter of curiosity, he visited the house of the aging Catholic writer Jules-Amédée Barbey d'Aurevilly. Barbey d'Aurevilly, a great novelist, literary critic, and dandy, whose fiction combined ultramontane sensibilities with a Sadean focus on perversity and sins of the heart, was to be the formative literary and intellectual influence on the young Bloy. Up until this point the latter had nursed violent revolutionary and anti-clerical sentiments; however, after a little time in the older writer's company, he re-embraced the teachings of the Catholic Church with a voracious lust. His spiritual formation was further shaped by the lay theologian Ernest Hello whose "mysticism of tears" was to inform his own theories on the universal redemptive value of suffering.

The circumstances that gave rise to this novel began in 1877 when Bloy met Anne-Marie Roulé, a prostitute who worked in the Latin Quarter not far from the indigent writer's lodgings. It's uncertain whether his initial contact with her was as a client, but, regardless, Anne-Marie soon became his mistress and moved in with him. She had been devout before family circumstances forced her into prostitution, having once even applied to enter a convent and now Bloy, seeing her as a new Magdalen, wasted no time encouraging his lover with great zeal to return to the Church. From that point on their relationship oscillated between passionate carnal love and periods of intense guilt over their inability to cohabit chastely.

In the course of her religious devotions, Anne-Marie began to experience ecstatic states and visions that both her and Bloy took to be indicative of prophecy. Soon Bloy and Hello treated her as a private oracle, subjecting her utterances to every form of symbolic and numerological interpretation. Over the years the tone of these prophecies grew more violent: echoing the prophecy of La Salette, an alleged Marian apparition from 1846, she announced that the corruption of the clergy and the materialism of French society had grown so great that an avenging Christ would soon return to purge the world and usher in the age of the Holy Spirit.

The two lovers planned fantastic pilgrimages and eagerly awaited the destruction of the society which had wronged them. But the promised apocalypse failed to arrive and Anne-Marie's behaviour began to grow increasingly erratic. Finally, in the summer of 1882, Bloy was forced to seek aid from doctors, who wasted no time in diagnosing a "progressive neurosis" and committing her to the asylum of Sainte-Anne. She died there twenty-five years later, never having recovered from the ordeal.

In the months that followed Anne-Marie's departure, the heartbroken writer began laying the groundwork for what would become *The Desperate Man*. The dead woman would appear therein as Veronique, their shared views on suffering and mystical symbolism informing it and the rest of Bloy's works. It was not Love, however, but Hatred, which provided the final motivation necessary to birth this novel—hatred for the Parisian literary establishment.

Success, at least in the commonly perceived sense of the word, was always illusory for Bloy. His violent, invective-filled style alienated most pious readers of the time and his vituperative manner won him few friends amongst editors and critics. At the start of his literary career in the 1870s, he had been exiled from *Le Universe*, the major Catholic newspaper, and no less a venue than *Le Figaro* had closed its doors to him. Even those who admired his combination of Catholic theosophy and obscenity thought him doomed to obscurity. Nor was he alone in his literary vagabondage. At this time he numbered amongst his friends two other greats of anti-modern decadence: Auguste Villiers de l'Isle-Adam, the quixotic author of *Contes Cruels*, and J. K. Huysmans, himself enjoying the frosty glare of establishment skepticism in the wake of his masterpiece *À rebours*. The three, collectively styling themselves the "Council of Paupers," would meet at Huysmans' rooms to dine and bemoan the state of French letters.

It was Huysmans who was to prove instrumental in *The Desperate Man*'s publication. Over the course of their meetings, the novelist had provided Bloy with a thousand scathing descriptions of fashionable salons and famous writers which were to form the basis of the banquet scene. In 1884, when Bloy announced that he was writing *The Desperate Man*, it was Huysmans' own publisher, Stock, who offered him a contract. The novel was handed to the printer in 1885, but Stock stalled the publication after threats of literary excommunication and the two were forced to make desperate efforts to find a replacement publisher. In the end, the book was published by A. Soirat, in 1886, to little fanfare, Stock strangely printing a second edition in 1887.

Notwithstanding some passages of fairly extreme anti-Semitism, *The Desperate Man* is no mere literary curiosity but a novel of great power. Part roman-à-clef, part satire and part mystical tract, it displays Bloy at the peak of his abilities. His "abominable scatological expressions" capture a dark x-ray of nineteenth-century Parisian culture, in which all the corruption, venality and degradation of the human spirit is laid bare. In the salon scene there is scarcely a writer of the 1880s who escapes having his infamies preserved in vitriol. Overlooked, partly because of its author's fanaticism, it is perhaps the pinnacle of a certain literary trend, "splenetic writing," inaugurated by Baudelaire. It is a masterpiece of inflammatory writing and as representative of the principles of Decadence as *À rebours* is, or any other piece of writing of that same movement and period.

Like Huysmans' autobiographical hero Durtal, Caïn Marchenoir, the novel's protagonist, is a stand-in for Bloy himself. He appears as a supporting character in *The Woman Who Was Poor* and as a protagonist in some of the *contes cruels*. Unlike Durtal, who undergoes change and spiritual growth throughout the novels in which he features, Marchenoir's nature is immutable and apparent: he is the Old Testament prophet who thunders bitter truths only to be spat on and ignored by society, the scourge of the powerful but himself powerless. Whereas the hero of *Là-bas* and *En route* is an interior character, an embodiment of all the doubts, dichotomies and tensions in his author's heart, Bloy's protagonist is a remarkably exterior character—his entire purpose is to give voice to the abhorrent suffering unjust society visits on the indigent and vulnerable. Far more so than Huysmans, Bloy was a revolutionary writer. No bomb-carrying Anarchist yearned for the cataclysmic abolition of the bourgeoisie order with more ardour than the author of *The Desperate Man*. The rich are "new wounds dealt to the Body of Christ," and the acquisition of wealth is a cannibalistic process by which they snatch food from the mouths of the poor and thus consume them. With this in mind his famous quip about awaiting only the corsairs and the Holy Ghost takes on a more sinister meaning. If the promise of Christianity is in vain, if Divine Justice is not meted out soon, then the work must be done by the Poor themselves—not as a revolution to create some impossible utopia, but an orgy of nihilistic destruction to expurgate the indignity of this world's very existence. In the "Stabat of the Modern Poor," an epic monologue reminiscent of the anarchists in Dostoevsky's *The Devils*, Bloy warns of this apocalyptic fury about to break upon modernity.

For Bloy nihilism is surmounted by the development of Catholic orthodoxy into an intensely personal mysticism. Like Huysmans, Bloy believed that through embracing our suffering we can redeem others, however, he develops this further with his theory of Reversibility, which holds that all souls are mystically linked, to the extent that any act an individual performs, good or bad, has hidden causal implications for an untold many.

Indeed, the relations one bears to others is so central to one's ontological identity that were God to annihilate that one soul, it would destroy all the rest of creation with it (here again we see the communitarian nature of Bloy's thought). This hidden web of relations makes possible "the great communion": Christ's Passion connects Him to all of us and paradoxically our suffering connects us to Him and is an opportunity to realise this connection. All these correspondences have existed eternally, for the successive character of history is an illusion resulting from our imperfect, fallen vision. This opens the way for Bloy's idealised mystical science of history. If we are images of God and our relations to others are essential then the whole of history is an image of the divine. The task of the sacred historian is to read events as symbols revealing something of the Divine Nature. Bloy's lapses into anti-Semitism are ironic as he arrives at a position close to the Jewish Kabbalists: the Messianic hope that behind all the filth, cruelty, and blood of history there lies the face of God.

THE DESPERATE MAN

LACRYMABILITER!
The Office of the Dead of the Carthusians.

PUBLISHER'S NOTE
FROM THE 1887 EDITION

Just as we wrote two years ago at the beginning of Monsieur Léon Bloy's first volume that we published, our intention has been simply to put before the eyes of the public an extraordinary talent,—leaving to the author the entire responsibility of his opinions or judgments that he believed necessary to express through the mouth of his novel's characters.

We have too great a respect for Monsieur Léon Bloy's literary originality to have demanded from him the slightest modification of the assessments or judgments that many readers will find excessive, unjust and perhaps even offensive. Besides, Monsieur Léon Bloy would very likely have been contrary to our advice.

It is then clearly understood that we leave to the author the entire responsibility of his judgments or assessments, keeping ourselves simply within our right as publishers and merchants of literary curiosities.

T. & S.

I

When you receive this letter, my dear friend, I will have succeeded in killing my father. The poor man is agonizing and will die, it is said, before daylight.

It is two o'clock in the morning. I am alone, in a neighboring room, the old woman who watches over him having made me understand that it was better for the moribund's eyes not to see me and that she would notify me *when it would be time.*

I feel no grief presently nor any clearly distinct moral feeling of a confused melancholy, of an indecisive fear of what will come. I have seen death already and I know that, tomorrow, it will be terrible. But, at this moment, nothing; my heart is still. I am knocked senseless as if from a blow to the head. Impossible to pray, impossible to weep, impossible to read. I write to you then because a soul left to its own emptiness has no other resource than the imbecilic literary gymnastic of expressing itself.

I am a parricide, nevertheless, such is the single vision of my mind! I hear from here the intolerable hiccough of that agony that is truly my work,— work of the damned that has been imposed on me with fate's despotism!

Ah! the knife would have been preferable, doubtless, the rudimentary knife of the filial stabber! Death, at least, would have been, for my father, free from the torments of the last years, free from the always disappointed resurgent hope of my return to the pig troughs of a bourgeois common sense; I would be fixed on the legally ignominious nature of a probable expiation; lastly, I would not be left with this hideous doubt of having been right to pass over the unfortunate man's feelings in order to hurl myself at the reprobations and diabolical public affronts of the artist's life.

You have seen me, my dear Alexis, with a cylindrical dustbin on my head, deprived of clothing, shoes, everything finally, except for the aperitif of hope. However, you imagined I had a conjecturable domicile, a semblance of intermittent stipends, a teat of some sort at the brass flanks of my bitch of destiny, and you had no idea of the irreproachable perfection of my poverty.

In reality, I was one of the Ten Thousand sempiternal withdrawers from the Parisian famine,—forever without a Xenophon,—who collect the levy of their ravenous hunger from the excrement of the wealthy and who season in the smoke of unattainable and penumbral *kettles,* the symbolic crust of bread harvested in a urinal.

Such was the vestibule of my writer's existence,—an existence that has hardly improved, moreover, even now that I have become somewhat famous. My father knew it and died of shame.

Excellent masonic theologian, adorer of Rousseau and Benjamin Franklin, the entirety of his critical jurisprudence was to measure merit by the gauge of success. From this point of view, Dumas père and Béranger seemed to him all that were necessary to satisfy every aesthetic thirst.

He cherished me, though, in his own way. Before I had stopped drooling in my swaddling clothes, before I had even entered the world, he had carefully marked out for me all the stages of my life, with the most geometric of solicitudes. Nothing was left out, except the eventuality of a literary penchant. When it became impossible to deny the existence of a chancroid, his confusion was immense and his despair unlimited. Discerning nothing but an *impious* revolt in the simple effect of an intransgressible law of nature, but absolutely imbued with his powerlessness, he gave me, however, a last proof of his most unilluminable tenderness by never damning me entirely.

My God! how horribly disgusting life is! And how easy it would be for wise people never to have children! What an idiotic madness it is to propagate! Would an eternal continence then be more atrocious than this onslaught of tortures we call the birth of a poor woman's child?

Already, in all imaginable conditions, a father and a son are like two mute souls who regard each other from either side of the maternal side of the abyss, almost never being able to speak to one another nor to embrace, because of, doubtless, the penitential filth of all human procreation! But if poverty trundles out its torrent of agonies in this profaned bed, and should the frightening anathema of a superior vocation be pronounced, how to express the opaque immensity that separates them?

For a long time now we have stopped corresponding, my father and I. Alas! We had nothing to say to one another. He did not believe in my future as a writer, and I believed even less, if that were even possible, in the competence of his diagnosis. Contempt for contempt. Hell and silence on both sides.

Only, he was dying of despair and therein lies my parricide! In several hours, I will wring my hands perhaps while crying, when enormous sadness hits me. I will be dripping with tears, devastated by all the tempests of compassion, fear and remorse. And yet, if I had to relive these last ten years, I do not know that I could do it any differently. If my Catholic pamphleteer's quill had been able to earn great sums, my father,—the most disinterested of fathers!—would have traveled one hundred leagues to sit before me and contemplate me at ease in the aureole of my genius. But it was my fate to make the voyage instead, and to do it without a sou for the abominable contemplation that we have here!

You have no idea, oh novelist full of glory, of this perfect malice of fate. Life has been kind to you. You received the gift of pleasing, and the very nature of your talent, so happily balanced, distances you from suspicion of the most vague dream of literary tyranny.

You are, without any effort, what I could never be, an amiable and fine writer, and you will never revolt anyone,—something I have spent my whole life doing, to my misfortune. Your books, carried on the wave of innumerable editions, come on their own into a multitude of elegant hands that propagate them with love. Happy man, you who have previously called me your brother, I am crying out to you then in my distress and calling on you to aid me.

I have no money for my father's funeral and you are the only rich friend I know. Put yourself out a little, if necessary, but send me in the next twenty-four hours the ten or fifteen louis plainly indispensable for making it decent. I am isolated in this town where I was born, however, and where my father passed his life making, I believe, some wealth. But he dies without resources and I would probably be unable to find a compatriot with fifty centimes in his pocket.

Trouble yourself to consider, my favored colleague, that I have never asked for money from you before, that the situation is grave, and that I count absolutely on no one but you.

Your anxious friend,
CAÏN MARCHENOIR.

II

This letter, as maladroit and devoid of juvenile illusions as it was, was addressed to the celebrated author of *Painful Mystery*, Monsieur Alexis Dulaurier, on the rue Babylon.

The relationship between him and Marchenoir went back several years. A troubled relationship, to be honest, by virtue of the prodigious differences of ideas and tastes, but it remained cordial for the most part.

At the time they met, Dulaurier, not yet having entered upon the surprising glory of today, lived obscurely on some nutritive lessons selected for him, with the greatest attention paid to sifting through his university acquaintances. He came to publish a volume of Byronic verse of little promise, but sufficiently oozing with melancholy to give to certain runny souls the mirage of Musset's "Saule" on the tomb of Anacreon.

Likeable and with abundant verve,—the same as he is today,—but without the erysipelas of vanity that has disfigured him since his triumphs, his small apartment near the Jardin des Plantes was at that time the meeting place of a fervent group and coterie of young writers, now dispersed in the soiled intercolumniations of fifteen-centime newspapers. The most remarkable of them all was that annoying gypsy Hamilcar Lécuyer, made so famous by his anti-religious churlish vaticinations.

Alexis Dulaurier, friend, by choice, of everyone and, by consequence, without principles as well as passion, loaded with the gifts of mediocrity,—that force capable of uprooting the Himalayas!—could reasonably claim every success.

When the time was right, all he had to do was touch with his finger Publicity's great walls of stupidity for them to come tumbling down before him and let him enter, like some Antiochus, the impregnable fortress of men of genius, with one hundred and twenty futile elephants laden with his literary baggage.

His preponderant position as a writer is now incontestable. He represents nothing less than French Literature!

Barded with three volumes of bluish and frigid poetry, made of excellent steel from the most highly-esteemed English factories,—through which he can defy anyone to come close to his heart; inventor of a polar psychology by the happy addition of several of Stendhal's procedures to the critical *dilettantism* of Monsieur Renan; already sublime on account of the haters of all intellectual virility, he finally scaled the highest chevaux-de-frise by publishing his two first novels in a series, the ending of which no prophet could divine, because he is persuaded to have found his true path.

One must think of the incredible anemia of modern souls of the so-called elevated classes,—the only souls who interest Dulaurier and whose approval he strives for,—in order to truly understand the eucharistic success of that evangelist of Nothing.

To erase every passion, every enthusiasm, every generous act of independence, every indecent vigor of affirmation; to split into quarters the shadow of a hair of a senile phantom of sentiment; to make, in three hundred pages, imponderable amorous delicacies macerate in the myrrh oil of a chaste hypothesis or in the spices of an elegant scruple; above all never to conclude, never to see the Poor, never to break off moaning with Lord Byron about the aridity of human joys; in a word, *never* to WRITE;—these were the psychological victuals offered by Dulaurier to that ruling elite fattened on all the revolutionary dumping grounds, but who expired precisely for an aristocratic lack of nourishment.

After that, how could this fattener of the elite be refused anything? Everything, instantly, was lavished on him: the authority of an oracle, publications constantly reissued, surcharges for old unsold copies, academic prizes, infinite money, and all the way up to that so polluted, but always desirable, cross of honor that a proud artist, supposing he could obtain it, would no longer even have the right to accept!

He still lacked the armchair of immortality. But he will have it soon enough, one would merely need to knock off thirty some odd academics in order for him to be assured of his chances.

Only one man of letters could flatter himself to have enjoyed recently as insolent a fortune. That is Georges Ohnet, the ineffable avaricious millionaire hunchback, the imbecile author of *The Owner of the Ironworks*, whom a strict justice should have forced to give pensions to talented men whose salaries he steals and whose audience he makes idiots of.

But however vomitive the universal success of this rascal might be, who in the final analysis is merely a sordid speculator and who perhaps considers himself a genius, that of Dulaurier, who ought to recognize his own poverty of spirit, is much more revolting still.

The former, in effect, saw in literature merely an appetizing harvest of acorns that his pig of a soul rejoiced over, and it is generally in this way that we can understand his function as a fabricator of books. The latter saw the same thing, doubtless, but, wisely, he confined himself to an influential clientele and thus arranged for himself a literary situation that the immense poet of *The Flowers of Evil* never enjoyed, and he quite frankly dishonors French letters.

This reservation made, the intellectual weighing is about the same on both sides, both having admirably understood the necessity of writing like coachmen in order to be taken for the Automedon[1] of thought.

The author of *Irrevocable* and *Painful Mystery* is, moreover, tainted by English obsessions. For example, after only ten minutes in his company you are already entrusted with the confidence that life has treated him with undue rigor and that he is more or less the most justified of all mortals to complain.

A decent fellow who had just seen dying in poverty and in obscurity a superior being, whose disappearance several newspapers had barely mentioned, grows indignant one day by the patter of this mediocre person who succeeded at everything. "After all," he tells himself, calming down, "maybe there is some sincerity in this terrible joke. The chap has a small soul, but he is not a sot, nor a hypocrite, and something of the monstrous iniquity of his happiness must weigh him down at times!"

III

The postal entreaty by this Marchenoir with the strange first name was therefore doubly inept. It exposed an utter and complete poverty, the most inelegant thing in the world in the eyes of such a dandy of the quill, and exposed in the last lines a vague but irremissible disdain, which the hapless petitioner, inexpert in the handling of vanities, and otherwise exhausted, did not perceive. He had even believed, in his extreme fatigue, that he had pushed the flattery too far and he told himself, with a gesture similar to that of dropping a treasure into the sea, that his frightening distress demanded a like sacrifice.

He and Dulaurier had practically not seen each other at all for many years now. A kind of curiosity of spirit had previously attracted them to each other. For several seasons they were always seen together,—the ardent misanthropy of the bohemian

---

1 Automedon was Achille's charioteer, in Homer's *Illiad*.

who passed for possessing genius, acting as a foil to the skeptical indulgence of the future arbiter of high literary finesses.

From the first moment of success, Dulaurier uncannily felt the danger of continuing to keep in tow this shark, with the howling entrails, who was going to become his judge, and, suavely, he let him go.

Marchenoir found the thing very simple, having already penetrated his soul. It was neither a declared rupture, nor even a quarrel. It was, on both sides, like a green growth of indifference through the ineffectual intentions with which their friendship had been paved. They had had few illusions and no dream was rent.

Every now and again, a handshake and some distracted words when they met. That was all. Otherwise, the radiant Alexis rose higher and higher in glory; he became empyreal. What had he to do with this rough, raggedy fellow who refused to admire him?

One day, however, Marchenoir having succeeded in getting several brilliant articles published in the *Basile*,—a pituitous newspaper with immense exposure, whose editor-in-chief had had a passing fancy of spicing up the feeding trough,—Dulaurier discovered, suddenly, a revival of tenderness for this old companion of unpleasant days, who appeared as a polemicist and who could become one of his most redoubtable enemies.

Fortunately, it was nothing but a flash of light. The immense journal, soon frightened by the scarlatinal temerity of the newcomer and by his scandalous Catholicism, hastened to sack him. The discharged Marchenoir immediately saw all the doors of the journals, sympathetically agitated by the same fright, close before him, and, famished, ousted from the royal feast of Publicity, for not having wished to put on the pimp revelers' nuptial dress of camaraderie, he plunged back down again into the external shadows from which two superior books were unable to draw him out, stifled without further examination by the concerted silence of the entire press.

The fateful Dulaurier, who had never thought of helping this refractory person with an iota of the credit he enjoyed as an influential serial writer, was certainly not the man to compromise himself by playing the Good Samaritan. In the little-desired encounters that their nearness made difficult to avoid, he limited himself to some admiring protestations, accompanied by melodious groans and affable reproaches on the, fundamentally fully unjust, intransigence that this disgrace had brought on him.

"Why make enemies for oneself? Why not love every good person? Besides, the Gospel, which you believe, my dear Caïn, isn't it there to teach you?"

He dared speak of the Gospel! . . . and nevertheless it was this man that the shipwrecked Marchenoir saw himself reduced to reach out for help from!

IV

The *young master* received the letter in bed. He had passed the evening at Baroness de Poissy's place, celebrated hostess of all sexes, together with a select group of scoundrels from *Premier-Paris* and promoters of comedians of the theater. He had been brilliant, as usual, and even a bit more so.

At five in the morning, the *Gil Blas* had spread the news among several wine merchants in Montmartre, and by eight o'clock every commercial clerk knew about it. The squamous nocturnal journalist had let it be known, with discreet diaphanousness appropriate to this type of information, that the presence of a young Norwegian woman from distant fjords, with a lily-white throat and ductile virginity, had been responsible for something in the improvisational erethism of the irresistible *leggero* tenor of "our latest literary salons."

Consequently, he found comfort in a bit of sleep, after that lyrical dilapidation of his fluid.

"Is that you, Francis?" he said in a languishing voice, while being awoken by the faint sound of the bedroom door that his domestic half-opened with care.

"Yes, Sir, it's an urgent letter."

"That's fine, put it here. Open the curtains and start the fire. I'll get up in just a moment . . . It feels like I've slept for a long time, what time is it now?"

"Sir, it just sounded half past eight, when the postman arrived."

Dulaurier closed his eyes again and, in the warmth of his bed, with the sound of the crackling fire, he submerged himself in the exquisite matutinal indolence of those colonists living on the happy shores of the world, for whom the day that rises is always without menace, without the abjection of commercial enterprise and office servitude, without the demoralizing fear of the creditor and the diaphragmatic trepidation of colics caused by due dates, without all the nightmare of the eternal expedient's overwhelming terrors.

Ah! how the Poor are absent from these awakenings that enfranchised men have, from self-sufficient souls' voluptuous yawns, when chanticleers announce the new day! How he is,—at that moment,—Cimmerian, telescopic, done away with in the ulterior tenebrosity of spaces, the doleful Skin and Bones, the dirty and great Poor, friend of the Lord!

The thinking flute that was Dulaurier vibrated still with the mundane bucolics of the night before. The Norwegian eiderdown undulated softly, around his mind, in the luminous grayness of a half-sleep. A gosling, from the North Pole, scattered chaste dreams over him, psychological snow on that frozen, floating imagination . . .

"What purity! What a fine soul!" he murmured while extending his hand toward the letter. "'*Very urgent, in case of absence, forward.*' It's Marchenoir's handwriting. I know it well. As if he had anything urgent in his life!"

He read, without any visible emotion, the four pages of this handwriting, upright and firm, in the style of dolmens, whose surprising readability has given joy to a great number of printers. Towards the end, however, a sudden alarm appeared in it, accompanied by signs of distress, no sooner followed by the interpretative outburst of a small nervous fury.

"What a bother, this misanthrope," he exclaimed, throwing aside his onerous friend's crucial prose. "Does he take me for a millionaire? I work for my living, I do; he can do the same! Eh! what the devil, his father won't be thrown into the refuse dump, maybe! Why not a funeral like Hephaestion's for this old imbecile?"

He got dressed, but unenthusiastically. His day was going to be ruined.

"I really needed that! Decidedly, there's nothing like melancholics and tender souls and this Marchenoir's hard like the devil . . . Caïn! it's the only spiritual idea his father ever had, to name him so. But what to do? If I don't respond, I make an enemy, which would be absurd and intolerable. I was able to blame him for his fanaticism and his violent outbursts which I vainly tried to show him the injustice of, most of all when he attacked in such a savage way that poor Lecuyer, whom he should have spared, out of friendship for me; I was forced, with great regret, to distance myself from him, all because of his insufferable character; but to the end I never attacked him, no, I even said good things about him at the risk of compromising myself and I let him see clearly enough the pity that his situation inspired in me. He's taking advantage of my feelings today . . . Ten or fifteen louis, that's good! I barely make two thousand francs a month. I can hardly go around stark naked. On the other hand, if I respond to him that I share his chagrin, but that I cannot do what he asks, he will accuse me of avarice. Everything is dangerous with this fanatic. I'm always too kind, I've said it often enough. It would be better to live in solitude, in the company of charming and incorporeal souls! . . . What lassitude I feel! . . . Already ten o'clock and five hundred lines of proofs to correct before going to Des Bois' who expects me for breakfast! . . . This letter exasperates me!"

He sat down before the fire, proofs in hand, and proceeded to consider the voluble effort of a bluish flame around a humid log.

"But actually it's very simple," he said, suddenly, in a low voice, responding to the interior interrogating thoughts more softly still. "Marchenoir is on very good terms with Des Bois who is rich. I will undoubtedly persuade the doctor to do something."

His face lit up, the cordial of this resolution having comforted his good soul, and he was able to reread, with the rapid clairvoyance of someone who despises little literary mistakes, the clinging and albuminous phrases expected by two thousand salons.

V

Doctor Cherubin Des Bois lives in a sumptuous apartment in the multimillionaire quarter of Europe, the most beautiful place on the rue de Madrid. He is the doctor of the exquisite class, the therapist of salons, the delicate exorcist of small distinguished neuroses.

At the very beginning of his brilliant career, he had already conquered the avenues and the boulevards. His personal airs, made of nothing at all, like his science even, are generally considered irresistible. His small ascendant and mobile consultant cassowary's head is habitually searching like a speculum for pleasant smiles. Medical casuist full of mysteries and conjecturing brocade weaver full of intentions, but hypothetical thaumaturge, he would be perhaps the first doctor in the world to heal people by setting foot in their homes, if he had not had the admirable gift of tranquilizing ulcerated Cyprians and thus attracting a vast clientele of aristocratic mucous membranes whom he has become the tentacular confidant of.

Curious about alchemy and about occult traditions, but without the archaic manipulation of substances,—gullibly enamored with every abstruse doctrine capable of travestying his nothingness, fanatic of decent literature and of correct art, respectable friend of powerful comedians, such as Paulus, or avaricious scribes, like Georges Ohnet,—accomplished prototypes of the acquaintances of his choice,—he gratifies with excellent dinners all the influential stomachs that he supposes accustomed to grateful digestions.

As was mentioned a little earlier, the lamentable Marchenoir had had his minute of celebrity. It was thought for a moment that he was going to find himself in a fantastic situation. The doctor dreamed immediately of annexing him.

Marchenoir was, at that time, as he was so many times, in one of his agonies, when the most impregnable lycanthropy gave way to the sweaty hand that wanted to seize it, instead of severing it ferociously in its jaws.

Furthermore, the miserable man, with his confusion and his inexpressible rage, was so made that the grimace of love had always vanquished him and that he was always disarmed by pretended expressions of the most manifestly adulterated kindnesses.

Des Bois having arranged the encounter as if by accident, knew how to enter, with a melting suppleness, into the feelings of the pamphleteer and removed, almost effortlessly, the incensed man's savage repugnances. He got Marchenoir to breakfast at his place, without witnesses.

"My dear Monsieur Marchenoir," he said on the spot, "I earn one hundred thousand francs a year and I spend them. In consequence, I am poor, poorer than you, maybe, because of the crushing expenses that result from my situation. I am therefore able to understand certain things quite well. Permit me to speak to you with total frankness. You have evidently before you a most brilliant literary future, but I know that you are momentarily in dire straits. Straight to the point. I am putting twenty-five louis at your disposal. Accept them without further ado as from a friend who believes in you and who would be happy to be able to offer you even more."

It was so perfectly said and with such surefire warmth, that the poor Marchenoir, ravaged by anguish on account of his lack of money, menaced by imminent catastrophes and believing the sky about to open up and swallow him, accepted without deliberation, with imbecile enthusiasm.

As for Des Bois, he was much too clever and complex to understand whatever there might be in the unbelievably rudimentary simplicity of such a man and he felt sure of having concluded a happy transaction.

This friendship, so strangely paired, was without clouds for some time. But, one day, Marchenoir having begun to stumble in the journals' vivifying esteem, Dr. Cherubin began to wax oracular.

With infinite measures, in circumspect exhortations, the latter made his guest understand that good sense was obliged to reprove the absurd inflexibility of his principles, that good taste was suffering, by his insolent writings, an intolerable grilling, that he should carefully guard himself from thinking that such a ferocious independence of spirit was a straight track to financial independence, and, finally, that he had expected much better of him and that some people were upset by all this to the point of tears.

At the same time, less humid and much more direct words were spoken to a third table companion who hastened to repeat them to Marchenoir. His improperly frequent visits were complained about and the private life of this defeated man was not exempt from blame. He was known to be living with a young woman and the defamatory word *affair* was mentioned.

That was it. Marchenoir gathered up all these words as if they were garbage and flung them, higgledy-piggledy, with the money, like a pile of treasures, into an incorruptible cedar chest, clad in vibrant bronze, in the deepest recesses of his heart!

VI

The law of "proportional attraction" should have, on the contrary, infallibly precipitated the one towards the other and soldered together Alexis Dulaurier and Doctor Cherubin Des Bois. Evidently, the two minds had been created to work in unison.

They had one thing to regret and that was not having known each other sooner. Unfortunately they had only just met. Even though they frequented practically the same salons,—the one strengthening and healing what the other was content to lubricate,—an inconceivable bad luck had long kept them apart . . . had long separated the occasions, which ought to have been innumerable, of their so desirable union.

This circumstance, regrettable from the point of view of the interlacing of their minds, had been providential for Marchenoir, whom the conscientious Dulaurier would never have permitted Des Bois to assist with such lavishness, had he been consulted.

If now Dulaurier was coming, on his own initiative, to incite Des Bois to new largess, it was only, as has just been seen, to maintain a friendship that was, although considered pointless, still dangerous, all the while keeping, as best he could, his perfect-child reputation from the stain of a suspicion of robbery.

It is always a time of exhilaration at the doctor's when Dulaurier makes an appearance. On both sides, the smiles go up, they parade about with affectionate flummery, they cover everything with the whitewash of a sepulchral sensibility.

It is an endless business of sentimental tow, hyperborean emotions, congratulatory frictions, apologetic whispers, crazed or peevish little confidences, anecdotes or verdicts, a mediocre fifty-trick orgy in the thimble of Caesar's irreproachable mistress!

For these marionettes are, *unbeknownst to themselves*, extremely jealous majesties and it is a question whether God himself, with all his power, could inspire any doubt in them of the irreproachable beauty of their moral life.

It is perhaps the least perceived effect of a French decline going on for fifteen years, to have produced these masters, unknown in previous periods of decadence, who reign over us without wanting to and without even realizing it. It is the superhuman oligarchy of Unconscious men and the Divine Right of absolute Mediocrity.

They are not *necessarily* eunuchs, nor wicked, nor fanatics, nor hypocrites, nor crazed imbeciles. They are neither egoists with assurance, nor cowards with precision. They do not even have the energy for skepticism. They are absolutely nothing. The world is at their feet and that appears very natural to them.

By virtue of the principle that something is destroyed only when it is completely replaced, it was necessary to fill the enormous hole through which the ancient aristocracy had escaped like filth, while waiting for them to ebb back like a pestilence. It was necessary to condemn at all costs this dangerous gate and the Acephalous were elected to straddle a decapitated people.

Also, the oldest Daughter of the Church, now Whore of the world, has selected them with an infinite solicitude, these impotent lilies, these blue lilies whose innocence reinvigorates its perverse decrepitude! If the Exterminating Angel had arrived at last, no longer would it find a living soul among the opulent quarters of Paris, nothing in the Champs-Elysees, nothing in the Trocadéro, nothing in the Park Montceau, three times nothing in the Faubourg-Saint-Germain, and doubtless, it would disdain angelically to strike with the sword the human simulacra loaded with riches that it would have discovered there.

VII

Dulaurier did not mention Marchenoir immediately. As a rule, he never spoke immediately about anything and he rarely, as a result, spoke with clarity when he did. He babbled conjectures and did not say much beyond that, leaving the vulgarities of affirmation to those who lacked delicacy.

This time, however, he had to come forward.

"I received a letter from Marchenoir," he began. "The poor devil wrote me from Périgueux that his father is at death's door. He was expected to pass yesterday morning. He asked me in a nearly imperious manner to send him fifteen louis, today even, for the funeral. He seems to believe that I have packets of bank notes to send through the mail, but he appeared tormented and I am quite at a loss on how to respond to him."

"I see no other response possible but silence," Des Bois pronounced. "Marchenoir's proud and ungrateful and you should give up trying to help him in any meaningful way. He despises and offends everyone, beginning with his best friends. I wanted to help him out and he very nearly ended up embarrassing me. I've had enough of it. I don't have the right to sacrifice my interests and my obligations as a man of the world to a person of bad company who'll finish by compromising me."

"He's got talent, it's really too bad!"

"Yes, but what hateful viciousness! If you knew the tone he used here! He seemed to have mistaken my house for a stable that had been annexed to a restaurant. Fortunately, I never received him when I had company. He took it upon himself to speak badly about all my friends. One day, despite my precautions, he encountered my old comrade Ohnet, whom he couldn't forgive for his success. Ah well! He treated him like a discarded potato skin. I'm sure you will agree that it was an unpleasant experience for me. Can you believe that he was in the habit of eating garlic constantly and that the vile odor reeked throughout my apartment and even as far as my consulting room? I was forced to forbid his entry and I believe he finally understood, because he stopped coming after two or three months."

"He's unhappy. He should be pitied. All my spiritualism is there, my good Des Bois. Divinity is nothing if not pity. I see Marchenoir just as you see him yourself, and I could make the same complaints. I have often and so many times in vain reproached his intolerance and injustice! He even accuses himself of having caused his father's death by sorrow. When he speaks with me it's always with disdain and insult. One time, didn't he go so far as to tell me that he didn't think enough of me to hate me? To tell the truth, I'd rendered him some services myself and he made me understand that I should be proud to have been solicited by a man of his merit. You must take his side, you see! This Catholic energumen is ungrateful, but not vulgar, and that is enough to be able to rejoice in. Do you remember that famous slave during the triumphal solemnities in ancient Rome, charged with tempering the apotheosis and insulting the triumphant? Marchenoir is like that. Only, his day being over and his basket of insults empty, he extends his hand humbly, for the love of God, to the very same people whom he has just inundated with his outrages. Don't you think it would be criminal to discourage this activity?"

Having gotten this off his chest, a breeze of contentment passed over Dulaurier's heart. He repositioned an unstable monocle beneath the arch of his eyebrow that under the emotion of discourse had fallen and, lifting his glass, he looked at the doctor like a man who was about to give a toast to eternal Justice.

"But what do you want me to do?" responded Des Bois. "I can hardly take him into my house with his garlic and his perpetual rages!"

"Assuredly, but couldn't you, one last time, help him out with some money? It's a matter of burying his father and the situation is grave, so much so that he wrote to me himself, with a small nuance of threat, the poor man! Pity should step in here. Unfortunately, I can't do anything or almost anything at this moment, what with my recent 'promotion' which has forced on me endless expenses. I don't want to hide it from you, Des Bois, I'd hoped to soften you towards him. In any other circumstance, I wouldn't have bothered you with this small matter. You know me. I would've done what he desires without hesitation and hemming and hawing, but I'm up against a wall and, precisely because he thinks I'm overwhelmed with the gifts of fortune, I'm afraid lest he should think himself justified of accusing me of a sordid harshness if I made no ostensible effort . . ."

Dulaurier's melodious voice had dropped from the soprano of vengeful subsannations to the deep velvety notes of a persuasive baritone.

He knew what he was doing, this legionnaire,[1] by drawing attention, in a single unequivocally detached word, to his decoration just now completely exposed. This decoration in a buttonhole was extremely effective on the doctor, for whom it represented an irrefragable sanction of the aesthetic preferences appertaining to his social standing; the author of *Painful Mystery* having acquired this distinguishing mark of grandeur above all by dint of his debasement of literature.

The lucrative success of his last novel—irreproachably glabrous—had been the occasion, long hoped for, of this national recognition which the holder, one fine morning, received news of,—at the same moment when one of the rarest writers of contemporary France received his forty-fifth weekly punch in the face while working as a trainer in an English boxing room, which position furnished him a salary of sixty francs per month,—whatever he could do to feed his son!

VIII

"So be it!" concluded Des Bois, after a long struggle. "In consideration of you, Dulaurier, I consent to make another sacrifice. But, keep in mind, this will be the last. I'd feel culpable if I encouraged the haughtiness and lassitude of this man who's distressed, but only by his own doing, as you know. Here are three louis. I cannot nor will not give any more. Send him this money as you think it appropriate. I'd be obliged if you'd make him understand that he should expect nothing more from me."

In consequence, the squire poet of high society's psychological discharges posted, that same evening, a message written as follows:

1 Legionnaire: holder of the French Legion of Honor

My dear Marchenoir,

Your letter caused me much pain. You know how much I value our friendship, in spite of the superficial differences of opinion that have appeared to alter it and you can't doubt with what sincerity I share your grief. I know too well what it is to suffer, no matter what you think, and nobody, maybe, has felt more painfully than I have, since Lord Byron, the suffering of existence. I've even called myself, in a poem of most distressing skepticism, a soul "at once exasperated and weary." Nothing truer, nothing sadder.

You've reproached me several times, quite wrongly, with what you call my indifference and my thoughtlessness, without considering the awful heartbreaks of a life torn into twenty miseries. Your request for money has put me in the most cruel and awkward situation. You believe me rich based on your faith in a much exaggerated success that's small compensation for my many years of obscure labor and continual effort to impregnate with idealism the most repugnant vulgarities.

Know that I'm very poor and, by consequence, very far from being able, even *if I feel badly about it*, to send you what you ask for. But I didn't want to send you so pathetic a response before making an effort. I've therefore visited Des Bois whom I apprised of your situation.

He's also quite fond of you, but you've offended him like so many others; take what I say amicably, my dear Marchenoir. Your inflexible character has always repelled the people most favorably disposed to you. I've defended you with all the warmth that my friendship has for you, without succeeding to overcome his prejudices. I was hoping to obtain the entire sum and it's only by virtue of wearing him out that he's consented to remit sixty francs to you, all the while charging me to warn you that all other attempts of this kind from now on would be useless.

I add to this money, by the goodness of my heart, another two louis, which makes one hundred francs, and I assure you, Marchenoir, that it was only because of the horrible urgency of your situation that I could commit, at this moment, to such a sacrifice.

However, I well imagine, you're going to say that I've done you a miserable service and you'll bitterly complain about what you couldn't do for your father, the excessive funeral arrangements that you dreamed of. But, my dear friend, nothing is impossible and there's no dishonor in sticking to the communal grave when you can't afford the expenses of a less modest burial.

I know that I afflict you speaking like this, but my conscience as well as my reason dictates this language and, as a Catholic, you have no right to dismiss an exhortation to Christian humility.

"Why," the doctor asked me, "doesn't Marchenoir stay in Périgueux? Assuredly, he'd be much better off than in Paris where he lives as badly as possible. He'd unfailingly find friends of the family, old school chums who'd be happy to help him procure the means of existence . . ."

I feel he's right and I can't refrain from giving you the same advice. Take it in the right way, as coming from a soul united by sadness with your own and who renounced, a long time ago, every illusion.

You're banned from literature. You've talent, that is clear, an incontestable talent, but it's of no value to you, an arid field. You can't submit work to any journal and you're without resources to subsist on while writing a book. To live by his quill, one must have a certain breadth of humanity, an acceptance of conventional forms and received prejudices of which you're unfortunately incapable. Life's flat, my dear Marchenoir, and you must resign yourself to it. You believe you were called to do justice, but everyone's abandoned you because, at bottom, you were unjust and lacking in *charity*.

Believe me, renounce literature and courageously take the first job that comes along. You're intelligent, you have beautiful handwriting, I believe you're destined for an infallible success in any other career. This is the disinterested counsel of a man who sincerely loves you and who'd be happy to learn of your having finally found your true calling.

Your devoted,
ALEXIS DULAURIER.

IX

An eternal movement in the same circle, an eternal repetition, an eternal passage from day to night and from night to day; a drop of sweet tears and a sea of bitter tears! Friend, what is the point of my, your, all of us, living? What is the point of our ancestors having lived? What is the point of our descendents living after us? My soul is empty, weak and sad.

These lines were written in the last years of the previous century by the historian Karamzin.

As one can see, strange Russia was already tormented by this notorious despair that descends today like a dragon of the apocalypse, from Slavic plateaus onto the old Occident, overcome by lassitude.

This Devourer of souls is formidable, in its slow but invincible progression, when all other menaces of political or social meteorology begin to seem like nothing before this theophanic Menace, whose frightening and trilogical expression is inscribed by bastard cannons on the black pennon of triumphant Nihilism:

Long live chaos and destruction!
Long live death!
Make way for the future!

But what future do they speak of, these wrongheaded hopefuls, these excavators of human nothingness? They do not make do with the *next life* announced by Catholicism and protest with rage against the intolerable denial of the justice of a thinking soul's imbecilic escape into matter.

What then? No one can say, and the poor mechanics of reasoning had never endured the torments of such an agony. One has hung on as best one could, one has tried all the ropes and clamps of rationalism or humanitarian mysticism to avoid falling as far as all that. Every philosophical vesicatory, supposedly capable of resuscitating in one instant the breath of Hope, has been applied to this phthisic, from the time of the hierophant St. Simon who spoke of redemption to the patriarch of nihilists, Alexandre Herzen, who spoke of it also.

"Preach the *good news* of death," said this last one, "show men each new scar on the chest of the old world, each progression of destruction; point out the decrepitude of its principles, the superficiality of its efforts; demonstrate that it cannot heal, that there is neither support, nor faith in itself, that nobody loves it really, that they persist by misunderstanding; demonstrate that each of its victories is a defeat that it brings on itself; preach *Death* as the good news, as the annunciation of the *next* REDEMPTION."

Such is the gravitating doctrinal Absolute that no religious jack will shift ever again!

Absolute negation of every present good and absolute certitude of recuperating Eden after the universal destruction. Enthymeme informer of life's emptiness by death's emptiness, last cornering of Pride, enjoining one last time the X of Justice, in the name of all terrestrial grief, to give finally something other than the *simulacrum* of a redemption or to erase,—like a solecism,—the inexpiable Infinity of our nature, together with the unfortunate human race!

This terrible thought, this covetousness at the back of the heart, has pounced on modern society and enveloped it like an octopus. The most myopic minds begin to understand that it is in the process of producing a real cadaver,—the very cadaver of Civilization!—as many as fifty nations, whose Godless dogs ready themselves to gnaw on the West's brain, while its putrefied feet will spread the pestilence into the heart of the East!

Expectans, expectavi, to wait while expecting. For a thousand years the Middle Ages chanted it. The Church has continued to chant it ever since the Middle Ages had its throat cut by the second-rate bourgeois scholars of the Renaissance, as if nothing had changed with respect to what could bring a little patience, and, now, one has had quite enough of it.

To wait fifty centuries in the illuminated margin of a book of hours saturated with poetry, like one of these expectant patriarchs, with the faithful smile, who sempiternally watch cedars grow out of their bellies—and it's still happening!

But, come from Sodom, to wait on a sidewalk, right in the middle of the electoral solicitation, in the immediate vicinity of the Américain or Tortoni's[1], with the ridiculous fear of stepping on the face of a prime minister or a journalist, that is decidedly above human power!

That is why everything that has some virile quantity, for three decades now, has been thrown frantically into despair. It makes a complete literature that is veritably a literature of desperate men. It is like a completely despotic law that seemingly no plausible poet going forward can escape.

---

1 The Américain and Trotoni's were cafés in Paris.

One must not look for this unprecedented situation of superior souls at any other point in history than at this end of the century, when contempt for all intellectual or moral transcendence has arrived precisely at a sort of counterfeit miracle.

Before Baudelaire, as everyone knows, there was Lord Byron, Chateaubriand, Lamartine, Musset, fake lamenters who watered down the soup of their glory with the incontinent tears of a melancholic *good girl* who shared her favors with them.

Now what is the *passionate vagueness* of the incestuous René, Rousseau's bastard, or Manfred's decorative frenzies compared to the tetanic slobber of reprobates like Baudelaire, Ackerman, Ernest Hello, Villiers de l'Isle-Adam, Verlaine, Huysmans or Dostoevsky?

They *no longer remember heaven*, according to the much-admired Lamartinian joke. They do not remember anything at all anymore. But they remember the tangible earth where they are forced to live, in the midst of human filth, in an irremediable *privation of the sight of God*—whatever their concept of that substantial Entity,—with an enraged desire for revelry and getting drunk at all hours!

At that depth of spiritual ill fortune, there is but one torture, in which all the others are reabsorbed to give it a dreadful energy, I mean: the need for JUSTICE, infinitely absent nourishment!

Gad! They know what Christians say, they know it even better than they do. But one needs faith in all the devils and that is not the view of modern Christians who would give it to them. So, they produce the literature of despair, so that sententious imbeciles can believe a very simple thing, but which is, in reality, a sort of mystery . . . herald of one knows not what. What is certain, is that all vigorous thought is now pushed, taken up, swept away in this direction, sucked up and swallowed up by this Maelstrom.

Could it be that we finally touch on some divine Solution whose prodigious vicinity would drive the human compass crazy? . . .

One of the least doubtful signs of this situation whereby modern souls are pushed to every extreme is the recent intrusion in France of a monster of a book, nearly unknown as yet, although published in Belgium ten years ago: the *Songs of Maldoror* by the Count de Lautréamont (?), work completely without analog and probably destined to have some effect. The author died in a hut and that is all we know of him.

It is difficult to decide if the word *monster* is here sufficient. That resembles some appalling submarine polymorph that an amazing tempest would have thrown onto the shore after having disturbed the bottom of the ocean.

The very mouth of Imprecation remains gaping and silent in view of this visitor, and the satanic litanies of the *Flowers of Evil* assume quickly, in comparison, a certain air of anodynic religiosity.

It is no longer the *Good News of Death* by that good man Herzen, it is something like the *Good News of Damnation*. As for literary form, it has none. It is molten lava. It is senseless, black and devouring.

But does it not seem to those who have read it, what this incredible defamation of Providence exhales, by anticipation,—with the unequaled authority of a Prophet,—the last imminent clamor of the human conscience before its Judge? . . .

X

Marchenoir was born desperate. His father, a tense middle-class man, an office worker at the General Revenue Office of Périgueux, had given him, on the advice of his Lodge's *Venerable* and by way of defiance, the name of Caïn, to the inexpressible horror of his mother who hastened to have him baptized under the Christian vocable Marie-Joseph. The maternal will having been, extraordinarily enough, the stronger, he was therefore called Joseph in childhood and the malefic name, inscribed in the civil registry, was not exhumed until much later, after long hours of solemn discontent.

Others have need of failures or crimes in their own life in order to feel nausea. Marchenoir, more gifted, had had nothing but the sadness of entering the world.

He was one of those beings miraculously bred for unhappiness, who have the air of having passed nine hundred years in their mother's belly, before lamentably coming to drag an hoary childhood through a decrepit society of men.

He was adorned, from his first day, with the deplorable faculty, quite rare for those who could recognize it, of carrying, around his intelligence, something like a fog of ancient and indiscernible things, something like a halo of bygone reveries that soon gave him a refracted vision of the ambient world. He had a reminiscence of his swaddling clothes, if one will allow this fashion of expressing what is naturally inexpressible.

"This anomalous ecstatic disposition," he recounted, "at thirty years of age, this absorbing despotism of the Dream that made me incapable of any application by binding me to a perpetual stupor, brought on me enough tribulations and terrors to defray a martyrdom of children. My father, hardened by imbecilic prejudices for education and resolutely locked up in the impregnable fortress of a very small number of uncompromising ideas, never wanted to see in me anything but an idle person and nearly killed me with a Lacedaemonian strictness.

"Maybe he was right. I even came to persuade myself that the intensive cultivation of the thinking reed is, in general, the spiritual result of a superficial ascendancy. Unfortunately, the poor man sterilized his thrashings by never following them up with any return to tenderness which would have intellectualized the baking of them. Naturally inclined to cherish, this ill-fated educator nourished on the rack of Plutarch, believed in making miracles by taking the advice of that ancient good-for-nothing and repressing his own heart, his modern heart scarified by anachronistic immolations, he imposed on himself never to caress his child, in the civic hope of safeguarding his paternal majesty.

"When he enrolled me in secondary school, it was a hell.

Numb already with fear, despised by the other children whose unruliness horrified me, ridiculed by ignoble prigs who made a laughing stock out of me in front of my classmates, punished non-stop and beaten by all hands, I ended up falling into a taciturn disgust of life that made me look like a young idiot.

"This perfect distress, this perpetual constriction of the heart, ordinarily passed down to melancholic children in the penitentiaries of the University, aggravated for me the impossibility of conceiving a more atrocious terrestrial condition. It seemed as though I had fallen, from what heaven I do not know, into an infinite pile of trash where human beings appeared as vermin to me. It was like that at fourteen years of age, and it is like that today, my conception of human society!

"One day, however, I revolted, my fellow students' malice having surpassed I do not know anymore what limits. I stole a kitchen knife, fortunately harmless, and threw myself, after an emphatic act of bravado, upon a group of fourteen young rascals, two or three of whom I wounded. They pulled me off, foaming with rage, knocked silly, superb. My knife had done little damage, a few scrapes if that, but my father had to remove me from that stupefying place and keep me at home.

XI

Marchenoir the father, having learned from his own experience of the emptiness of administrative expectations, had decided to push his son towards industry. Railroads were being built everywhere with a furor. Périgueux was at the center of this network of lines, which speculation had thrown like a net over the center of France and was called, for that reason, the *Grand Central of Orleans*.

The industrial spider, sated today, and even busted, had fixed its laboratory there and sucked the financial juices from many provinces, previously tranquil, that it had promised to enrich. The Californian frenzy, the prostitution, the civilizing gullibility was in full swing. The little old Roman city invaded by many armies of dusty engineers and prolific Limousin natives had doubled in size in several years and now threatened, by its inundating obesity, the low-lying mountains that had contained it for twenty centuries.

Consequently, the poor employee of the State had made the Buddhist vow to immerse the son of his secret, disillusioned ambitions in this golden Brahmaputra.

From this point of view, it was doubtless a good thing that he had not risen to the bait of the *humanities*. Apparently, the stomach of his spirit had been reserved exclusively for the digestion of mathematics. It was a matter of force-feeding him with this new alimentation without delay.

The poor boy bit at nothing else. The preliminary hypothesis, the primordial act of faith, planted like basil on the sill of every natural science, sufficed to extinguish, at first blow, the timid flame of curiosity that his father's solicitous exhortations had appeared to arouse in him. The young Périgourdin's insufficiency of cerebral equipment became manifestly obvious from the moment that he had to visualize the impossible romance of a conjectural line problematically engendered by the dubitable copulation of a multitude of inexistent points! . . .

He had to resign himself to a mediocre future and become a copyist. Caïn Joseph, from this moment forward having been abandoned like an uncultivated tract of land, having surrendered to a nearly manual task that no longer repressed his faculties, returned of his own accord, by an unsuspected slope, to the first studies of which he had seemed prodigiously incapable of. Only, effortlessly almost, he learned in two years what the stultifying despotism of the pawns of the earth could not have taught him in half a century. He found himself suddenly full with ancient literature and began to dream of a literary future.

In fact, what the devil do you think an adolescent, who modern disciplines exasperate and who commercial abjection makes vomit, could possibly dream of today? The crusades are past, as well as noble, distant adventures of any sort. The entire globe has become reasonable and one is certain to encounter English excrement at every intersection of the universe. Art is the only thing left. A proscribed art, it is true, spurned, subordinated, scrawny, ragged and catacombal. But, all the same, it is the unique refuge for some very noble souls condemned to drag their suffering carcasses through the rotting crossroads of the world.

The unfortunate young man had no idea what tortures he would have to undergo for this independence of spirit. Nobody, in his stupid province, would have been capable of instructing him on it and the ironic scorn of his father, resolutely hostile to every ambitious plan he had not thought up himself, could not help but be even more of a stimulant. Besides, he believed he possessed a martyr's heart, able to endure everything.

One day then, having, after many steps, obtained in Paris the most miserable of employments, he came docilely close to dying, like a hundred thousand others, in that promised land of an Ergastolum where the human flower is soaked in Circe's chamber pot. The hideous Ghoul of souls, who has but to whistle and they rush to her dirty feet from the extremities of the earth, once again, had been obeyed.

XII

He was eighteen years old, one of those rural physiognomies in which the atavistic muzzle had not yet had time to wage its last battle against the invasive intelligence that soon rose, to ennoble everything, from the intimate valleys of the heart.

From his mother, who had passed away long ago, he had a romantic ridiculousness of Spanish origin, shared moreover by that multitude of infamous priests whose same shortcomings can be read about in the majority of anticlerical novels.

That origin,—just a little refuted by his eyes which were so naïvely blue that he always gave the impression of using them for the first time,—was overabundantly attested to by the extraordinary energy of all his other traits without exception. Only, it was the contemplative energy of these lovers of heroic action who do not consider whether vulgar action is worth the expense of other energy.

Hirsute and dark, silent and miserly of gestures, sacrificial execrator of banal phrases and hackneyed expressions, he carried on the tip of his tongue a catapult to launch erratic monosyllables that instantly pierced a conversation of imbeciles. Closed mouth, vibrating nostrils, eyebrows nearly crossed and crossing one into the other at the least commotion, he exhibited sometimes mute, repressed rages, white with sedition, that would have given colic to a disemboweled despot. At these encounters, the cannibal emerged from the dreamer instantly. The faraway eyes with an almost childlike tenderness,—alone capable of tempering the habitual hardness of the whole,—changed color then and turned black! . . .

Years of humiliations and tortures filtered, little by little, through the fallow of this visage, the fertilizing powder of several inevitable compromises. The complexion of his face, already bilious, took on that burning lividness of a badly stoned Christian who, from the very beginning, would have become sacristan of the catacombs.

He had the gift of tears, a sign of *predestination*, say the Mystics. Those tears were the hidden joy, the occult treasure of one of the most deprived and tragic existences of this century.

After he had swallowed one of those grass snakes the size of a *divine* boa that were so often his only nourishment, he scattered about him, in his solitary room, with the prudence of a miser, that liquid gem which he would not have exchanged for the desiccating consolations of a more solid wealth.

Because he had the strange habit of cherishing his sadness, that *incanabulum* of melancholy, which had fallen into his cradle as if into a barathrum[1] and which his stupefied mother watched

---

1 Barathrum: a pit in ancient Athens which criminals were thrown into as punishment.

bawling, for days, on her knees,—silently! Just a baby, he had concupiscence for Grief and lust for a paradise of tortures, in the manner of St. Madeleine de' Pazzy. That was not the result of education or setting or any mental lesion, as oracular idiots tried to explain it. It had nothing to do with any discernible operation of the nascent mind. It was the mysterious core of his soul a little less unconscious than another of his abyss and naïvely enraged with an absolute of sensations or feelings that corresponded to the absolute of his entity. When Christianity appeared to him, Marchenoir rushed to it like Eliezer's camels to the nuptial watering place in Mesopotamia.

He had been dying of thirst for so long! His incredulous father did not believe he should oppose this semblance of religious instruction that sham priests, stuffed with formulas, wrung out like dirty seminary linen on young uninterested faces. He had taken his first communion without malice and without love. The only two faculties that appeared alive in him,—the only two handles by which one could hope to seize him,—memory and imagination had quite simply received that vague *literal* imprint of Christian symbolism that sacrilegious entrepreneurs deem sufficient for admittance into the skiff of the Eucharist. Because no spouter of formulas had bothered to inquire into his heart, the poor child was unable to keep down the badly baked bread and, like so many others, vomited it up again almost immediately on that verdant path of his fifteenth year when Puberty, that great lion with a pig's head, prowls about.

XIII

It was not until much later,—after ten years of an impure novitiate in the latrines of philosophical examination, being already on the point of pronouncing stercoraceous vows,—having skimmed through, for the first time, the New Testament, during the leisurely warming of his feet one night on the front line, in 1870, that he had the immediate, violent apperception of a divine Revelation.

He always remembered the immense agitation, the superhuman stupefaction of that moment on the wings of the eagle that carried him away in the hurricane of uninterpretable delights. He was drawn up into the new feeling of an unknown force, arteries beating and heart aflame; drunk with certitude, shaken by the rocking of a hope mixed with anguish, ready for all the acceptances of martyrdom. For that divining and synthetically ardent soul, leaping by bounds above the intermediate lessons of the faith, was carried, from the onset, to the decisive concept of immolation.

It seemed to him to come from one of those rare dreams, with determinable contours, which made believe in some sensible vision of Conscience, reflexively manifested in the extralucid intussusception of sleepers. He believed he had appeared himself, unimaginably transmuted in order to resemble himself even more, but horrible, dripping with abominations and sad beyond all hyperbole.

This impression adjusted well enough with the fearsome, inspired scrutinies of certain mystics,—in regards to Hell and to the paralyzing hideousness of the Irrevocable,—which he had read about, a long time before, and which had left on his memory something akin to burnt enthusiasms and the ecchymoses of poetry . . .

A double abyss opened up in this being, dating from this prodigious instant. Abyss of desire and of fury that nothing could gratify any more. Here, essential, inaccessible Glory; there, undulating, inexterminable human boorishness. Infinite fall on both sides, simultaneous failure of Love and Justice. Hell without counterweight, nothing but hell!

Christianity gave him its word of honor of blessed Eternity, but at what price! He understood now that raging hunger of tortures of his entire childhood. It was the presentiment of the terrible Face of his Christ! . . . Face of the crucified and face of the judge on the impassible pediment of the Tetragrammaton! . . .

Wretches have writhed and died for two thousand years before this inexorable enigma of the Promise of the Kingdom of God that one must always ask for and never attain. "When such things begin," it is said, "know that *your Redemption is near*." And how many hundreds of millions of human beings have endured life and death without having seen anything begin!

Marchenoir considered this lifting of innumerable arms perpetually supplicating and perpetually unfulfilled and he understood that this was the most enormous of all miracles.— Nineteen centuries already, he thought, that this has gone on, this request without response from a Father who reigns *in terrâ* and who gives deliverance. The human species must be terribly constant if it has not gotten tired of it already and if it has not given up in the cave of absolute despair!

He concluded on the conditional despair of millenarians.

He had felt Love come through, spiritual love, absolute love. He had, also, like all the others, poured his heart into that unfaithful riddle of the Lord's Prayer and . . . he had been saturated with perfect joy. There was something after all beneath the grave mounds, beneath this Curse of ashes that suffering hearts felt, something at the bottom of God's chasm of silence,—a principle of some sort of resurrection, of justice, of future triumph! By dint of amorous faith, he made eternity thrilling with a handful of time, molded in his hand, and fabricated hope from the most bitter pessimism.

He persuaded himself that it was a matter of a Lord God who was voluntarily a eunuch, infertile by decree, bound, nailed, expiring in the inscrutable reality of his Essence, as he had been symbolically and visibly in the bleeding adventure of his Hypostasis.

He had the intuition of a kind of divine powerlessness, *provisionally* concentrated between Mercy and Justice, with a view to some ineffable recuperation of squandered Substance on the part of Love.

Unheard of situation, invoking in an abject patois. The Ternary *Reason* suspends its payments for a number of centuries and it is up to human Patience to assist it with its own resources. The solvent Master of Eternity needs but Time, and time is made of the desolation of men. That is why the Saints and the Doctors of the Faith have always taught the necessity of suffering for God.

The burning neophyte, having divined these things, ripped out the thorn from his lame foot, that of a Catholic who had come so late, and,—pouncing on Grief,—made a sword of it which he plunged into his entrails after having gouged out his eyes.

More than ever, he was a desperate man, but one of those sublime desperate men who fling their heart into the sky, like a shipwrecked person who launches his fortune into the ocean to avoid drowning immediately, at least before having caught glimpse of the shore.

Besides, he thought the catastrophe of the secular tragic farce of Man to be too near. Certain surprising ideas about the history of the universe came to him, and when he followed them to their extreme consequences, they made him conjecture, with a quasi-prophetic authority of exegesis, the imminent accomplishment of scriptural Vaticinations.

The exaltation of humble men, the drying of tears, the beatitude of the poor and the damned, the paradisiac primacy of thieves and the regional crowning of prostitutes, and, finally, this very solemnly announced advent of the liberator Paraclete,—everything that the fratricide deafness of the rozzers of tradition had decried, everything that keeps orphans and captives from dying of horror,—he did not believe it possible that one would have to wait for long and he gave his reasons . . .

But only the famished were in on the little secret, not out of fear of being judged ridiculous or insane,—in that regard, there had been nothing to gain or to lose for a long time now,—but out of the horror of the visceral goodwill of happy digesters who would have listened to it.

XIV

Such was Marchenoir's doctrine. A doctrine that did not separate him from Catholicism, since the Roman Church permitted anything that did not alter the canonical Nicene Creed, but judged singularly audacious by the vendors of celestial countermark who vociferated their Sulpician patter on the muddy sidewalk of consciences.

A believer who wanted to compel second-hand sellers of salvation to re-weigh their merchandise before him and whom Christian pride revolted more than the Pharisaic crucifier of the Torah, could not make many friends among the priesthood.

He could only find one among them, a gentle and humble priest in the manner of that unknown emulator of St. Vincent de Paul, whom the people of Paris named the *Poor Priest* and who, one day, pressed by the all-powerful Cardinal de Richelieu who wanted to ask him some important favor, gave him this simple response:

"Your Eminence, please give the order to put new boards on the cart that carries those sentenced to death to their place of execution, so that fear of *falling onto the road* does not distract them from commending their soul to God."

Marchenoir had the unexpected fortune of unearthing a priest of this sort, but only for a short while. In general, the French Clergy loves neither saints nor apostles. It venerates only those who are long dead and returned to dust. Ligneous offshoot of the old Gallican stump and legatee of its coriaceous pride, it abhors above all the superiority of the spirit, naturally incompressible like water from the sky, and, by consequence, dangerous for sacerdotal equilibrium.

The Abbé T*** worked himself to death, not long after having made the acquaintance of the Périgourdin. Painstakingly kept aloof from any pulpit where his rare faculties as an apostolic preacher could have served for something, distressed by the cesspool of stupidity in which he saw the Catholic world engulfed, brought down with sorrow at the foot of the altar, he had barely had the time to sow the seeds of doctrine in this viviparous man whose immediate, monstrous fecundity would have been enough perhaps to make him die of terror.

It is certain that Marchenoir got from him the best that he possessed intellectually. The deceased had transmitted to him abstruse methods of sacred interpretation which had become straight away a universal algebra in the ardent mirror of that spirit concentrator. The pupil, more robust than the master, had violently repercussed from the first stroke, in all imaginable directions, the burning esotericism of an *integral* of divine Beauty, which the timid apostle, of a less incendiary nature, confined himself to covet with the resigned gentleness of a saint.

Marchenoir accomplished this marvel of surpassing all audacities of investigation or conjecture, without obliterating in himself filial submission to the sovereign authority of the Church. This wild colt, who confronted abysses, did not break his halter and stayed within the guard rails.

Only, he had succeeded to such escalations that contemporary Catholic society could no longer hold the least prestige for him. Obedience was a decree of his reason, a completely military homage and of pure confinement to the Eunuchs of the Seraglio of the WORD. Nothing else needed to be asked of him.

The *salt of the earth*,—to employ the sacred liturgical Text adopted by the *commonalty* of Doctors,—he saw it devoid of flavor, incapable of salting a slice of pork even, sedimentary gravel good at best for sanding old bottles or drying the paths of a fashionable park under the vast feet of the disdainful "Madame's lackey."

Invested with the most transcendental conceptions, he considered with horrific fright, this oecumenical college of the Apostolate, this famous clergicature that had really been "the light of the world,"—so formidable as yet that derision cannot touch it without splashing up onto God something like a tempest of mud,—having become, however, the mudscraper of the people and the foot mat of hippopotamuses!

He told himself that this here was justice, and that the great sacerdotal Prevarication was doubtless about to begin again, as the obduracy and theological turgidity of the Synagogue was returning,—with the aggravation, for lonely executioners, this time, of universal contempt.

From nascent Christianity's ignominy to expiring Catholicism's ignominy, the translation was finally drawing to an end in this chariot of glory that had trundled on for nineteen centuries, all over the earth!

The Lord had nothing else to do but to show himself. Pastors of souls were going to settle their accounts, more surely even than Princes of priests and Pharisees of the old law, who *did not know what they were doing*, according to the Gospel.

Systemic emasculation of religious enthusiasm by mediocre spiritual alimentation; hatred without mercy, Punic hatred of the imagination, invention, fantasy, originality, all the independence of talent; congenerous and concomitant absolute forgetfulness of the precept to evangelize the poor; finally, gastric and abdominal adhesion to the most repugnant sludge in front of the most powerful men of the century: such are the pustules and poisoned mushrooms of this large body, otherwise so pure! . . .

Marchenoir pressed his ear to all the doors of his hell in order to hear the coming of this God whom his own servants were going to murder.

XV

He had little consolation to hope for from the Christian laity. They are made in the image of their pastors and that is all one can say about it. Here, like there, innocence is almost always imbecilic when, alas, it is not corrupt.

The virile boldness of his faith and his religious probity's too eloquent indignations revolted, in the beginning, this wooly flock who went out grazing, under the guidance of parochial shepherd crooks, with the automatic roaring of small Dominican cataracts. Moreover, he was poor and, by consequence, prunable . . . He lived alone, in the neighborhood of a friend, a little less indigent, who had saved him from death fifteen or twenty times.

The ten years before his *conversion* had been similar to all his poor, goofy, timid, ambitious, melancholic, misanthropic, epiphonemic and brutal adolescent years. But he had brought from his province, in addition to the common baggage, the particular viaticum of powerlessness that I have mentioned above. This sempiternal dreamer could not see things for what they were and there was never perhaps a man of so little resource, less ambidextrous and lacking the nerve to take possession of the moment.

His only feeding trough, the copyist job that had been the pretext and means of his employment for the Parisian battle, to which he was so marvelously unfit, he lost at the end of several months. The office manager, a fat and favorably-disposed old man, but full of principles and without weaknesses, revealed to him one day that the administration was not going to pay him for doing nothing and saw him tranquilly to the door with incredible dignity.

It was the classic and very well-known poverty, so many times explored and described. The poor young man was absolutely good for nothing. He was one of those wild fruits, of a terrible bitterness that even cooking does not lessen and which must ripen for a long time on the vine of the poorhouse, as Balzac has judiciously observed in his ripe old age.

He had later made the calculation based on approximate deductions that he had undergone at that time, eight entire years out of ten, without taking any nourishment nor wearing any sort of clothing! . . .

Later, repulsed by every bit of cunning and every trick suggested by the ambition to subsist, he saw himself reduced to condescend to the most rudementary expedients. Diurnal collector and noctambulant investigator, he devoted himself half-starved to a quest for anything that could be gleaned or pecked at, on the mournful steppes of universal egoism, by the most flexing of needs, in view of appeasing his intestinal vociferation.

Forced to adjourn indefinitely his literary debut, he buried his precious head under the debris of his illusions and took off to agonize at the crossroads of indifference. "This tenebrous epoch was the Middle Ages of my era," he said, the day after his Christian *renaissance*.

The world of letters, to be honest, did not miss much. This spirit as knotted as a vine stock, condemned to search and hope for quite a long time, was to develop literarily only much later, under the emphyteutic watering of tears.

Public libraries having become for him a habitual refuge, he met that already-mentioned friend, the only friend he had ever had. He was a kind maniac of ecclesiastical history and pontifical monographs, a serene soul and mostly unbelieving, altogether the opposite of Marchenoir.

Deprived of fortune, as befits lapidarists of erudition, this didact lived poorly on a grayish bibliographic bulletin published in an important magazine. In this way, he saw pass before him the torrent of books launched into the world by contemporary foolishness or vanity.

Providentially, he was menaced with a deluge of work around the time he began to grow interested in this vagabond who had the air of walking in a glory of miseries and whose sorrowful physiognomy appeared extraordinary to him.

One day then, moved by compassion, he invited him to dinner and led him back to his place, that he might help him to clear away, he said, some of the heap of brochures whose sale alone could be useful. It is from the date of this blessed instant that Marchenoir launched himself into the envied career of *friend of the critic*, the only career that, for a rather long period of time, one saw him perform advantageously.

But, more importantly, he had a friend, finally! "A faithful friend, *medicamentum vitae et immortalitatis*,"[1] as the Holy Bible says mysteriously,—as if true friendship weighed as much as the billions of worlds necessary to counterbalance the transubstantiated bread crumb that these expressions recall!

---

1 *Medicamentum vitae et immortalitatis* is Latin for "medicine of life and immortality."

XVI

Women did not appear in Marchenoir's life until the end of this first period, that is to say, after the war and after that decisive jolt of the soul that had suddenly restored his religious feeling, the unknown predeterminations of which he had carried within himself, from birth.

Before then, he had been chaste in the same manner as prisoners and sailors, who do not ordinarily view love except as a desirable dirty friction, in the obscurity of costly dens. A stoical Tantalus before a feast of filth, he had resigned himself, as best he could, to the privation of unimaginable garbage. On one side, absolute deprivation, on the other, the most unbelievable timidity for such a violent man, preserved him more efficaciously than religion even, when the latter intervened to soften his heart . . .

Deep thinkers who professionally decree sweeping away any notion of religion, have the amusing contradiction of demanding that Christians whose faith withstands their scouring and potash should be, at minimum, saints. Above all, they want them pure. They tell them things as strong as this: "You sin, therefore, you're hypocrites;" a lacustrine enthymeme which has a certain authority on the palms and squamae of the anti-religious swamp.

This would still not be too silly, if it were merely a question, for the thinking soul handed over to invisible Devourers, of a difficult battle in which continual heroism were in order. After all, it is a judicious policy and barbed like experience even, to pile up on someone else's shoulders the crushing burdens that one would not wish to move merely with one's finger tips.

But religious feeling is a passion of love and behold what they will never comprehend, these pedagogues of our last childhood, when it would rain keys of light in order to open their understanding.

Now, this firebrand, thrown all of a sudden, from the most inaccessible of summits, into the miserable human cob, through the plowed thatch,—it would be necessary, however, to take it into account, if one wanted to be reasonable and just, at the last day of judgment! . . .

Marchenoir was, more than another, Love's conquest and his heart had been the evangelist of his reason. The punishments and rewards mentioned in sermons, in which the most selfless transports are explained so meanly, had no influence on him during his spiritual exodus. He had pounced on God as if on a prey, as soon as God had shown himself,—with the rudimentary spontaneity of his instinct.

Then, as if his destiny had been fulfilled at that instant, a sudden and correlative revelation was made, to him, Sorrow's chosen one, of his own affective power, until then unbeknownst to him, enveloped and floating in the amnion . . . A surprising avidity of human tenderness was the immediate accompaniment of this virgin heart's supernatural appetencies.

From the first moment, without having gone through the cesspool of intermediary concupiscent feelings, he found himself ready for the great passionate tribulation. Everything that poverty and a retractile pride's defiances had kept down until then, exploded: ignorance, silly prudery, gullible credulities, lyrical outbursts, dangerous demonstrations of tenderness, the sudden need to split his soul from top to bottom, in the midst of sexual whinnying even, and finally, all the naïve outbursts of a belated and grandiloquent cherubimism. Eternal squandering of the same treasures in order to arrive at the fatal fire of satisfied passion!

This eighteen-year-old ephebe, supercilious and badly dressed,—who carried his heart like a cockchafer in a lantern and whose redoubtable spirit, like a flower out of place on a cactus, was just beginning to smooth out the wrinkles under his membranous wrappings,—was too easy a prey for the busy libertine curiosities to leave alone.

Marchenoir made ecstatic love in filthy beds, with a lacerated conscience, detesting himself,—following the example of ancient Egypt's dusty anchorites whom the prodding of the flesh constrained sometimes to visit unclean cities in order to heal their mortified carcasses, but who ran away afterwards, filled with horror.

Feeling more guilty still, this assiduous relapse of incontinence left his foul rejection of the Bible, like so much dog's vomit, simmering in contemplation of feeble changes of heart. Torn between God and women, grieved by the perpetual fiasco of heroic purities that he had dreamed of,—equally incapable of hunkering down into a granite bias for unperturbed debauchery, of exterminating the interior voice that was springing up under the knife of penitential holocausts, he saw himself slapped around by imperturbable nature just as many times as he had prematurely hoped to dominate it.

Feeble penitent, without a doubt, but ashamed and humiliated. He confessed, at least, his distress and did not padlock exclusively his ignominy in the strongbox of confessionals and tabernacles. It would have been difficult to encounter a fornicator further from hypocrisy or from the slightest hint of self-satisfaction.

It must be said again, this adolescent was unlike any other. He was born for despair, and Christianity *deranged* his life, by filling it up,—too late!—with the afflictive famine of love, superimposed on the other famine. Short of a miracle that God would not perform, dazzled by the Face of the Lord,—mystical Icarus with melting wings,—how could he escape the vertigo that sucked him up toward the clayey creatures conditioned to this Resemblance? . . .

Evidently it would be crazy to expect that Monsieur Zola's contemporaries, for example, will have the kindness to concede that these infantile prolegomena possess the very rare moral grandeur about to be recounted. The deliquescent literary psychology at this end of the century will also not accept that so few perverse premises could ever engender a concluding esthetic delectation.

Finally and above all, the porcine congregation of free-thinking sycophants will be able to grant themselves the facile triumph of contemning,—right up to the vertical defecation!—the exact genesis of this Catholic tossed about by impure waves over absurd abysses . . . No matter!

XVII

Marchenoir wept beside his father's body, when he received at the same time two letters from Paris: one from Dulaurier and the other from his friend the bibliographer. He opened the last one straight away:

> My afflicted friend, here are five hundred francs that I was able put together, as best I could, rushing about like a madman just after your departure, and I send them to you with an infinite joy. No thanks are in order, above all. You know how I hate them, right?
>
> Dear suffering heart, do not let yourself be eaten up by your disappointment. You have your book to write. You have great things to say to certain souls, to whom nobody speaks anymore. Pull yourself together. I have no other words of consolation to offer you. Your unfortunate father, whom you no more killed than I killed my own, has much more need, at this hour, of your active *approbation* than of your tears. You must, it seems to me, understand this language.
>
> You did not write to me,—naturally!—and I did not expect it, despite your promise. But, on the other hand, you wrote to Dulaurier asking for money, as if I did not exist! I bumped into him just today, while I was in the process of putting some

money together for you, and he informed me of everything.

You are a traitor, my poor Caïn, and an imbecile thrown into the bargain. How could you hope that that puppet of letters, that Harpagon-Dandy, would act willingly to help you? Did you by chance descend into definitive senility by supposing that that so-called thinking compiler of every commonplace and every cliched inanity could have been able to even recognize the immense honor that you have done him by imploring him? It is too idiotic and if you were not so miserable, I would knock you senseless with insults.

He played me all the sounds on his mandolin, the wretch! He felt sorry, as always, for your disappointments, for your literary bad luck, etc. Then, taking my silence for approval of everything he was pleased to tell me, that eunuch,—for whom fanaticism consists in saying *yes* or *no* to whatever question is asked,—spoke, one more time, of your very regrettable intolerance and of your unjust, denigrating rage; he gave me his word of honor that your absurd principles were incompatible with the idea of a level-headed person and that acting like this you would amount to nothing. Fundamentally, he is terribly afraid of you and would like it if you remained in Périgueux.

I sensed perfectly that he wanted above all to defend himself in advance of any suspicion of miserliness. It appears that he pushed the limits of friendship by going to ask for alms on your behalf from the Doctor, who parted with several coins of one hundred sous, from what I could understand. It must not be much. Quite a nasty little affair, that there! I truly hope you will immediately return them their dirty money.

This Dulaurier made an admirable gesture: "Do you want my watch?" he said to me with a faint voice. "You could bring it to the pawnshop and send the money to that unfortunate man."

Me, never saying a word, I saw the onion[1] come out and then go back into the fob, finally to disappear, like some poor disdained heart. Then he turned at the Palais-Royal.

That grotesque oblation reminded me, however, that the hour was late. I hurried to congratulate him on his red ribbon and on the prize of five thousand francs that had been awarded him, entreating him gently going forward to extend his protection over several writers better than himself whose names I mentioned, and who never received any recompense for their work. He looked at me then, rolled his eyes, and immediately disappeared. I hope that I have rid myself of him again for quite some time.

Now, my dear friend, weep at ease, as much as you can, all at once, and when you have done, do what I ask of you.

Go to the Grande Chartreuse and ask for hospitality for one month. I know these excellent religious men, confide in them your ideas, your plans, they will make life pleasant for you and if you know how to please them, they will not let you return to Paris without resources. Do not hesitate, do not deliberate, I know what I am telling you. I will even write to the Father General to announce your arrival and introduce you. Staying on that mountain will be a poultice for your heart, and you can then resume your fight with new vigor which will disconcert many a sage.

---

1 "Onion" refers to a pocketwatch that is shaped like an onion.

Do not fret over Véronique. The good girl is killing herself praying for you eighteen hours a day. You can flatter yourself knowing that you are loved in a most extraordinary way. Her impatience to see you again is extreme, but she understands that I am giving you good counsel sending you to the Chartreuse.

You have nothing to worry about when it comes to beef stew and all that. I am here and you ought to know me by now, right? I embrace you.

GEORGES LEVERDIER.

XVIII

This Georges Leverdier, barely known in the world of letters, was in reality the only man Marchenoir could count on. Tight-fisted destiny had given him just this one friend and, even then, it had chosen someone who was poor, as if to empoison the act of kindness.

One must experience poverty to understand the horrible jest of an exquisite emotion struck by powerlessness. The crucifying archaic joke on love's wainscoted and trimalchionesque consolations in indigence, would not appear a less insupportable irony when it was a question of simple friendship. It is perhaps the most enormous of sorrows, and the most suggestive of hells, this quotidian necessity to elude reciprocal aid that might sometimes be bought at the price of one's life,—as if the miserable life of the Poor could ever have the weight of ransom!

Leverdier, crazy about Marchenoir, whom he regarded as a man of the rarest genius, and whom he was honored to be the *discoverer* of, had achieved marvels of devotion. He considered himself worth nothing before him and esteemed himself only in proportion to the services he could render him.

He had met him in 1869, fourteen years ago already,—when the wintry superiority of his surprising friend had not yet shown any sign of imminent maturity. But he had very effectively disentangled him, under the greedy foliage, from chimeras and prejudices that were retarding his development. He had even, as a horticulturist full of diligence, practiced, with a trembling pair of shears, some respectable pruning.

Marchenoir was in part his work. Cold by nature and not very enthusiastic, nevertheless this original critic had given his soul in slavery to this bronze Galatea who would have exhausted the fervor of a less intellectual Pygmalion. This gift of his entire being had gone as far as voluntary bachelorhood!—this devoted follower's piety not permitting him to step back before any advantageous immolation for his prophet.

It is true that he had nearly saved his life during the war. They were members of the same battalion of sharpshooters and, in the horrifying every-man-for-himself moment of retreat from Mans, the puny Leverdier, worn out by fatigue and twisted by the cold, would have died on the snow, in the middle of universal indifference, if his companion, endowed with an extraordinary vigor, had not carried him in his arms for more than two leagues and had not finally succeeded, by supplications and threats, to have him admitted onto the first cart they came across and which he nearly killed the driver of.

Also, Leverdier could not forgive himself for not being a millionaire. Voluntarily, he accused himself of his poverty as if it were treason.

"I detest money for its own sake," he said, "but I would gladly be a bag of crowns in Marchenoir's hands. I would thus have a plausible excuse for obstructing his way."

And, nevertheless, he was hardly assured of a future triumph! His mind, highly ablaze when it was fixed on his friend, became singularly lucid and cold when he lowered it to the contemporary public. The hope of a less somber future was for him inversely related to the height of genius that he assumed and this calculation was not without heartbreak.

Marchenoir, older than him by several months, had entered into his forty-first year, he had already published two books judged to be first-rate, but glory with her hands full of gold was not imminent. She prostituted herself in the urinals of journalism.

Leverdier had made unheard-of approaches to the managers and editors in chief who always refused to launch a writer whose independence outraged their abjection. What is more, this latter had never hidden his absolute disgust for them. Literarily, he shat on them. He let his faithful slave act on his behalf so that nobody could reproach him for having absolutely refused to help himself, but he would have chosen to have both arms and legs cut off with a horse-shearer's scissors and been sawn between two well-soaped boards balanced on bottles by a maniacal centenarian drunk for three days, before he would have consented to approach them in person in view of receiving, from their hands stinking of rotten eggs, a quarter of that arch-putrified carrion which they are procurers of and which they sell for real glory!

One could not reasonably prognosticate a more brilliant success for the new work he was preparing. Marchenoir always exasperated himself in his unbridled way, which evoked the superhuman invective of sacred Prophets. He made himself more and more torrential and a dike breaker.

Leverdier who admired him precisely because of this, could not, however, hide from himself that he was heading toward inevitable catastrophes. He ended up by siding with him and made himself the resigned pilot of the tempest and despair.

XIX

Leverdier's munificence dismayed Marchenoir without surprising him. For a long time now, he had gotten used to these wonders of devotion that racked him with inquietude. He did not bring it up, knowing that he was strapped for cash but capable, nonetheless, of skinning himself alive and tanning his own hide, if he could, to procure for his friend a little money. Although he knew perfectly well Dulaurier's affectionate egoism and elegant sordidness, he had hoped that, this one time at least, he would not dare to shy away from him and that the exceptional monstrosity of such a refusal would frighten him by its possible consequences. He had not foreseen the ruse with the doctor.

He laid, for a moment, the two letters on the dead man's face, as if to make him the judge, then he went to occupy himself with the funeral preparations, not without having sealed with care, in a new envelope, Dulaurier's one-hundred-franc bill which he sent back to him, the same evening, without adding a word.

He had a terrible need for a feeling that would protect him from his gnawing thoughts, and the message from his friend was, in every way, a deliverance.

His father was dead without recognizing him, or, what amounted to the same thing, without showing any sign that he recognized him. The silence of many years of separation and dissatisfaction had not been interrupted, even at this extreme moment. The last two hours of agony, he passed next to the moribund, on his knees, penitent, full of prayers, carrying his heart,—like a chalice,—in his trembling hands and hoping for a word, a glance or even a gesture of pardon to appear. The mystery of death had entered, without consulting them, and sat between them on a throne of enigmas . . .

This Queen of Sheba who perambulated ceaselessly with her frightening treasures of divination, Marchenoir knew well! He had called on her at ill-fated hours, and she had come and struck beside him,—so close that he smelled her breath and tasted her sweat. It left him with a rotten taste in his mouth and fissures in his heart.

But it seemed to have hit him harder this time. He had un-covered in himself an unknown filial palpitation and this new death, after so many others before it, seemed to him an enor-mous injury, out of proportion to the remainder of energy that he had left to go on.

At one moment, he forgot everything, the two living beings who loved him, the vast projects in his mind, even the cadaver that was going blue under his very eyes; a chilling blast of isolation came and whirled around in this mortuary room clouded over with fear; he felt "alone and poor," as in the story of the terrible Sabaoth, and he sobbed to himself like an abandoned child in the dark.

But, soon, the thorn of revolt, from black flowers, which he had transpierced his own hand with, renewed his throbbing pain. "Why such a hard life? Why this invincible aridity of the social humus around a wretched man? Why these gifts of intelligence, so similar to efficacious maledictions, which seemed to have been allotted to him expressly to torture him. Why, above all, this almost inevitable trap of his rational faculties in perpetually unequal conflict with his affective faculties? . . ."

Everything he had undertaken for the glory of truth or the comfort of his brethren had turned to his confusion or his misfortune. The impulses of the flesh, he had expiated them infernally enough! It was finished, now, all that, it was very far behind him, it was effaced by all the canonical penitences that erase Christian culpability. The torrent of filth had passed without returning, but the vase of memory had kept the most exquisite lees of ancient griefs, which had almost been immeasurable.

The cadavers of two women, formerly washed by his tears, appeared to him stretched out to the right and left of his father's, and a fourth, one hundred times more lamentable,—it was that of a child,—lay at their feet.

Of these two women whom he had adored to the point of madness and by whom he had accomplished the miracle of being loved exclusively, the first, wrested from a den of prostitution, had died of consumption,—after two years of shared poverty,— in a hospital bed where the ill-fated man, having no more than a sou, had been forced to carry her. Administratively advised of her decease and wanting, at minimum, to give the poor girl a proper burial, he had swallowed, in the momentary absence of his friend, swells of filth in order to acquire the several francs needed for the funeral procession that is given to the poor and he had arrived one minute before the statutory expiration date.

This deplorable naked corpse, thrown onto the tile of the amphitheater, disemboweled by autopsy, surrounded by unimaginable detritus, already exuding hideous charnel house fluids, had set in motion for this devastated contemplative the dangerous pedagogy of the Abyss!

XX

The experience of the second death had been no less tragic. This time, Marchenoir had not married her on the pallet of dejections, in the epithalamion bawl of a disgusting act of two drunken pigs in rut.

She was one of those poor women with a spirit of debauchery,—a tough case for Justice!—one of those irresponsible huntresses, ordinarily empty-handed, thinking with their kidney, wine waitresses without vocation, inept at tapping the human cask.

He had found her one night, on the street, distressed and without shelter. Her story, infinitely vulgar, was the upsetting story of one hundred thousand others just like her. Seduced by some faceless rascal who had disappeared almost immediately into thin air, chased out by her priggish family and not knowing which way to turn, like a piece of flotsam, she had fallen under the absolute domination of one of those sinister destructive louts, half pimp, half fink, who monopolize for their own profit the stuff of innocence.

Having been forced, for months, to transmute her flesh into lust's victual, under the quotidian menace of beatings, the unfortunate girl, decidedly unsuited, dying of horror and no longer daring to return to the horrible cave where she lived, accepted without hesitation Marchenoir's offers of service, his having possession in this particular instance of several one-hundred-sou pieces.

Incapable of taking advantage of a similar distress and full of evangelical intentions, he slept on a chair for several nights in a row, hiding in his room and in his bed this desirable creature who trembled at the very thought of going outside. He had to fall in love and he had to become passionate. In the end, the fragile Christian interrupted his cathedral slumbers and an unexpected pregnancy soon recompensed his fervor.

He was earning a little money at that time, at the State Archives, as a harpooner of unctuous documents, on behalf of a whale oil manufacturer, historic of the Institut de France. This enormous aggravation of his poverty did not frighten him. Practitioner of heroic concubinage, the circumstance of a newborn child, far from troubling him, appeared to him a providential addition of tribulations that ought to be blessed.

One evening, her pregnancy already well advanced, his mistress was brought back to him half dead and giving birth to the child. The mother had run into her old boss, been given a thrashing, and savagely trampled on, in plain view of a group of shopkeepers not one of whom intervened. The unfortunate girl died in the night, having given premature birth, leaving behind to the only friend she had ever had a crucifying souvenir of the most deliciously naïve feelings.

Like a wild beast, he lavished all his attention on his son. In this ancestral soul, altered by tender love, the paternal sentiment broke out like a fire.

It was a new sort of deliriousness, composed of all the precordial agitations of the past and all the anterior tempests, a sublime epitome of all the stormy vehemencies of passion, finally clarified, spiritualized, concentrated and hurled uniquely on the cradle of this debile little infant.

Fearing the murderous abominations of nurseries far from home, he wanted to keep him next to him and, by dint of loving energy, managed to keep him alive until the age of five. What this cost him, he himself would have been unable to say! But he wanted to be happy to suffer and took exquisite delight in railing against all his agonies. For his son, he would have accepted walking on a Milky Way of sorrows!

When, after having completed any of the fifteen or twenty humiliating employments that necessity had suggested to him, he would pick him up at an old neighbor woman's who was watching him in his absence; it was a cry and an ecstasy! . . .

He took up this little being as Hercules must have taken up the great Antaeus, son of earth, with an embrace that the crumbling of heaven could not have disentwined. He brought him into his room, like an abductor, and rolled him passionately on his chest. Mad kisses, babblings, cataracts of tears . . . He exhibited such penetrating outpourings of love that the child had no fear whatsoever of all these furies and only trembled because of the gentle trembling of those fearsome arms!

Seeing his father always in tears, he wiped his eyes with the ends of his too pale, feeble fingers,—"Poor little father, don't cry, you know that your little André doesn't want to die without your permission," he said to him, the *last time* they saw each other, with a precocious and surprising light of compassion in the two sepulchral lamps that were the wide eyes of the child marked for death.

This frail creature in normal circumstances should have expired immediately on the chest of the unfortunate man who was unable to be the thaumaturge that he needed to be to prevent his death. Even this redoubtable consolation was not granted to him! Destiny, until then merely pitiless, manifested itself suddenly menacingly atrocious, so demonically hideous that the very howling of an eternity of damnation could be defied to express the suffocation of despair of a more hermetic hell!

How did it happen exactly? This lost soul never succeeded in finding out. After three days of disappearance that nobody could explain, the body of the poor little fellow was discovered by Leverdier, at the Morgue, between a drowned man and woman who had been beaten to death and who vaguely resembled the mother. It was established that the *subject* had died for lack of nourishment.

How and why? Questions without response, unsolvable mystery that nothing could shed light on . . .

The good Leverdier endured some beautiful times! Marchenoir had fifteen days of frenzy, to put it mildly. The superintendent of police had to intervene at the burial and eight pairs of robust arms were needed to pull him away from his son's body. He only recovered at the end of two months from a sort of turbulent fever, his powerful organism having vanquished,—him alone, alas!—death, which had been judged almost inevitable for him, a half dozen times.

XXI

One imagines now what could have been Marchenoir's thoughts and feelings, on seeing the cadaver of his father whom he accused himself of killing. The spectral return of his own thoughts of paternal beatitude threw a fantastically desolate light,—similar to a moon going down and grazing the ocean on the horizon,— on the vengeful coalition of his remorses. The expiatory remonstrances of his past made it, once again, undeniably manifest for him, the stainless equity of swords in hearts that are ready to be run through.

It was true, however, that for him, the swords were judged too noble. What he had endured, it was a transfixion of wooden piles, embedded by the blows of hammers that weighed down the world, with one hundred thousand men at the capstan.

But in this instant of meditative retrogradation of his consciousness, invaded by the quasi-divine greatness of paternity and comparing the presumable sufferings of death to his personal sufferings, he persuaded himself that an infallible Justice had been exercised, here and there, as always, in irreprehensible arrests; although he proclaimed that he was lacking the intelligence to penetrate the indecipherable preambles. Having arrived by this route to a complete softening, the tears had redoubled in the precarious silence of his mind and the postman had had to deliver his punctual registered letter at the finest moment of a tempest of tears.

In his present disposition to magnify everything, the canine faithfulness of his friend appeared immense, superhuman to him and, by an unexpected stroke of good luck, he was not mistaken. Leverdier was truly unique. One could believe he had been created specially for this need of dedicating himself to an exceptional being who, without him, would have been completely alone. To employ an extravagant and monstrous image, this devotion was like a genital appendage of the virile superiority of Marchenoir, probably infertile without this providential testicle!

His letter was to him, then, a soothing balm, an electuary, a celestial refreshment. Without hesitation, he resolved to accomplish the voyage recommended to him by a man whose practical discernment he had had many occasions to experience. Moreover, this retreat to the Grande Chartreuse had been, for a long time, one of his vows and strangely appealed to him.

He was, certainly, quite far from cenobitic vocation. After the death of his child, two years before, he had had the idea of experiencing a Trappist order and he had sounded it out at Maison-Dieu. The experience, full well completed, had produced a superabundantly negative result and no one had bothered to tell him that an excessive activity of imagination was in opposition to the architecture of that rigid and pious acephalousness that one calls a Trappist.

But several weeks of contemplation in the more intellectual domain of St. Bruno seemed extremely desirable to him. He could, in the sedative peace of that desert, verify at ease certain metaphysical inductions still insufficiently elaborated, for a book he had undertaken in the drawn-and-quartered torments of his existence in Paris. Above all, he would press his extenuated soul against that monastic oak of silence and prayer which would communicate to him, doubtless, something of its tranquil vigor.

As for the woman whom Leverdier called Véronique and who was not Marchenoir's mistress, although she lived with him and through him, the pelican[1] solicitude of his Mameluke delivered him from any gnawing concern, on the subject of quotidian subsistence during his absence. What you have here is a story as simple as it is improbable.

Véronique Cheminot, known, formerly, in the Latin quarter by the expressive name of the *Suction Cup*, was a splendid wench whom ten years, at least, of prostitution out of twenty-five was unable to wither. And yet God knows the frightening journey of that ship of turpitudes!

Born in a Breton port, of a prostitute to sailors who had been mistakenly impregnated by an unknown cosmopolite, nourished, one knows not how, in that sewer, polluted since childhood, prostituted at ten years old, sold by her mother at fifteen, she was seen retailing herself in all the fish markets of lust, itemized by hand at all the counters of debauchery, hung up on all the hooks of the great tripe shops of licentiousness.

The Boulevard Saint-Michel had also known her, this audacious redhead who gave the impression of wearing on her head all the fires she was lighting in the juvenile loins of schoolboys.

She did not generally pass for a *good girl*. Even though she would have had strange crushes on men she claimed to have loved, this avid warrioress gave herself over to terrific depredations that rendered her infinitely redoubtable to families. With the exception of some rare and singular caprices that caused her to bed homeless vagabonds sometimes,—and which was explained inexactly by some abject nostalgia of particular submission to these refractory types,—her most authentic caresses were of an escalating venality, which approached lyricism. She had preserved this ingenuity of firmly believing that these men who desired her were all apoplectics of money that no bloodletting could ever make anemic.

---

1 A pelican, symbolizing a father's love for his child, the Christ being the most extreme example.

Her much-to-be-feared cupidity was not, however, hideous. She easily emptied her wallet into the hands of less patronized comrades and, sometimes even, she would indulge in the fantasy of brusquely inviting the first ragged beggar she came across, to the bloke's inexpressible consternation, exasperated by this dinner guest and menaced,—if he so much as ventured a seditious word,—by the appearance of Adamastor.[1]

XXII

Marchenoir had been designated to retire this Maelstrom from circulation. He hardly thought about it, however, when the thing happened. He was just beginning to recover and mend himself of the enormous emotional torment that has been recounted. He in no way felt disposed to renew these acts of rescue, these redemptions of captives that had cost him so dearly and which had been so numerous in the last ten years, although only the two most serious have had to be mentioned, because of their duration and their tragic denouement.

Besides, a great revolution had taken place in him, much earlier than the recent catastrophe. He lived according to the most ascetic continence, and sophisms of the flesh no longer had any part in his will's victorious determinations. Having arrived finally at the plenitude of his intellectual and physiological strength, he was, of all men, the most tender and least likely to be seduced.

No dramatic circumstance marked the commencement of his relations with the Suction Cup. Having ceased, since Leverdier, the ragged vagabondage of his beginnings, almost earning a living for himself and, also, often for others, by divers industries of which literature was the least lucrative, known already for the newspaper scandals and even a bit famous because of them, this somber individual, so different from everyone else and who never spoke to anyone, strongly intrigued the bohemian woman who

---

1 Adamastor: a fictitious Greek god of the sea.

saw him habitually breakfasting several paces away from her, in a little restaurant at the corner of the Observatory.

The outflanking maneuver was banal, as was fitting, and completely unworthy of the majesty of the story. In response to the ridiculous remarks that she believed she could initiate a conversation with, she obtained from Marchenoir, very gentle under his mask of a fanatic, by way of reply, without even looking at her, inanimate monosyllables that one would have believed painfully drawn by a pulley from the bottom of a well of silence.

Exasperated by this mediocre result, she said to him one day:

"Monsieur Marchenoir, I like you and I desire you, do you want to sleep with me?"

"Madam," responded the other with simplicity, "you have really come at the wrong time, I never sleep."

And it was true. He was working furiously day and night and did not sleep but a few hours in an armchair, which he explained laconically.

This redhead, very stupefied, then undertook something quite new for her, an outpouring of sage remonstrances. She spoke like a prudent mother of the necessity of a better hygiene, of the number of hours in the day and of the need for repose at night, which was made for sleep, she assured him. Finally, she recognized that *a man of thought* needed to have someone to take care of his little affairs, etc. and Marchenoir paid for his breakfast and never returned.

One month later, coming back home one cold midnight, he found her squatting and shivering on his doorstep. Not asking for an explanation, he let her into his room, lit the fire, showed her his bed and went to work. Not a word was said.

She came and wrapped her superb arms around his neck.

"I love you," she whispered. "I'm crazy about you. I don't know what I have. I don't want to think about it any longer, this caprice I've had to hold you in my arms, but this evening, I dragged myself on my knees to come here. I see quite clearly you're not like the others and you must proudly despise me. That's fine, tell me what you want, but don't push me away."

And the shameless vanquished woman, afraid she might displease him with a kiss, fell to the floor at his feet and broke down in tears.

Marchenoir felt a shiver of death. "Will it never end?" he thought to himself. He bent over and, parting the thick hair of this Salamander of the depths, streaked with flames,—with a gentleness that approached tenderness, he recounted to her his poverty and his immense mourning; he represented to her, without hope of understanding, the impossibility of knotting and tying together two existences such as their own and his horror, up until then insurmountable, of any sharing of lives, in the past or in the future.

At this word *sharing*, the beautiful girl lifted her head and, without wishing to get up, placed her hands as a supplicant on the knees of the master whom she had chosen for herself:

"Forgive me for loving you," she said, in a singularly humble voice. "I know I'm worth nothing and I don't merit your attention. But there can be no sharing. I'm taken by you and I can't do without you, you only. The infamies of my past, I blame myself for them as if they were infidelities I've committed against you. You're a religious man, you'll not refuse to save a wretch who wants to repent. Let me be near you. I don't ask for anything, not even a caress. I'll serve you like a poor domestic, I'll work and I'll become maybe a good Christian in order to resemble you a little. I beg you, have pity on me!"

Marchenoir had never been so affected in his life. He did not believe he had the right to send her back to market, this slave who appeared to offer herself even more to his God than to him. All the dangers that can result for a strict Catholic from so imminent a habitual opportunity to lack continence, he accepted them, with the resigned certainty of compromising and overwhelming his life abominably.

Several months later, he set Véronique up in a little apartment for working-class people on the rue des Fourneaux, at the end of Vaugirard. Then began that so calumniated cohabitation of two absolutely chaste beings, so perfectly united and so profoundly separated at the same time. The formidable machine for winnowing men that was called the Suction Cup, became, miraculously, a very pure girl and an ever-burning thurible before God. The religious practices, at first begun in view of identifying herself with the man she loved, soon became a necessity of love, her love even, transfigured, transported into the infinite!

XXIII

There were few people at the burial, the coffins of the poor not being, in Périgueux as elsewhere, escorted by multitudes. It is true that Marchenoir, having forgotten the names of most of his fellow citizens from the past, limited himself to having inserted into the *Echo de Vésone* a paragraph of general convocation to the obsequies of the deceased. Besides, the funeral Liturgy of the Church,—the greatest thing on earth in his eyes,—acted on his entire being, in this circumstance, with an unprecedented force, and he was the only person who did not notice the exiguity of condolent cattle.

For a man disillusioned with life such as he was, who had known only the most atrocious rigors, and who seemed to have been born a eunuch to the joys of this world, there was in the religious ceremony of death a vertiginous force that completely confiscated him with an absolute despotism. It was the only majesty that this rebel did not resist. He was often seen following the funeral processions of people he did not know and he needed to be urged not to enter a church when its doorstep was draped in black advertising some funeral ceremony. How many hours he had passed in the cemeteries of Paris, at infinite distances from the din of society, deciphering the old tombstones and the superannuated epitaphs of adolescents in ash, whose contemporaries were ancestors today and whom no one in the world remembered any more!

In the eyes of this universal contemnor, Death was really the only sovereign that had the power of ennobling the human riff-raff for good. The most abject mediocre people became august to him as soon as they began to rot. The carrion of the filthiest bourgeois settling comfortably into and confining himself to his bier for a serene deliquescence, appeared to him a surprising testimony of the original dignity of man.

Because of this irrational induction, ebbing back internally onto the syllogistic plexus of his mind, Marchenoir had always been full of conjectures before all the funereal signs. Without doubt, oracles of the faith touching on the final aims and ultimate retribution of the responsible animal, sufficed for this believer. But the visionary underneath the believer had quite other exigencies, that God alone, without doubt, would have been able to satisfy.

It just so happens that this word exigency riled him. He, whom death had so torn apart, stiffened, transported by rage, against the rhetoric of resignation, which calls *repose* or *sleep* the liquefaction of the eyes and the gnawing of the hands of the loved one, and the teeming of helminths in its mouth, and all the inexpressible violations of matter on this so pointlessly spiritualized clay. He found that the exigency was not really the man's, whose wife or child had been taken away, in order to do he did not know what with, and who was asked to wait for them until the consummation of the centuries!

If this was not a derision to make the stars fall down, it was terrible to ask in exchange for such precarious gifts! Even if we knew everything, it would be intolerable, and the truth is that we know nothing, absolutely nothing, except what Christianity has wanted to tell us.

But whatever! It is an atom of hope to weigh against a mountain of terrors! Religion alone gives the certainty of immortality, but it is at the price of a *possible* hell, of disfiguration without return, of the eternal monster!

This poor creature that he weeps over, this miserable child, whom he calls out to in desolate clamors in the late hours of his nights,—who was his terrestrial paradise, his tree of life, his refreshment, his light and the peace in his struggles,—he did not have to imagine, at least, that it was enough for him to have seen him die and to have handed over his deplorable corpse to the hideous devouring things that lie under the earth. If his soul is deep, all that is just the beginning of sorrows.

There is,—and let him not forget it!—heaven and hell, that is to say a chance for beatitude against the seventeen hundred thousand maledictions and sempiternal wailings, as St. Thomas Aquinas teaches us, whose doctrines the Good Shepherd did not seem to have predicted.

The irresistible impulses of the heart that threw the ill-fated woman into his arms, the nearly chaste, but not permitted, caresses, that made him forget, for an instant, the abomination of his misery,—while he waited comfortably under the flowering chestnut trees,—she is probably in the process of expiating them in a way that one could not, without dying of laughter, see him undertake to conjecture.

All divine power is armed in order to torture this sweet little girl who drank the tears from her eyes and who got down on her knees to wash his bleeding feet, when he had walked too much for her redemption. There is now pitted against her a complete Xerxian army of fears. The innermost essence of fire will be drawn from the active core of the most enormous stars for an inconceivable flagrance of tortures that will *never* end. This dreadfulness of sepulchral putrefaction that is to make the horses of the Apocalypse rear up,—ah! it is nothing, it is beauty even, compared to the supernatural infamation of the image of God in this burning pit of rottenness! . . .

The desolate Catholic had often had these thoughts that knocked him to the ground, howling, epileptic, foaming with horror. "Ten thousand years of separation," he cried, "I will take it, but at least let me know where they are, those whom I have loved!"

Extravagant obsecration of an ardent soul! He would have accepted everything, the diadem of toads, the moving necklace of snakes, eyes of fire shining at the end of verminous arcades, viscous arms, swollen, sucked at by snails or spiders, the frightening belly full of antennas and undulations,—in short, appearances that would slay him on the spot,—if it would have been possible to learn something at the cost of this monstrous profanation of his memories!

And now, at the edge of the pit where, the preacher having gone, the shovelfuls of earth fell like shovelfuls of centuries on eternity's new intern, he did not find, after all the reckoning, any other refuge than Prayer. This wearied soul no longer exhausted himself with useless somersaults and convulsions. A surprisingly faithful Catholic, he managed to retain the Tridentine dogma of everlasting hell, by removing the *irrevocability* of damnation. He had found the means to set it upright and to give it the breath of life, this perfect antinomy that so resembled a contradiction of terms, even though it became a singularly plausible opinion when he explained it. But prayer alone truly worked wonders,— the infinite simplicity of prayer by which a powerful and hidden life welled up from deep within him, above the most unknown abysses of his thoughts . . .

He remained for a long time on his knees, so long that the gravediggers had completed their duty and, full of astonishment, let him know that they were going to close the gates to the cemetery. He had the satisfaction of leaving alone, having had a great fear of the crocodiles of sympathetic regret. His departure from Périgueux was scheduled for the following day and he decided that he would see no one. He returned then immediately, had a meal prepared for him, and passed a portion of the night writing the following letter to his friend Leverdier.

XXIV

I received your money, my faithful, my one and only Georges. I will do what you counsel, as if it were the divine Third Person[1] who had spoken, and all thanks to you. I have just returned from the cemetery and I leave tomorrow for the Grande Chartreuse.

I write to you in order to confide in you my emotions of the last few days. They were great and terrible. A virginity of heart has been remade for me, I think, precisely so that I might see my father expire whom I do not believe, certainly not, that I loved all that much. You know how little a place he wanted to have in my life. We were hardened against one another, for a long time, and I was expecting nothing more than this obscure trepidation that gives mortals the immediate and sensible vision of death. It happened that I needed to take an ax and sever the cables in order to escape from this dead man who has been buried in the earth . . .

I am saturated, knotted with sadness, my friend, something that changes me not in the least, you will be convinced, but the great crisis is past and tomorrow's trip appears to me like one of those frozen and soothing dawns that I saw break, two years ago, from my bed when I was feverish, after a night of phantoms. They have hampered my life ever since, the phantoms! They surround me, they press against me like a crowd, and more frightening still, alas! are the innocents and the very pale ones who look at me with their pitiful eyes and who do not reproach me!

---

1 Third Person, of the Trinity.

I have just arrived, moaning, here at my father's poor house where I was born, where I was raised and which must be sold in order to pay old debts, as has been explained to me. The melancholic sonority of these empty rooms, hemmed in, for my imagination, by so many ancient memories, has echoed profoundly inside me. It seemed to me that I was wandering in my soul, deserted forever.

Pardon, my good Georges, this last word. I believe that I will never be able to say exactly just what you are for the somber Marchenoir. I have an older brother who died very young, in the same year as my mother. Just now I found children's playthings that belonged to him. I have spoken about him with you already. He was called Abel and it is, without a doubt, what made my father rig me out with the name Caïn that I am so proud of. I would have been able maybe to love him a lot if he could have lived, but I do not represent him to myself as you, and I would not voluntarily call you my brother.

You are something else, a little more and a little less, I do not know exactly. You are my guardian and my roof, my holocaust and my equilibrium, you are the dog on my doorstep, I do not know what you are any more than I know what I am myself. But, when we are dead in our turn, if God wants to do something with our dusts, he must knead them together again, that architect, and he must look at it three times before employing the strange cement that his hands of light will apply to it!

You are of course correct to reproach me for having written to Dulaurier and I am also correct, very probably, to have done it. He thought it suitable to respond to me with a letter that dishonors himself. Is that not a good result? Everything you wrote to me about him, he took pains to write to me also. The poor boy, he can barely hide the terror that I inspire in him.

Frankly, I had believed that this sentiment that I am well aware of, for want of magnanimity, would have conquered his avarice and made him render me the simple service I had asked him for. He had the goodness to recommended to me the *common grave*, reminding me of Christian humility. To be so imprudent, he must believe me completely vanquished, otherwise it would be too stupid to outrage a man with a good memory and who has a quill to revenge himself with!

As for the doctor, I did not anticipate his getting involved in this business. Ah! they are right to think of themselves, and to cherish themselves, these slave traffickers of friendship who have thrown me overboard at the moment they are given chase, and who would lay at my feet treasures of their devotion if I obtained a success that made me formidable! With what joy I have sent back their money, you can easily divine.

But let us leave that behind. I have received a visit by the family notary. I suppose he has other clients, for he is fat and shiny like a sea lion. This authentic individual brought me infinite explanations that I did not understand anything about, except that my father, living only on a retirement pension, left absolutely nothing but his house and the furniture, neither one of much value, which I knew as well as he did. But he revealed to me certain debts I was not aware of. Everything must be sold and a buyer has already been found, it appears. I believe even to have disentangled that I could take with me not much more than the wind coming out of a large bellow. No matter, I signed what I had to sign, the knave having prepared all the paperwork in advance. The poor do not have the right to a hearth, they have no right to anything, I know, and I bind my heart with the best metal of my will to sign more firmly.

I hope to receive several hundred francs that will be sent to me, once the jiggery-pokery is consummated. That will be my inheritance. If your Father General of the Carthusians wants to gratify me from his side, it will not hurt me any to receive the alms from his hand. We will be able, then, to make acquisition of a new battle horse for revenge or for death. I have the presentiment that it will be more likely death and I truly believe that I would need to bless him, because I begin to grow furiously tired of playing the Tantalus of justice!

Tell my dear Maria the Egyptian that she should continue to pray for me in the desert of our arid lodgings. She could do nothing more useful for me. You do not understand too well all that, my poor minion. You only know how to suffer and how to sacrifice yourself in my service, as if I were a Manitou of the first order, and the unrivaled wonder of this girl consummated by mystical love is almost entirely lost on you. All the miracles of the Exodus from Egypt were accomplished in vain, in your eyes, in the person of that escapee from the ergastulum of cat worshippers and eaters of the onion-vomitings of Lust.

For me, I grow each day in admiration and I consider myself infinitely honored to have been chosen for the recuperation of this lost drachma, this evangelic pearl scented and contaminated by the groins of so many swine.

It is strange that I should be the very man needed to bring together two beings so exceptional and so perfectly different. In your emulation to cherish me, it is you, the man of ice, who sets me on fire and it is she, the enflamed, who tempers me. You will never be satisfied with what you call my audacities and she trembles sometimes for what she naïvely calls my *justices*. At the same time, you reproach each other for exasperating me. Dear and unique witnesses of my most hidden tribulations, you are both quite extraordinary and we make, the three of us, quite a surprising assemblage!

Today, you send me off to Chartreuse with the same oracular air that you used, previously, when you wanted to divert me from going to the Trappist monastery. Only, this time, I obeyed you without discussion and even with as much joy as possible. Such is the progress of your genius.

You make yourself guarantor of the restorative and intelligent hospitality of the Carthusians. I believe it willingly. However, it is improbable that I will write much from their quarters. But I will put some order to the shambles of my thoughts and I will make the river of deepest meditation pass through the Augean stables of my mind.

What book could be mine, however, if I birthed what I have conceived! But what an oppressive, what a formidable subject! The *Symbolism of History*, in other words, providential hierography, finally deciphered in the innermost arcana of facts and cabala of dates, the *absolute* meaning of chronic signs, such as Pharsalia, Theodoric, Cromwell, or the insurrection of March 18, for example, and the *conditional* orthography of their infinite combinations! In other words, the linear calculus of the divine plan rendered as sensible as the geographic delimitations of a planisphere, with a complete corollary system of conjecturable apperceptions in the future!! . . . Ah! this is not yet the book that will make me popular, supposing I could even write it!

I leave you now, my friend, fatigue crushes me and time gallops furiously onward. I must make haste to flee from this town where I have only memories of sorrow and perspectives of disgust. Now, I have much to burn, before my departure, in this house that will be sold. I do not want any profanations. But, it will not be fertile in gaiety, either, this execution of all the remains of my childhood! . . . Good evening, my dear faithful friends, and see you again in several weeks.

MARIE-JOSEPH CAÏN MARCHENOIR.

XXV

Two days later, Marchenoir began his ascent of the Desert of the Grande Chartreuse on foot. When he had crossed what is called the Fourvoirie entrance, the imperceptible groove between two monstrous rocks, above which modern life appears brusquely interrupted, a sort of joyous peace melted over him. He was going to find out what this famous House of Christianity was all about,—so foolishly seen, these days, through the fumes of democratic alcoholism,—an alpine hive of the most sublime workers of prayer, whom an old writer compared to the Burnings of heaven and whom he called for the same reason, "Seraphims of the Church Militant!"

People whitewashed with a light coat of Christianity, who want pilgrimages to be easy, affirm under oath that the monastery is inaccessible during the snowy season. The happy effect of this prejudice is a periodic restitution of the antique Carthusian solitude so desired by St. Bruno for his monks.

The enormous influx of travelers, in what is usually called good weather, must be, for the hermits, a very heavy importunity. The faith of the greatest number of these curious people would certainly not have the evangelic strength to enable them to scale the mountains, and many come and go who do not have any other spiritual baggage than the stupid tourist diary without ingenuity. It does not matter! They are received as if they had fallen out of the sky,—worldly aerolites of little fulguration, who never disconcert the welcoming resignation of the hospitable monks.

The Grande Chartreuse must therefore be visited in winter by those who wish to have an exact idea of that marvelous combination of the eremitic life and the communal life that characterizes the essence of the Carthusian order, and whose triumphant experience has lasted, now, eight centuries.

Founded in 1084, the order of St. Bruno,—a glorious oak that covered the Christian world with its powerful foliage,—alone among all the religious orders, merited this testimony from the Papacy: "*Cartusia nunquam reformata, quia nunquam deformata*, the Carthusian order, not having been deformed, never had need to be reformed."

In a century as disposed as our own to the lampreys and morays of a final anarchy that threatens to feast on the world, it is at least interesting to contemplate this unique monument of Europe's Christian past, still standing and intact, without wavering and without stain, in the middle of the torrent of centuries.

A contemporary Carthusian author has written:

> Where does that come from? From the wisdom that accompanies necessarily the resolutions of the Definitory, since their Ordinances are not obligatory until after they have been put to the test; since their Constitutions must be approved by those who did not make them. What saved us is the free, impartial, always independent Definitory, because the

monks who can and must compose it arrive at the Chartreuse ignorant of, or uncertain of, their nomination; they come there without any preconceived ideas, free from bias: intrigue and cabal would be impossible.

At the annual sessions of the General Chapter, the first occupation of that assembly is to form the Definitory, composed of eight *Definitors* named by secret ballot and not having belonged to the definitory of the preceding year. This definitory, presided over by the R. P. General, is charged with the property of the whole Order and exercises, conjointly with the dean, the plenitude of power, with respect to ordinances, statutes, and definitions.

What saved us is the energy of that type of council, composed of members from different nations who, for the most part, have not lived with and ought not to associate with those on whom they will pass a just sentence. Perfectly free, it has never receded, on any occasion, before an energetic attack. Never, in the entire Order, never, in a Province, has an abuse been approved, not even tacitly; we can even say, history in hand, that no serious breach in the fundamental Rules of the Carthusian life has ever been tolerated in any Chartreuse. The Definitory warned, waited, insisted, menaced; finally, it took an extreme, but decisive, view of the common good. It has cast out such house that no longer observed the Rule in its entirety and refused to amend and to submit; it cast it out, declaring that neither people nor property belong to the Order, leaving to the refractories, edifices, rents, properties, everything, except the Carthusian name and the Rule of St. Bruno, *Cartusia nunquam deformata*, because from the moment the Order expanded, at the beginning of the twelfth century, our ancestors knew to give us a Constitution as strong as it was broad, as wise as it was protective of the only true liberty that consists, not of being capable of doing evil or good, but, on the contrary, of being in the happy necessity of doing nothing but good, while choosing, from among what is good, what seems to us best.

For the rest, it suffices to traverse the barriers of that celebrated Desert in order to feel the sudden absence of the nineteenth century and to have, as much as possible, the illusion of the twelfth. But, the route must not be encumbered with the noisy caravans of curiosity. Then, it is truly the haughty and formidable Desert that God himself, they say, had designed for his servant Bruno and his six companions so that their spiritual posterity might chant there, for eight hundred years, at least, in the august peace of the elevations, the Jubilation of the earth before the face of the Lord King, *Jubilate Deo omnis terra . . . Jubilate in conspectu Regis Domini!*

Marchenoir had never savored so profoundly the religious and calming beauty of silence, as in that ascent to the Grande Chartreuse, between Saint-Laurent-du-Pont and the monastery. It had snowed heavily during the night and the entire passage, covered with white like a Carthusian monk, blinded the eyes under the gray matte of a low and heavy sky that seemed to lean against the mountain. Only the torrent that rolled at the bottom of the savage gorge cut into, with its fracas, the immobile taciturnity of that sleeping nature. But,—in the manner of a single voice in a very solitary place,—that clamor below, which mounted while dissolving into space, was devoured by the dominating silence and made it appear deeper still and more solemn.

He leaned over—to regard while dreaming that wild and bounding water, which is inappropriately called the *Guiers-Mort*, and whose color, like blue steel when it rushes forward, resembles an undulating green moire of foam, when it gathers, while trembling, in a conch of rocks, for a more furious outburst and more irremediable fall.

He began to think on the enormous duration of that river's existence which has flowed thus, for God's glory, for thousands of years now, much less uselessly, of course, than the many men who lack its beauty and who seem to be fleeing and groaning in order not to have their own image reflected in it. He remembered that St. Bernard, St. Francis of Sales, and many others, after St. Bruno, had come to this place; that the poor and the powerful, having escaped from the world, had passed by here, for half of Christianity's history, and that they must have been enticed, as he was, by that image of leaving everything of the century behind them forever . . .

A meditation of this sort and in such a place is singularly powerful on the soul and recommended for those who are tired of life and groping along. Marchenoir, as wounded and also bloody as a miserable man could be, felt an infinite sweetness, the calm of good death, unsuspected until that instant. He bathed in the forgetfulness of his immortal sorrows, alas! and which would, a little later, seize him again. The more he climbed, the greater his peace grew, his entire being melting and evaporating in an almost superhuman mellowness.

An adorable page of naïvety that he had previously learned by heart, so beautiful did he find it, came back to his memory and sang within him, like an Aeolian harp with the Virgin's strings animated by sighs of seraphim.

This page he had found in an ancient *Life* of the celebrated Father de Condren, whose doctrine was so sublime, it appeared, that Cardinal de Bérulle wrote down all that he heard while kneeling. See for yourself in what terms that astonishing personage expressed himself on the Carthusians:

> These are men chosen by God to express, in the most naïve and exact way possible by human creatures, the state of those whom the Scripture calls *the*

children of the Resurrection, and to live in a mortal body, as if they were pure immortal spirits. They are then lifted out of themselves non-stop into a contemplation of divine things; there is no night for them, for it is during the darkness of the earth that they perform the saintly operations of children of light. They are all honored with the saintly character of the Priesthood, since St. John testifies that all the saints will be priests in heaven. Their habits are the color of those of Angels, when they appear to men; their modesty and their innocence is a painting of sage simplicity and the righteousness of the Fortunate.

Their habitation in the mountains of the Grand Chartreuse is not a sojourn for worldly people; one must have nothing but the spirit to subsist in such a dwelling place. Also, one can leave the tombs of all sorts of monasteries to come and revive among the resuscitated saints, but when one has arrived in this Paradise, there is nothing else to hope for on earth. One can come here from any place in the world, even the most sacred, but when one has arrived in this *House of God* and this *Gate of Heaven*, one must be a saint or one will never become one!

"To be a *saint!*" cried Marchenoir, as if delirious, "who can hope for it? . . . Job, whose patience is celebrated, cursed his mother's womb, four thousand years ago, and it would take four hundred million desperate and exterminated men to compensate the sufferings that the birthing of a single elect might cost old humanity! . . . Will it always be like this, O celestial Father, who have promised to reign on earth? . . ."

XXVI

The ensemble of constructions of the Grande Chartreuse cover an extent of five hectares and its buildings are protected by forty thousand square meters of roofing. From the topographical point of view alone, these numbers sufficiently justify the epithet *grand* inseparable from the name Chartreuse, when one wants to designate this *caput sacrum*[1] of all the chartreuses on earth.

First crushed by an avalanche, the day after its foundation, and reconstructed almost immediately in the same place, less exposed to the fall of snow masses; devastated twice from bottom to top by the Calvinists and the revolutionaries, this admirable Metropolis of contemplative life has been burned eight times in eight centuries. These eight trials by fire, symbol of Love, recall in their own way the eight evangelical Beatitudes, which begin with Poverty and finish with Persecution.

Finally, on 14 October 1792, the Grande Chartreuse was closed by decree of the national Assembly and only reopened 8 July 1816. For twenty-four years, this solitude became mute again, silent as it had been for so long, mute and desolate like the impious cities of the East depopulated by the Lord's anger.

It had to pay for an insolvent people who were pressed by retribution's sting, in accomplishment of that transcendental law of supernatural equilibrium, which condemns the innocent to acquit the ransom of the culpable. Our limited notions of equity cannot accept Justice's distribution of Mercy. *Each man for himself*, our baseness of heart says, *and God for all*. If, as it is written, the hidden things must be revealed to us one day, we will know, no doubt, in the end, why so many weak people were crushed, burned and persecuted throughout the centuries; we will see with what infinitely calculated exactitude were divided, in their time, the prosperities and the sorrows, and what miraculous equity necessitated temporarily the appearances of injustice!

---

1 Latin for "sacred head."

A thing worthy of remark, the Grande Chartreuse continued to be inhabited. An infirm monk remained there and was never disturbed, even though he always wore the habit. April 7, 1805,—it was Palm Sunday,—he was found dead in his cell, on his knees at his oratory: he had given his soul up unto God, while praying. A few days later, Chateaubriand visited the Grande Chartreuse.

In his *Memories from Beyond the Tomb* he wrote:

> I cannot describe the sensations that I feel in this place! the buildings bathed in the sun under the surveillance of a sort of farm in ruins; a lay brother resided there to take care of an infirm recluse who was about die. Religion had imposed on friendship fidelity and gratitude. We saw the narrow grave, freshly covered.
>
> We were shown the convent's enclosure, each of the cells accompanied by a garden and a shop; we noticed there joiners' workbenches and the wood-turners' lathes, and a chisel that had been dropped on the ground! A gallery displayed portraits of the Superiors of the Order. The ducal palace of Venice keeps the series of *portraits* of the Doges, diverse places and memories! Higher up, at a distance, we were conducted to the immortal recluse Lesueur's chapel. After having dined in a vast kitchen, we took our leave.

Today, the Grande Chartreuse is as prosperous as ever. The innumerable visitors can give testimony to the surprising vitality of this last root of the old monastic trunk, which four revolutions and four republics were unable to extricate from French soil.

It would be childish to undertake a one-hundred-and-first description of that celebrated City of voluntary renunciation and real joy, known today by all who read and think in the universe. Moreover, Marchenoir was not visiting the Grande Chartreuse as an observer, but as a sick man and, later, he would have been seriously embarrassed to give an account of his hours of sojourn that lasted nearly a month.

He had simply resolved to bury himself, if he could, in the silence, in that contemplation, in that silver twilight of prayer, which heals anger and which heals sadness. He knew in advance how important solitude is to men who want to live, more or less, a godly life. God is the great Recluse who never speaks but to the recluses and who does not share his power, his wisdom, his felicity, but with those who participate, in some manner, in his eternal solitude! Without doubt, solitude is realizable everywhere and even in the midst of the common pack of men,—but what souls that demands, and what exile for such souls! Now, he had one foot in the country of exiles: the Carthusian order of Saint Bruno, the most perfect of all monastic conceptions, the great school of imitators of God's solitude!

Marchenoir found there precisely what he had come looking for, what he had already begun to find on the way there: peace and charity.

"*Levavi oculos meos in montes*," he said to the father who received him, "*unde veniet auxilium mihi.* [1] I bring you my soul to be resoled and cleaned. I hope you can tolerate these expressions of a cobbler. If I employed anything less noble, I would express even better the immense disgust that fills me, the indigent artist who comes to implore hospitality from the Grande Chartreuse."

The other, a long-pacific monk, with a joyous tonsure, regarded the hirsute and responded to him with gentleness:

"Sir, if you are miserable, you are the dearest of our friends, the *mountains* of the Grande Chartreuse have ears and whatever help they can give you they will not fail to give you. As for your spiritual footwear," he added laughing, "we sometimes

---

1 "I lifted my eyes to look on the mountains . . . whence help will come to me."

95

work in an old-fashioned way, and perhaps we will succeed in satisfying you."

The jubilant physiognomy of this fully intelligent monk pleased Marchenoir immediately. In the several pressed and rapid words of this preliminary conversation, he exposed to him his entire earthly adventure. He told him his labors and the ambitious petitions of his thought. "I want to write the history of the *Will of God*," as he formulated it, with that arresting precision of oratory discobolus that seemed the most surprising of his gifts.

To mention it here in passing, Marchenoir, at the time of the Roman Republic, would have been a tribune, like the Gracchi Brothers, and he would have walked on an equal footing on the antique face of the earth. The world's mistress willingly took her masters from among the thunderbolt bearers, those men, who boomed when they spoke, whom the human species,—mute with stupefaction since its fall,—has always pricked up its ears to.

This faculty, completely superior in him, had had a delayed development compared to his other faculties. For a long time, his mouth was stitched shut and his tongue was thick. His natural timidity, a then repressive education, the dampener of all the miseries of his youth, had exceptionally prolonged his childhood hesitations and stammering. He needed the decisive encounter with Leverdier and the new existence that followed from it in order to untie at the same time his heart, his mind and his tongue. One day, he rose armed to the hilt . . . never having waged battle before,—the orator's only vent in modern times, that is to say, parliamentary politics, horrified him.

This thundering should have darkened his window panes. Only, sometimes, he flashed out and it was superb. As an imprecator, particularly, he was unprecedented. He was heard roaring like a black lion, in the newspaper managers' offices, whom he accused, justifiably, of giving the bread for men of talent to the imbecilic thugs of letters and whom he reprimanded as the most vile of riff-raff.

But at the Grande Chartreuse he had no need for this prestige, nor any other. It sufficed, as Father Athanase had told him, from the first instant, that they knew he was miserable and suffering in spirit. Even the habits of this Parisian artist were taken into consideration, as much as was possible, by virtue of a discrete and vigilant goodness that permeated him. This unwell man was not required to submit to the discouraging rigor of any rules of retreat. Anything that was not incompatible with the monastery's regularity was accorded him, without his even asking for it, including permission to smoke in his room, a favor almost without precedent. They left him to think at his leisure. His exasperated soul, vibrating like a brass instrument, loosened up and softened,—deliciously,—in the flame full of the incenses of this charity . . .

Each day, Father Athanase, his friend now, came to see him, bringing him joy whenever he could. And there were infinite conversations, when the monk, formerly educated in the world's stupefying disciplines, was instructed, once again, in their emptiness, at the school of this massacred man, and who filled him, Marchenoir, with a tranquil sadness of being unable to escape them in the luminous Rule of these released men.

These Carthusians who were so austere, so racked, so tortured by the *rigors* of penitence,—for which, legendarily, the idiotic cowardice of worldly people have pity on them,—he saw clearly that they are the only free and joyous men in our society of intellectual convicts or galley slaves of the imagination, the only ones who really did what they wanted to do, accomplishing their privileged vocation in that happiness without illusion that God gives them and which has no need of any fanfare to attest to itself that it is anything but a secret desolation.

"Father," he said one day, "do you believe, in good conscience, that the regular religious life should be decidedly and absolutely forbidden to me? You know my whole history, all my unearthed dreams, and my clairvoyant disgust of all secular promises. The bonds that still hold me can be broken. The book that I carry in me, if it is viable, could be born here, as you are a writing order. You see how much I have been exposed to perish in the vain battles, where it is nearly impossible that I should triumph; how fatigued I am and tired of my grievous ways. My soul, which cannot take any more, is half-open like a riddled vessel that has been too long at sea . . . Do you not think that this unforeseen retreat is, perhaps, the work of Providence that wanted, for a long time now, to conduct me and settle me in your house's Havre-de-Grace?"

"My dear friend," responded the Father having become very serious, "since the time of your arrival, I have been waiting for this question. It comes late enough that I have been able, in studying you, to prepare an answer for you. *In all honesty* before God, of whose designs I am as ignorant as you are, I do not believe you are called on to share our life, at least not at present. You are forty years old and you are *in love*. You do not see it, you do not know it, but you certainly are and it is plainly visible. Your friend could tell you, if he is not blind. I want to believe in the purity of your passion, but this circumstance is adventitious and does not change your character. You are so in love that, at this moment even, you are shivering at the core of your soul.

"Now, I say it again, you are forty years old. You have spoken to me about the symbolic value of numbers, study that a little. The fortieth year is the age of irrevocability for the man who is not condemned to an eternal infancy. A direction will open up before you, I do not know which way, but, in my judgment, it would be miraculous if it carried you to a cloister. Then, you are a man of war and perpetual inquietude. All that is not very monastic. It is still a romantic foolishness that you must get rid of, my dear poet, to believe that disgust of life should be a mark of religious vocation. Up to now you have been our guest, you come and go as you please, you dream on the mountain and in our beautiful forest of green pines, in spite of the fifty centimeters of snow that seems to you all the more enchanting, but, believe me, the apparition of our Rule would fill you with horror.

It is then that you would feel the strength of the bond that you believe capable of breaking at will, and which would appear to you no more fragile than the immense bronze chain that bars the gate at Carthage. At the end of a week of confinement, our postulants' black coat would burn on your back, like the famous tunic, and you would become yourself a Centaur in order to escape us . . . my poor child!"

Marchenoir bowed his head and cried.

XXVII

He was right, this father. The poor man was terribly smitten and he felt it, now. But it was quite strange he had to make so distant a voyage to learn it, that his feeling of security had been, until then, so perfect and that nothing for many months had warned him of it. That traitor Leverdier, why had he not mentioned it? Ah! it is apparently because he judged the evil without remedy and, from there, what good can come from inflicting this revelation on a friend already overcome with pain? Maybe also, he had sent him to the Carthusians for this reason, doubtlessly believing that they would see this ulcer that was so obvious and which could not escape their notice.

Equipped with this torch, Marchenoir descended into the darkest crypts of his conscience and his stupefaction, his horror, were unlimited. Nothing held steady any longer. The buttresses of his virtue fell apart around him, the wooden beams and iron stanchions of his will, with which he had believed to have flaunted all the rotten and worm-eaten deficiencies of nature, literally crumbled to dust. Everything sounded hollow and in ruins. It was a miracle that the collapse had not happened. He was going, therefore, to have to live above this chasm, haphazardly among the debris. It was impossible to foresee the disaster and there was no means to escape it. The evidence of danger came too late.

Triple imbecile! He had imagined friendship was attainable between a man and a woman who are not at least two hundred years old and who live every day together! That superb creature, whom he realized he thought of nonstop, he had believed foolishly that she could be like a sister to him, nothing more than that, that he could be like a brother to her and that one would proceed, thus, down chaste paths of divine love,—indefinitely. "I am done for," he thought, "without remission, this time."

Effectively, it became terrible. The first dirty little pig who came along would have found this situation perfectly solvable. He would have decided to sleep with her, no problem. Marchenoir did not see the means to extricate himself so cheaply or, rather, this solution, detested in advance, seemed to him the most feared among all shipwrecks.—Impetuously, he distanced himself . . .

After several years, he had placed his affective life so high that this idea, by itself, profaned it. He was proud of his Véronique, as much as a fine book he might have written. And it was a really sublime one, in fact, that his religious faith guaranteed imperishable to him. She did not have a feeling, a thought, or even a word, that she did not receive from him. But all that, passed, sieved, filtered through a soul so singularly candid, made it seem that her very person was an angelic translation of this somber living poem that called itself Marchenoir.

This skank of a girl, seeded and harvested in filth,—who revived, in the full decrepitude of the most lapsed of all centuries, the Thaïs and Pelagies from Christianity's adolescence,—had transformed herself, all of a sudden, by the miraculous occasion of the most profane love, into a lily with diamond petals and with a pistil of gold burnished by the most splendid tears that had ever fallen, during the centuries of ecstasy that she inaugurated. Madeleine, as she wanted to be called, but Madeleine of the Grave, she had so volatilized her love for Marchenoir that he practically no longer existed for her in the state of an organic individual. By dint of seeing in this disinherited man nothing but a lacrymal argument for perpetual prayer, she had finished by losing, when it concerned him, the discernment of an exact boundary between spiritual and sensual nature, and,—even though she busied herself, zealously but mechanically, with the materiality of their unusual household,—it was above all the soul, the soul in and of itself, that this dove of prey claimed to delight in.

Since the Gospel, this word dove invokes precisely the idea of *simplicity*. Véronique was inexplicable as long as this idea of simplicity never came to mind. Never had a more simple heart been seen. Modern language dishonored, as much as it could, simplicity. It is at a point that one does not even know any more what it is. Vaguely one imagines a type of corridor or tunnel between stupidity and idiocy.

"The conversation of the Lord is with the simple folk," says the Bible, which supposes, however, a certain aristocracy. Here, it was a complete absence of anything that can have a relief, an embossment of any sort of vanity or the most instinctive self-love. The hypothesis of a very profound humility, engendered by an infinite repentance, would have poorly explained this innocence of moonlight.

The past was so abolished that to remember it required imagining a copy of the subject, a recommencement of nativity, a re-creation of the same being, an in-kneading, this time, of a little more than human essence. She herself, the predestined, did not understand anything. She had childlike wonders, a widening of her limpid eyes, when a circumstance forced her to look into her past. "Was it really me who could have been like that!" Such was her impression and, almost immediately, that impression was rubbed out . . .

To make a mistress of this former courtesan by whom he was adored Marchenoir would have been forced to seduce her like a virgin, passing through all the infamies and drinking all the shames of the profession, without any hope of assistance by the intermediary spasm that ends, ordinarily, by throwing onto the horns of the goat the unpolluted virgin's inexperienced mucous membranes.

The devil knew, however, whether the penitent's impurity had been ardent and other men, in large numbers, knew it also, who were nowise equal to this Prince with the crushed Head! What had become of the wealth of this treasurer of foulness? No one knew. The rhetoric of alchemists was needed to implore, to claim that one was in the presence of a mysterious crucible, recently ignited to melt a heart, and whose inferior flames, after transmutation, were extinguished. The fact is that nothing was left of it, absolutely nothing.

Marchenoir living quite retired from the world, at the end of a deserted quarter frequented by very few judges, was able for a long time to escape the sentences, maxims, apothegms, moral reflections, admonitions or counsels of wise men. He did not encourage inquisitors into his private life. But it eventually became known that he lived with the Suction Cup, whose disappearance had remained unaccounted for, and several old clients had even attempted to recover her.

Marchenoir, to put an end to it, did something that only he could have done. One evening while returning home in the company of his so-called mistress, quite alone on the boulevard de Vaugirard, and having been insulted by three of them, he threw the first one into a vague terrain, over an enclosing wall and so thrashed the other two that they begged for mercy. They left him alone, after this beating, and the ignoble gossip that was produced had no effect on this proud spirit, who declared himself a pachyderm as far as calumny was concerned.

"Ask me," said Véronique to Leverdier, "how I could love my poor Joseph, and how I could love the Savior Jesus. I'm not learned enough to tell you, but when I saw our friend so unhappy, it seemed to me I was looking at God suffering on earth."

In this way, she confused the two feelings, until they became one, so extraordinary in her practices and with so consuming a lyricism of expression that Marchenoir and Leverdier began to fear a fracture in this vessel of praise, which seemed too fragile to them to resist for long the exorbitant pressure of infinity.

XXVIII

All these thoughts besieged the Grande Chartreuse's distraught guest simultaneously. He remembered that in a fit of enthusiasm and without thinking about what he was doing, he had offered to marry Véronique. She had responded in her own words:

"A man like you shouldn't marry a girl like me. I love you too much to ever consent to it. If you've the misfortune of desiring the putridity that serves as my body, I'll ask God to heal you or deliver you from me."

She said it with such clear resolve that he never brought it up again. On reflection, Marchenoir had understood the heroic wisdom of her refusal, and internally blessed the saintly girl for this act of virtue that saved him from infinite torments.

At that time, he did not feel he was in love. But now, what was he going to do? Impossible to marry the woman he loved, impossible and hideous to make her his mistress, impossible above all to live without her. No expedient, even remote, appeared. To continue the false concubinage, while condemning himself to silence, where would he find the strength? Even if he accepted this shirt of flames like a penitence, like an expiation of so many things that his conscience reproached him for, it was still an absurdity to pretend to win the crown of Christian martyrdom on the beveled edge of a cistern of desires.

He would be accorded no resting place then, not one hour even of assured repose, not a pillow of granite to lay his head on and truly sleep! And the means of working with all that? For he could not dispense with giving out his fruit, this apple tree of sadness that extracted its sap anymore from the heart of the dead. He would need, soon, as before, to discover how to write while holding up with his two hands several walls forever crumbling, to take up again and brood over all the old bases of a hopeless misery, to pull again sempiternally, with bloody shoulders, the hand cart for relocating his old, arch-decrepit, cracked, dusty, shivering, but clinging still and unable to be torn away, illusions.

The only abomination that he would have lacked at this point: love without hope, that treasure of supererogatory snubs, from now on he no longer lacked them. He was admirably complete! Once again, what was going to become of him? He took a hammer to pound this question into himself, until it broke his heart, and the response did not come . . .

So-called amorous literature has dipped quite a bit into the old bag of *delights* of the pain of love. Marchenoir found only suggestions of despair there. He had truly believed, however, that they were behind him, the years of servitude, having paid such royal ransoms to the blind pirate who captures every variety of human animal indiscriminately! He was no longer in the mood for grazing on love's mast. By way of elegies, he had hardly anything to offer but the bellowing of a tapir fallen into a pit, and the only bouquets to Chloris that one could expect from him would have been harvested, by an ugly hand, from among the pale vegetation of a slaughterhouse for horses.

By means of treading on this thorn bush, he finished by having to raise an idea, three times darker than the others, a sort of flying frog of an idea that began to suck his soul. *His beloved had belonged to everyone*, not by desire or the beginning of desire, as was his case, but by a shared caress, possession, and bestial embrace.

As soon as this filth had touched him, the miserable lover wallowed in it, like a buffalo. He had an immediate vision of Véronique's past, a quite actual vision, inexorably precise. At that time were revealed to him, at the same moment, the imperial despotism of this new feeling that flagellated him with scorpions, from the very first day, and the genuine childishness of previous enticements to restrain his liberty.

He saw, with terrible clarity, that what he had believed, two times, the extremity of passion, had been merely a surprise of his senses, in complicity with his imagination. Without a doubt, he had suffered from always picking up the castaways, and his offices of reliever had seemed to him, many times, a very bitter fate. He recalled the grim hours. But at least he could still speak as the master and command the monster to leave him alone.

Today the monster returned to him and slowly crushed the bones in his face. Ah! He had given himself airs of scorning jealousy and he believed himself in love! But true love is the most incompatible of anxious passions. It is a flesh-eater stricken with insomnia, mottled with eyes, and with a pair of telescopes on its back.

Pride and its bastard, Anger, allow themselves to be grazed on by their flatterers; peaceful Envy licks the inside of Avarice's stinking feet, who likes it immensely, and who gives her mortgaged benedictions with instructions on how to make use of them; Drunkenness is an ever-penetrated Sphinx, who consoles himself by going to get smashed with his Oedipuses; Lust, with her honey belly and brass loins, dances, head down, before the Herods, so that she is served the beheaded men she needs, and Sloth, finally, who exits the vagina like a worm, winds itself with a viscous indifference around all the pilasters of the old human city.

But Love froths with anger at the mere mention of the word "shared" and jealousy is his house. He is a snail without a country, who enjoys himself, alone and without visitors, in his dark spiral. He has eyes at the tips of his horns and, if one so much as lightly grazes them, he goes back inside to devour himself. At the same time, he is ubiquitous, in both time and space, like the true God of whom he is the most frightening disfiguration.

With a nameless and unbounded anguish, Marchenoir apperceived that this diabolic misfortune was going to be his own. There was already no longer the *past* for him. All was the present. All the instruments of his torture weeped at one time, around him, in the humble room of this monastery where he had hoped to find peace.

The poor girl, he saw her a virgin, a complete child, exiting the belly of her mother. Then they mounted her, depraved her, spoiled her in front of him. That budding soul, that *green girl*, as they say in polite England, was mocked by a pestilent wind, trampled on by filthy brutes, contaminated before blooming. All the world's base infamy was unleashed against this tender reed shoot, who had not yet thought, who would doubtless never think.

Then, a sort of adolescence came for her, as if for an infant gorilla or an archduchess of the Holy Roman Empire and, from the open ruche of her corsage, a swarm of alluring indecencies fanned out. Men formed a line and passed her from hand to hand like a pale of water to put out a fire, this impure body, this vessel of pleasure, irreparably profaned. Existence for her was from that time forward no more than an interminable night of debauchery that lasted ten years, and which supposed the revocation of all suns, the extinction forever of all light, celestial or human, capable of dissipating it.

Appalled confidant of this nightmare, Marchenoir perceived distinctly Lust's sighs, murmurings, cracks, rattles, gulps. Still, if this lost soul had been only one of those lamentable victims—he had known so many!—all of them fallen, crying out with horror, from the belly of misery into the silver mouth of licentiousness! . . . But she was licking her lips in her debauchery and, gorged on infamies, she had indefatigably asked for more. Her dress of shame she had made her dress of glory and the queenly purple of her prostitute's joy!

There was no means of doubting it, alas! and it was precisely what crucified this unfortunate man the most! Try as he might to tell himself that all these things no longer existed, that repentance had erased, crossed out, scrubbed, destroyed them, that he owed it to himself, as he owed it to God, to the weeping angels, to all of Paradise on his knees, to forget what infallible Mercy had pardoned. He could not do it, and his soul, despoiled of enthusiasm, but invincibly enchained, rested there, naked and shivering before his thought . . .

It was in this school of agony that he learned decidedly what Flesh is worth and what it costs to throw this bread into the garbage! For the first time, his Christianity rose up in him to defend it, this miserable flesh that no mysticism can suppress, that one cannot disturb without upsetting the spirit and that no crumbling of the tomb will prevent from resuscitating at the day of last judgment.

He saw her invested with a mysterious dignity, precisely attested to by the continent ambition of her most ascetic contemners. Evidently, it was not the feelings or the thoughts of before that he could be jealous of. Irresponsible Nothingness would have descended from its empty throne to testify on this point, in favor of the accused, before the most rigorous tribunal. Her soul's retaking of her body was not in doubt. It was solely then the sullied flesh of this body that caused her so much suffering! An inexplicable bond of destiny against which he had stiffened, in vain, made him a spouse of this flesh which was retailed like a commodity and, by consequence, measured on the same scale, in the perfect ignominy of the same counters . . .

On this day, Marchenoir assumed all the throes of *conjugal* jealousy, empress of human torments,—that loveless beings alone have the right to be ignorant of, and that can grow into smutty passions, in hearts capable of experiencing it!

XXIX

The desperate man passed a part of the night in the chapel, in the gallery for outsiders. The night office of the Carthusians, which he followed with intelligence, calmed his yearnings a little. This celebrated office, which few visitors have the courage to listen to until the very end, and which lasts sometimes more than three hours, seemed to him not long enough.

It occurred to him at that time to pick up again the thread of a sort of superior life that his horrible present existence would have interrupted for an indeterminate period. Otherwise, why and how was there this internal flinching, these raptures, these flights of soul, these burning tears, each time that a flash of beauty fell on him from it did not matter what point of ideal or sensible space? It was quite necessary, after all, that there should be something real in the eternal platonic old tune of an earthly exile. This idea came back to him, without cease, from an atrocious prison in which he had been locked up for some unknown crime, and the literary ridicule of a hackneyed image did not overcome the obsession. He let this reverie float on the waves of hosannas that mounted from the choir towards him, like a tide of resignation. He forced himself to unite his sad soul with the joyous souls of these perpetual hymnologists.

Contemplation is the ultimate aim of the human soul, but it is very specially, and pre-eminently, the aim of a solitary life. This word contemplation, degraded like so many things in this century, has hardly any meaning any more outside the cloister. Who then, if it is not a monk, has read or would like to read, today, the profound treatise *On Contemplation* by Denys the Carthusian, also called the Ecstatic Doctor?

This word, which has one of the closest relationships with the name God, has undergone the bizarre fate of falling into the mouth of pantheists such as Victor Hugo, for example,—and that makes an amusing spectacle for thought, to be present at a poet's genuflection before a pinch of excrement, that his insane lyricism commands him to adore and to serve in order to obtain, by this means, eternal life!

At an immeasurable distance from the corpuscular contemplators similar to the man just mentioned, and who have a notion of God appropriate to the sensation of some fantastic myriapod on the lethargic pulp of their brain, there exists then in the Church contemplatives by *state*; these are the monks who make a profession of tending, in a most exclusive manner and by the most special means, toward contemplation, which does not mean to say that, in these communities, everyone is raised to contemplation. They can all be, just as it can happen that nobody is. But all tend with fervor and *depute* their entire life toward this unique object.

Marchenoir told himself that the people there do the greatest thing in the world, and that the law of silence, among the monks devoted to a contemplative life, is superabundantly justified by this exceptional plenipotentiary vocation for all the spirituality on earth.

"At a certain height," said Ernest Hello, referring to Rusbrok's *The Admirable*, which he is translator of, "the contemplator can no longer say what he sees, not because his object lacks words to describe it, but because the words lack an object, and the silence of the contemplator becomes *the substantial shadow* of things that he does not say . . . Their words," adds this great writer, "is a voyage of charity that they take for other men. Silence is their fatherland."

At the time of the Reformation, a large number of Carthusian monasteries were ransacked or suppressed and many monks suffered martyrdom, such as the Calvinists and other artists of tortures knew how to administer in that renascent century, with such a prodigious esthetic thrust.

"Why do you keep silent in the midst of torments, why don't you respond to our questions?" said the soldiers of the ferocious Chareyre who, for many days, inflicted atrocious sufferings on the venerable father Dom Laurent, vicar of the Chartreuse of Bonnefoy.

"Because silence is one of the principal Rules of my order," said the martyr.

The tortures were a lesser anguish than speaking, for this contemplator whose silence was the *fatherland* and who did not even need to be reminded of obedience.

Night has singular privileges. It opens hideouts and hearts, it unleashes ferocious instincts and base passions, at the same time that it dilates souls amorous of eternal beauty. It is during the night that the skies can *recount* the glory of God, and it is also during the night that the angels of Noel announced his most astonishing works. *Deus dedit carmina in nocte*[1]. These words by Job, do they not affirm, in their way, the mysterious symphony of nocturnal praises around the Well-Loved in the holy Bible, so *dark* and so *beautiful*, which the night is a symbol of, according to some interpretations.

But it is not just to praise or to contemplate that the Carthusians hold vigils and chant. It is also to intercede and to *satisfy*, in view of the immense Guilt of the human species and in participation with the sufferings of Him who assumed everything. "Jesus Christ," said Pascal, "will be in agony until the end of the world; one must not sleep during this time period."

These words of the poor Jansenist are sublime. Isolated in the cold and distant gallery, he remembered them, those tighteners of his guts, while he listened to men overcome with love chanting prayers and begging for mercy on the universe's behalf. He thought that at that same instant, on all the points of the globe saturated with the Blood of Christ, innumerable beings made in the likeness of the Most High God were being slaughtered or oppressed; that the crimes of the flesh and the crimes of thought, dreadful in their enormity and in their number, made, at that very minute, a circle ten thousand leagues in circumference around this focus of supplications, under the same constellated cupola of this long winter night . . .

The Holy Spirit recounts how the seven Maccabee children "each exhorted themselves with their mother to die courageously, saying: 'The Lord will consider the truth and he will be consoled by us, according as Moses declared in his canticle with this protestation: *And he will be consoled by his servants*.'"

These Carthusians, dead to the world for being the most faithful servants, hold vigils and chant with the Church to *console* the Lord God. The Lord God is sad to death, because his friends have abandoned him, and because it is necessary that he kill himself

---

1 Latin for "God gave songs in the night."

and reanimate the ice-cold heart of these infidels. He, the Master of Anger and the Master of Pardon, the Resurrection of All the Living and the Older Brother of All the Dead, he whom Isiah called the Admirable, the strong God, the Father of the Century to come and the Prince of Peace,—he agonizes, in the middle of the night, in a garden planted with olive trees, that have nothing else to do, now, than to produce their fruits, as the Light of worlds is about to be extinguished!

The distress of this unconsolable God is terrible, when the Angels which are called columns of heaven, would fall in innumerable clusters to the earth, if the traitor should delay a little longer to arrive. The Strength of Martyrs is one of the names of this divine Agonizing One and,—if there are no more men who have control over their flesh and who crucify their will,—then where is the kingdom, of what century will he be Father, of what peace will he be Prince and how will the Comforter be able to come? All these redoubtable names, all this majesty that fills the prophets and their prophecies, all precipitate at once on him to crush him. Human Sadness and Fear, lovingly intertwined, make their entry into God's domain and the antique menace of Sweat is finally fulfilled on the face of the new Adam, from the beginning of this feast of tortures, when he begins to get drunk on the best wine, according to the steward's precept at the wedding of Cana.

The angel come from heaven can, of course, "recomfort" him, but it belongs only to his servants on earth to *console* him. It is for this reason that the solitary children of Saint Bruno do not want to know anything other than Jesus in agony, and that their life is a perpetual orison with the universal Church. This is the price of the Lord's consolation, and the Strength of martyrs would default perhaps, entirely, without the heroism of the indefatigable Vigilantes.

XXX

Marchenoir tried to pray with them and to collect his poor soul. The victorious supernatural poured into his sad heart laid bare. The eyes of his faith made him aware of the terrible things that theologians and mystic narrators explained or recounted, when they spoke of the religious soul's rapports with God in orison.

An ancient Father of the desert, named Marcellus, having risen one night to chant the psalms as was his ordinary practice, heard a noise like that of a trumpet that sounded the charge and, not understanding where it could come from in so solitary a place, where there were no men of war, the Devil appeared to him and told him that this trumpet was the signal that warned the demons to prepare themselves for combat with the servants of God; because he did not want to expose himself to danger, he went back to sleep, to avoid having to sustain a very rude shock.

Marchenoir thought he heard the immense sound of this charge. He saw each monk like a war tower defended by angels against all the demons, which the prayers of God's servants is in the process of dispossessing. By generously renouncing the worldly life, each one of them carries deep within the monastery an immense equipage of supernatural interests for which he becomes, in effect, by his vocation, the accountant before God and the intendant against taskmasters without justice. Interests of edification for one's neighbor, interests of glory for God, interests of confusion against the Enemy of men. All that on a scale that is no less vast than Redemption itself, which continues from the beginning to the end of time!

Our liberty is united with the equilibrium of the world and that is what one must understand in order not to be surprised by the deep mystery of Reversibility, which is the philosophical name of the great dogma of the Communion of Saints. Every man who produces a free act projects his personality into the infinite. If he gives grudgingly a sou to a poor person, this sou pierces the hand of the poor person, falls, pierces the ground, burrows through suns, traverses the firmament and compromises the universe. If he commits an impure act, he may obscure thousands of hearts that he does not know, who correspond mysteriously with him and who need this man to be pure, like a traveler dying of thirst has need of a glass of water of the Gospel. A charitable act, a motion of true compassion sings divine praises for him, since Adam to the end of the centuries; he heals the sick, consoles desperate men, appeases tempests, redeems captives, converts infidels and protects the human species.

All Christian philosophy is contained in the inexpressible importance of the free act and in the notion of an enveloping and indestructible solidarity. If God, in an eternal second of his power, wanted to do what he has never done, to wipe out a single man, it is probable that creation would turn to dust.

But what God *cannot* do, in the rigorous plenitude of his justice, being voluntarily *bound* by his own mercy, feeble humans, by virtue of their liberty and within the measure of an equitable satisfaction, can accomplish for their brethren. To die to the world, to die to oneself, to die so as to speak to a terrible God, destroying oneself before him in the frightening solar irradiation of his justice,—that is what Christians can do, when the old machine of earth cracks under the appalled heavens and has almost no more strength to support sinners. At that moment, that which the wind of mercy blows away like dust is horrible creation, which is not God's, but man's alone; it is his enormous treachery, it is the evil fruit of his freedom, it is all a rainbow of infernal colors over the bright chasm of divine Beauty.

Lost in the half-obscurity of this chapel drowned in prayers, the doleful man ravaged by terrestrial love saw pass before him the apocalypse of the great battle for eternal life. The world of souls moved before him like Homer's Ocean with innumerable sounds. All the waves clamored towards the sky or fell back frothing onto the rocks, mountains of waves rolling one against the other, in a tumult and a chaos that is effable in the painful human tongue. The dead, the agonizing, the wounded of the earth or wounded of heaven, those lost in joy and those lost in sadness, defiling in infinite troops, raising millions of arms, and, alone, that peaceful vessel where the untroubled conscience of several elect genuflected, navigated while chanting in a profound calm that one could believe to be eternal.

"O holy peace of the living God," said Marchenoir, "enter me, appease this tempest and walk on these waves!" More than ever, alas! he would have liked to have been able to throw himself into that life of ecstasy, which all the bloody sediments of his heart forbade him.

"I do not believe," he wrote to Leverdier toward the end of the first week, "that, among all our abortive impressions of art or literature, one can find something as powerful, by half, on the intimateness of the soul. To visit the Grande Chartreuse from bottom to top is a very simple thing to do, one can be very able assuredly to furnish the memory with some souvenirs and, even, fortify one's Christian understanding with some virile notions of the evangelical letter and spirit, but one does not know it in the full flower of mystery if one has not seen the nightly office. *There* is the true perfume that transfigures this rigorous retreat, of so dreary a sojourn for the poseur of religious sentiment. I am not afraid to abridge my sleep. Such a spectacle is for me the most refreshing of all reposes. When one sees that, one realizes that one knew nothing about monastic life. One is surprised even to have known Christianity so little, not to have seen it, until that hour, save through the literary exfoliations of the tree of proud science. And the heart is taken in hand by the celestial Father, like an icicle, into the center of the furnace. Eighteen centuries of Christianity begin anew, like an extraordinary poem that one did not know existed. Faith, Hope and Charity rain down together like *three twisted bolts* of lightning from old Pindar and, were it just for one instant, a single minute in the duration of a life spilled like the blood of a flayed prodigal on every path, it would be enough to remember and never again to forget that, that night, then, it was God himself who spoke!"

XXXI

Marchenoir, the least curious of all men, was in no hurry to visit in detail the Grande Chartreuse. He found it passably ridiculous and vile the obligated exhibition of a such a tabernacle to imbecilic tourists, for whom it is the program to pass by there while coming from somewhere else, to then go some other place, where their stupidity will not fail, up to the moment they have gotten their fill, more cretinous than ever, in their bureaus or at their shops. He could not get used to the idea that a solicitor, a manufacturer of detachable collars, a seller of bandages or a State engineer, would have any sort of opinion, even unexpressed, while promenading their flatulence in this Eden.

In the eighteenth century which was, without comparison, the stupidest of centuries, one had been persuaded that all monks lived in delight, that the hypocritical penumbra of cloisters hid tortuous conspiracies against humankind, and that the thick walls of monasteries muffled the groans of uncountable victims by ecclesiastical arbitrariness.

In the nineteenth century, universal stupidity having been channeled in a different way, this lugubrious facetiousness became unsupportable. The horror changed into pity and the criminals became pitiable hermits. This romantic trend endures still. Nothing is more grotesque, and at bottom, more lamentable, than the attitudes of haughty mercy or sorry compassion shown by those who stuff and gorge themselves, towards these penitents, who protected them deep within their solitude and without whose intercession, maybe, they would not even have the security of a digestion!

Of all the religious Orders that have been the finery of the Church, when this humbled queen was nowise a poor woman, two alone, the Carthusians and the Trappists, succeeded at being pardoned because they were not gambling joints or houses of prostitution. Marchenoir already knew the Trappists. Now that the Carthusians, in turn, held no more secrets for him, he felt the unusual humiliation of being forced to accord to the rabble this twofold exception of the only two Orders that had remained truly monastic, and, although Carthusian life appeared to him superior, he confessed the near absolute impossibility of finding a veritable monk who was neither a Trappist nor a Carthusian.

To tell the truth, to judge them, he had another criterium than the evildoers who gobbled up the anticlerical patter. But he saw clearly that, on this point, the besieging instinct of hate had been as discerning as the most jealous solicitude. In fact, for enemies of the faith, it had to do with blocking it as tightly as possible, and, certainly, the best equipped and most expertly geared theologian would not see more clearly the vital importance for Christianity of these last citadels of the evangelic spirit.

The siege army, moreover, recruits its soldiers from the mass of modern Catholics, who have been completely sick and tired, for a long time now, of this spirit. Admirable and providential reinforcements! Religious sentimentality running to the rescue of modern persecutors! Poetry, the novel, history, theater even, the *charity balls* and beneficent societies, subscriptions for victims of flood or fire, the immense movement of the bowels that make the glory and fortune of the reporters of courts of assize, and finally the lyrical emotions of all the press on all genre of catastrophe, sufficiently attesting to Christian sensibility's unforeseen return to youth.

This marvel, more easily observed from the heights of the Grand Chartreuse, reminded Marchenoir of a famous article that was taken for irony and was entitled: *The Court of Miracles of Millionaires,*—designating thus the interesting multitudes of fortunate people full of charity, whose substance the indigent devours and whose sweat he drinks of. It seemed to him, now, to not have said enough and he bitterly regretted being unable to add anything more to it.

The thing is that, in effect this drove is a people, it is a state within the State. Never had such an affluence of misunderstood pelicans been seen before, nor had a more Diocletian-like persecution been executed on more shredded martyrs.

Time is too precious to spend it remarking on marvels disinterestedly, unspeakable generosity, the surprising freshness of soul of modern day patricians of wealth and power and, in general of any personage, of whatever title, having an influence on this wicked world unworthy of possessing it. Everyone knows that these intendants of public joy wear themselves out to swell the heart of the poor and run themselves down to make misfortune idle.

An indisputable universal prosperity is their work, and the exclusive ambition to render it perfect is their daily concern. It is rare today, that indigence, when it implores, goes unheeded and that happy individuals wish to be happy all on their own. It is not at the point, so to speak, that captains of industry and politicians, risen up diligently, forget to tender a helping hand to the man of merit passively registered for a somber destiny, or that they refuse opportunely to give water to languishing virtue.

One knows not to what benign sidereal interference it is appropriate to relate this unhoped-for shortage of egotistic human calculations, this favorable aridity of the old cactus of avarice, this surprising withering of the crocodilian egg of traditional usuries. But it is certain that an unprecedented emulation, a veritable delirium of charity is in the process of ravaging the rich,—the Catholic rich mostly,—whom the ingratitude of those dying of poverty dares venomously to qualify with the epithet of horrible *cads*.

In the practice of religious things, this exquisite sensibility is manifested through various accompaniments of the most suave precaution. One is expected at the foot of altars, one weeps sweet tears over the *dear deceased* whom one believes to be in heaven, which shifts the fatigue of praying for them to the liturgical masses that have to be paid for; one makes very small fraternal alms, in order not to expose the poor to the temptations of debauchery and so as not to grieve their souls by the ostentation of excessive pomp; one amorously abstains from speaking of God and the saints, out of regard for the obstinateness of disbelievers who could be exasperated by it, and one speaks even still less of the heroism of penitence to a crowd of tempered Christians who would respond, doubtless, that God *does not ask that much*. The question of distant or difficult pilgrimages, as that to Jerusalem, is delicately dismissed, by the same instinct of benevolence that would like to spare those who work in piety the umbrage of trouble or inconvenience. Finally, religious sentiment fulfills, today, the ideal of that great Catholic thinker, enemy of exaggerations, who is called Molière, who wished that devotion were "human, tractable," and that one should not kill anyone with *holy iron.*

Opportunely aided by this happy deliquescence of Catholicism, powerful moralists of free examination and literary coryphaei of slovenliness, all the broken-jawed Corybants of modern art and all the honest grocers of an inimical Voltairianism of art, have, with a common voice, approved the cenobitism of Trappist and Carthusian monks. These politicians being firmly persuaded that Catholicism ought, in the near term, to be swept away from civilization like garbage, it seems appropriate to them to treat it mercifully and not to despair of the imbeciles who still cling to it, by according them absolutely nothing. They accord them then these two Orders. A young bard of recent celebrity, Hamilcar Lecuyer, had said one day to Marchenoir that he didn't understand how with his faith, he dared to remain in the world, wondering whether he shouldn't run off instantly and *bury himself* among the Trappists. The hirsute responded by counseling him to get away from him and to go to the devil.

The existence of these places of refuge is still useful, for other reasons, to those tacticians of free reign. In their invincible ignorance of the profound solidarity of Christianity, they think that a kind of life of proverbial austerity is opposed to other less rigorous Orders approved by the Church and, by consequence, to the Church itself. The poor who do not know anything about Christianity or its history, guzzle down gluttonously this enormous howler.

Let us not speak to them any more of the cunning children of Loyola, nor of the sanguinary Dominicans who would want to restore the Inquisition, nor of the carnal Capuchins who amuse themselves within their Capuchin seminaries! How could their life be compared to that of these admirable, albeit outmoded, monks, who conserve themselves today by their integrity, the antique tradition from the first centuries of the faith? And this fastuous Roman Church, with all its pomp and its incalculable riches, and all these so redoubtable prelates, and all these innumerable curates spread out in the cities and countrysides, so powerful, so respected, and so perverse!—who would dare to compare these honest cenobites who eat nothing, say nothing, and so little bother the rapid development of republican civilization?

Marchenoir saw more clearly than he had previously how much there is of the bitterly veritable in those base sophisms spoken by louts whom he had, for a long time, renounced to get indignant over. He heard, from afar, the Church crumbling, not stone by stone, but in enormous masses of dust, because it no longer had any stones, and this Chartreuse, it also, this last counterfort of Christ's residence, polluted by Curiosity's intrusion, seemed to him to vacillate on the edge of these eight centuries.

It was necessary that Father Athanase, a confidant moved by the vibrations of this cymbal of grief, escort him, one afternoon, into the interior of the monastery,—that extraordinary guest having declared his repugnance for such a touristic visit.

"So be it!" the father had responded, going along with his guest's delirium, "we will march forward reciting our psalms of penitence, if you wish, and I assure you, my dear friend, that that will set you quite apart from all our tourists."

Despite the torment of his thoughts, Marchenoir could not defend himself from a shock, while walking through the immense cloister, lit up by 113 windows and measuring 215 meters in length, a little longer than Saint Peter's in Rome. A third only, having escaped the fire of 1676, had conserved the ancient ogival form with its symbolic exfoliations in the stone, whereby the piety of the Middle Age wanted to constrain by acts of grace the brutish and inanimate material.

They visited successively the chapter hall; the chapel of the dead,—remarkable from the threshold because of a very handsome bust of death draped in a shroud and, from its skeleton hand, making a perverse gesture to those who pass; the cemetery; the curious Saint-Louis chapel; the refectory,—that famous refectory where the monks reunite to give the impression of eating; and finally, the library ruined so many times and, by consequence, quite devoid of those magnificent vellum manuscripts that were the glory of so many monasteries before the Revolution, but possessing, nevertheless, more than six thousand volumes, ancient for the most part.

The Carthusians are known, besides, for being vigorous writers. An exclusively Carthusian library would have a list of at least eight hundred authors and this list would still remain an understatement of the truth. "Some of our Fathers," one of the ancient Carthusians said with candor, "who made excellent manuscripts that could serve the public exceedingly well, nevertheless used all that material to kindle their fire when it was cold, after matins, warming their bodies with what had warmed their spirits."

What affected Marchenoir the most was the sight of one of these numerous cells, all exactly identical, where the Carthusian, still more solitary than a cenobite, passed the greater part of his life. He collected himself for several instants as best he could, in that corner of peace, in that solitude amidst the solitude, and enjoined, with a gesture, his guide, to abstain from any description,—considering doubtless the perfect inanity of any language, in the presence of this ideal and *internal* deprivation which cannot be felt but from within one's very soul, not by a curious or a lettered person, but by a straightforward Christian whom the Lord Jesus inclines gently towards his feet worthy of adoration.

For wandering stallions of an always harnessed Imagination, this uniformity is a complete boredom and must appear a platitude that, by condescension, they would well want to call divine. There is no room to hope that they could be otherwise edified by it. But Marchenoir discovered there, on the contrary, a clarified source of poetry, infinitely superior to the black incarnation of his despairs. Beneath this Rule so severe and so cold in appearance, behind this impassable *insulator*, shined out, for him, the magnificences of a secluded life in God. Life perpetually transported, by a superabundant joy, by a celestial drunkenness, by an inexpressible peace, by an infinite *variety*!

These enfranchised monks receive with full heart, in the silence of all earthly affections, the plenitude of grace corresponding to the plenitude of their liberty. The celestial Father breaks for them himself the daily bread of supernatural felicity, in exact proportion to their detachment from all other felicities, and it is confidentially that the Spirit communicates to them the revelations of great love. The mystic life is, here, on the same footing with the other life, and these white souls pass from one into the other, alternately, like faithful and diligent housewives among the diverse apartments of an adored master.

The Carthusian spirit is contemporaneous with that of the catacombs, and the Chartreux is, itself, the great modern catacomb, more deeply buried and more secluded than that of the martyrs. But it is a catacomb in heaven! . . . In the distance, rumble the chariots of the world's conquerors and the insane tumult of popular acclamations; the terror-stricken nations flow like rivers, under the colossal arches of the bridge to the donkeys of universal Disobedience, and all these loud sounds of human glory, all these fanfares of victorious frivolity, disappearing and dying away through the thicknesses of this soil that must engulf everything tomorrow, come within earshot of the contemplatives of Life, like an imperceptible trepidation of the earth in the silence of its depths.

"Look," said the Father to Marchenoir, as he escorted him back to his room, "look at what a merchant who has account books to manage does, where he goes with all his possessions and with all his fortune. He locks himself up in his office without consenting to receive any visitors. He says that it is a bother if someone from his family approaches to speak with him about some other affair . . . We are the merchants in whose hands God has placed his goods in order to make a profitable transaction. He gives us the position and the duty when he says in the Gospel: *Negotiate while waiting for me to return.* And he points out to us, in a terrifying fashion, in the parable of the talents, the profit he wants us to make, the amount that we owe him and the punishment that the servant must undergo by way of chastisement, if he does not find his books in good order. If then, this merchant, to settle an account that involves a perishable good, voluntarily keeps to himself and pays no heed to conversations, how much must we esteem the solitude that is much more necessary for us in order to keep forever ready those accounts of our soul when it is a question of our eternal salvation?"

Marchenoir, silent, listened to this paraphrase and imagined himself listening, under the architectural crown of this old cloister, which would have retained the echo of it, to the hundred-year-old voice, infinitely remote and almost extinguished, of one of these humble men from times gone by, buried two paces away, in the cemetery!

XXXII

Precisely the very same evening, he was informed that on the following day, after mass, a brother was going to be buried who had died the day before, whose panegyric, imperceptibly murmured, had glided to him, like a shiver, along the walls of this imperturbable residence, where all is silence, until the joy of death. No spectacle could more strongly attract an individual so accustomed to funereal sights,—a sort of human crossroads, always obscure, where phantoms held conciliabules in the perpetual tragic midnight of memory.

Something that had often exasperated him, this passionate acolyte of all bereavements, was the absence, ordinarily absolute, of prayers over the caskets, at the most sumptuously executed so-called religious burials. Flowers abound and also tears, but the frightening supernatural episode of an appearance before the Judge and the even more glaciating incertitude of the ineluctable Sentence,—how few recollect it or are capable of thinking of it!

People gather in groups with doleful attitudes, they are informed of the exact age of the deceased and assured, with a polite benevolence, that he leaves behind him, at the same time as the pleasant recollection of his virtues, sufficient consolations for those who "will come to feel the sorrow of losing him." If this emigrant to the place of putrefaction attained some success in life, some note-takers sent by the large newspapers can be seen hastening through the crowd, like acarids in a fleece,—rapid jackals attracted to the odor of death. If the illness has been long and painful, they are seen to be more accommodating than the Sacred Congregation of Rites and they *beatify* him willingly, declaring that he is *very fortunate*, now, and that he does not suffer any longer.

Throughout this time, the terrifying Liturgy mutters and weeps without an echo. It is the Liturgy's business to speak before the Judge, that is included in the expenses that weighs heavily on, alas! every succession, and the banal funeral procession soon moves on,—thank God!—with certainty, in a fog of immortal regrets.

At the Chartreuse, what a difference! What could these loving mutes learn, who do not speak but to praise the Lord and who have never had the thought of judging their brothers? They know that the companion of their solitude is now a soul before God and they know also, better than anyone, what it means to be a soul and what it means to be before God!

A simple wooden cross, without any inscription, guards the Carthusians' tomb. A stone cross is given, by exception, to the Superior General. It is a mark of respect employed since the beginning of the Order. Marchenoir, ignorant as yet of the prodigious longevity of the Carthusians, is surprised to see their cemetery take up so small a space. It appears that the victims of Carousing are a thousand times more numerous than those of Penitence, and that the austere Rule is the surest of hygienes. He got proof of this by learning that the register of the deceased at the Grand Chartreuse would be a list of centenarians for the most part. One can see some of these interminable monks who are more than seventy years old by profession and it is rare that a recluse does not live fifty years at the Chartreuse before passing away.

At this moment, however, Marchenoir hardly thought to ask the age of the man he saw put into the ground, and nobody, perhaps, would have been able to say with precision. For these souls bent over the abyss, life represents a certain weight in merit and that is it. From an absolute point of view, "Time has nothing to do with" Eternity. What is essential is to be confirmed in grace, at the end of a century or at the end of a day.

But such funerals can be desired by the proudest helots of passion or glory. Except for the Pope, no Christian receives, upon death, any more prayers than the least known and last among the Carthusians, and what prayers! Marchenoir was profoundly affected by this simple, but so little known fact, that each Carthusian is buried, as in a battlefield, without bier or shroud. He is buried in the poor white habit of his Order, which color corresponds symbolically with the Resurrection of Our Lord, just as the color black for the Benedictine Order represents the holy mystery of his Death. He is thus restituted to the dust, while his assembled brothers weep and pray over his remains.

Ten months earlier, Marchenoir had seen Paris inter a famous man who had declared war on all the monks in France and who wanted to exterminate Christianity in mortal combat. This personage, come from below, had had almost no need to rise in order for his revolutionary cyclops' feet to be exactly at the same level as the majority of his contemporaries' heads.

For more than ten years, Léon Gambetta, continuing the games of his charming childhood, was able to stay astride the shoulders of the first-born Daughter of the Church, who thus received compensation for her apostasies and who drank the shame of shames,—while waiting for the last drunkenness, which will be in all likelihood "what the eye did not see, what the ear did not hear and what the heart of man could not understand," in the inverse sense of what God reserves for those who love him. That is why Paris gave him obsequies befitting a king. Never, perhaps, in any Western country, had more enormous pomp been deployed on the pitiable remains of any man . . .

Marchenoir remembered the three hundred thousand heads of human cattle, accompanying the putrescent Xerxes the Great to his subterranean residence, while the parade chariots and innumerable funereal discourses rumbled, and he compared this deception of buriers with the veridical interment of this unknown Carthusian, in the humble cemetery filled with snow where fifty brothers in tears asked God to resurrect him for eternal life.

This last spectacle appeared to him grander than the other and the prostituted cannonades at the dictator's inhumation had on him the effect of a strangely stupid and mean noise, next to the intelligent and grandiose religious clamor of these clairvoyant souls, who know themselves to be the heirs of Solomon's magnificence, in the face of the sepulchers' misery, and who wear the mourning of death much less than they do the mourning of life on earth!

In truth, Gambetta's obsequies were, themselves, quite a mediocre solemnity in comparison to Victor Hugo's apotheosis, which Marchenoir was led to contemplate, two years later.

This time, it was not only Paris, nor even France, but the entire world, it seems, that rushed in supreme pursuit of the deceased Cosmopolite. The modern world, tired of the living

God, gets down on its knees more and more before rotting carcasses, and we gravitate toward such funereal idolatries that, soon enough, the newborns will go off to wail in the recesses of the famous graves that their mothers' milk will, henceforth, whiten. Patriotism will have so many illustrious putrefactions to deplore that it will not be worthwhile any more almost to move out of the necropolises. It will become like a new national cult, sagely tempered by the final garbage dump where the carcasses of liberators and the residues of apostles, as they become successively less popular, will be transferred without fanfare, to make room for others,

When Marat had finished his ignoble existence, "he was compared," Chateaubriand said, "to the divine author of the Gospel. This prayer was dedicated to him: 'Heart of Jesus, Heart of Marat! O sacred Heart of Jesus, O sacred Heart of Marat!' Marat's heart had for its ciborium a precious pyx taken out of storage. His divine bust, bath, lamp and writing case were installed in a grassy cenotaph that had been erected on the Place du Carrousel. Then, the wind changed. The filth, poured from an agate urn into *another vessel*, was emptied into the sewer."

Modern poetry, having become the friend of the rabble, ought to finish like the *Friend of the People*. Madam is dying, Madam is dead, Madam is buried, not in the purple nor in the azure decorated with the fleurs-de-lis of monarchies, but in the verminous old cast-offs of the sovereign *populo*, and here are the quite hideous undertaker's assistants to carry her off to the grave. All the villains in the universe, in person or represented, defile for six hours, from the Arc de Triomphe to the Pantheon!

It would have been so easy, however, and so simple, to have made this cadaver's funeral procession on foot, binding cables three kilometers in length to its feet and yoking ten thousand men to it, who would have dragged it through Paris, singing the *Marseillaise* or *Derrrière l'Omnibus*, until each paving stone, each curbstone, each public urinal baluster inherited its scrap, for the delight of errant pigs!

126

The *material* horror of this posthumous expiation would have had the effect, at least, of moving the world's heart. An immense choir of sobs would have broken humanity's old breast for several days. An absolution of real tears would have fallen from the eyes of innocents and from the eyes of prostitutes, onto the impenitent Procurer of the Ideal, and until the most incensed souls would have made him a *better* Pantheon from their eternal forgetfulness.

One preferred to drag these remains into the cesspool of democratic apotheosis. A profanation that was a thousand times more certain, because it was accomplished on the *intellectual* cadaver, and because it is without hope of repentance!

The author of *Les Misérables* having absurdly promulgated the equality of the Arm and of Thought, the imbecile Arm wanted to manifest its recognition all on its own and the floating soul of the poet was obliged to fly off, moaning, out of range of this homage.

The school battalions, the Friends of the A.B.C. of Marseille,[1] the employers' union of hotel owners, the francs-tireurs from the Batignolles, the Libre Pensée of Charenton, the *Grelot*[2] of Bercy, the Fraternité of Vaucresson, the chorale from the Allobroges and the Espérance of Javel;[3] the *Printemps'* department heads, the Éden Théâtre ticket collectors, the band players from Nogent-sur-Vernisson and the corporation of bailiff clerks; the cooks, herbalists, florists, chimney sweeps, dentists, packers, plumbers, brush dealers and all the "bone merchants of Paris": such as they were, with two hundred other no less abject groups, the escorts to the *Savoy cake* of this overly satisfied mendicant of the most anti-literary popularity.

---

1 A fictional association of revolutionary French republican students featured in Victor Hugo's *Les Misérables*.
2 *Le Grelot* was the name of an anticleric, antirepublican satirical magazine published in Bercy, a quarter of Paris. It was founded in 1871.
3 L'Espérance de Javel was apparently the name of a hotel in Juvel, a quarter of Paris. Apparently it had a large hall where balls were held.

Victor Hugo had succeeded in dishonoring poetry so much, that France had to discover how to dishonor itself a bit more than before, to put itself in a position to prepare a final adieu that would shatter, as appropriate,—in the unsurpassable ignominy of a solemnity of disgust,—the complicity of their debasement.

This monument, which he himself denounced as ridiculous, fifty years ago, could, without doubt, suit God who put up with it in silence, for the ridicule of men is the majesty itself of the interminable Passion of the decried King; but the greatest poet in the world,—supposing Victor Hugo should merit this title,— absolutely cannot put up with that cupola, which is much less respirable for his glory than the pine tabernacle of the most humble of all tombs . . .

Of all this exultation of contemporary churlishness, the Carthusians probably knew nothing. The deluge of journals has not yet scaled their solitude. They continue to pray for the very humble and the very glorious, for the poets who prostitute themselves and for the imbeciles that hurl filth into the melancholic face of Poetry, and when it is their turn to die, it is enough to inundate them with joy, to hope that the invisible angels will hover over the narrow grave where they are interred without a shroud!

XXXIII

Marchenoir soon felt the necessity to work. He was not the kind of man to rest for long wallowing in a sorrowful thought, however atrociously exquisite it may have seemed to him. He disdained the Sardanapalus types and their pyres, and he would have defended himself, with blood-pouring stumps, right up to the sharpest edge of the last wall of its crystal palace. A surprising combination of dreamer and man of action, he had always been seen to bound from the bottom of his despairs and he uprooted himself from the dung of his disgusts as soon as he began to feel good enough to graze.

The only two books that he would have yet published: a *Life of Saint Radegund* and a volume of criticism entitled *The Powerless*, which he had written while tied to a stake reddened by fire, right in the middle of the raft of the Medusa, without hope of encountering a publisher who would accept him, with the continual fear of becoming enraged.

The first and most important of these two works had been, without comparison, the epoch's most immense failure. Decked out with the most scarlet Catholicism, this eloquent restitution of Merovingian society had been viewed, from the moment of its appearance, enveloped and wrapped up, with infinite attention, by Catholics themselves, in multiple bandages of the most Egyptian silence.

Yet this hagiographic story, as he had conceived and executed it, was truly a grand thing! Such a book, if the press had only deigned to mention it, would, perhaps, be powerful enough to start a historic trend,—at the favorable hour when Michelet, the conscienceless old evoker of several images of the past, left, dying, the field open to cultivators of the weeds of exclusively documentary history. Because that is all that has been seen, since the death of that sorcerer: idolaters of the document, in history as well as in literature and in all the speculative genres,—even in love, where sadism has embarked, recently, to document libertinism. It is the modern inclination attested by scientific bulging of the most turgescent universal vanity.

Marchenoir, of intuitive mind and far-reaching apperception, consequently always aspiring to somewhere before or after his time, could only have an absolute contempt for the sawdust history provided, each day, by mediocre cabinetmakers of the School of Charters in the historiographical guillotine's basket where Tradition's great concepts are decapitated. He had taken it on himself then to protest against this reduction to dust of all the past, by the integral resurrection of a society as defunct as antique societies and whose *physical* debris, one thousand times transformed over the course of ten centuries, could serve as all the geological or edible verifications of man's emptiness.

In this golden Legend of French history, which he always imagined he heard whispered into his ear, like a great tale full of wonders, and which seemed to him the most synthetically strange, the most centrally mysterious of all histories,—nothing had fascinated him more than this enormous, terrible and infantine epic of the Merovingian period. France was leading up to, at that time, the apostolate of western monarchies. The bishops were saints, in the hands of which the barbarous Gentiles, softened slowly, like virgin wax, to form, with the heterogenous mass of the Gallo-Roman world, the mystical rays of the hive of Jesus Christ. From the midst of this chaos of wailing peoples, above whom hovered the Spirit of the Lord, one saw rise up, through the tragic fog of the prolegomena of the Middle Ages, a candid row of human candles whose flames, hurled toward the sky, began, in the sixth century, the great illumination of Western Catholicism.

Marchenoir had chosen Saint Radegund, one of those tranquil luminaries and, perhaps, the most pleasant of all. In the light of this feeble, not yet faded lamp, he had sought the souls of the ancient dead in the least explored crypts of those very old ages. By force of loving will and of art, he had drawn them into the light and had given them the colors of a renewed life.

The most difficult effort that a modern writer could attempt, the transmutation into the *future* of all intermediary past, he accomplished, as much as such miracles might be operable on the human mind always oppressed with present images, and he had arrived at a sort of hypnotic vision of his subject, which nearly equaled contemporary and sensible vision. This work, positively unique, generated such a sharp sensation of backlash, that the oceanic swelling of thirty previous generations became a *conjecture*, a horoscopic theme, a dubitable reverie of some naïve Gallic monk that the sudden thirst for conquest would have pushed over a cliff of desperate vaticination.

The angelic or atrocious figures of this century, Chilperic, the monarch with the finesse of a mastodon and his venomous female, Fredegund, the Jezebel of the slaughterhouse; the growling kennels of liegemen; the bishops with powerless, miraculous hands, Germain de Paris, Gregory of Tours, Praetextatus of Rouen, Medardus of Noyon; some pale privets pushed, by God's grace, through the cracks, Galswintha, Agnes, Radegund, rudimentary types of the all-powerful *dame* of chivalrous times; finally, the ultimate Virgilian blowtorch, the voiceless poet Venantius Fortunatus;—all these arch-bygone dead men, Marchenoir had evoked them so sovereignly that it was as if one could have seen and heard them in the sonorous air of a crystalline morning in winter.

And that was not all. There was the fresco of concomitant adventures of the universe, painted in the umbra or penumbra, but rigorous in its plan, for the orientation of this vast drama: Justinian and Belisarius and all the dirty glory of the Lower Empire; the Goths and the Lombards trampling on Roman manure in Italy and Spain, and the precarious Papacy of this world in ruins; then, from a distance, from Asia, the immense ferocious rumbling of the barbarian reservoir, that each oscillation of the planet caused to flow a bit closer to unfortunate Europe, without overrunning it, until Genghis Khan, who came back and, in a one sweep, overran Western civilization, that basin of fifty peoples!

For this book of nearly three hundred pages, that cost him three years, Marchenoir became a scholar. He did a thorough job of gathering documents. But he thought that the documents were, like wine and, in general, like all things that make one drunk, as much a foolish master as an intelligent servant. He had often noted mutism and infidelity in them. Consequently, he used them with a haughtiness full of defiance, rejecting them with disgust when they violated, stammering, the integrity of a general conception that experience had demonstrated to him to be more reliable;—a working method that a viper-headed boss at *The Review of Historical Sciences* had strongly reprimanded him for and which would have made him decry all contemporary criticism, if that castrated yoke of a boneshaker Monsieur Renan was suitable to reflect on a masterpiece.

Besides, the hagiographic nature of his subject could hardly attract to his book anything but Catholic readers or religious admirers. Now, the chief editor of the most considerable Catholic paper in Paris having himself published, previously, on the subject of the Merovingian saints, an inert brochure fallen almost immediately into a most vertical forgetfulness, he ought not, for his own glory, to accord the least assistance of publicity to this temerarious newcomer who could supplant him. To tell the truth, if it were not for this excellent reason of literary State, the infinite contempt Catholics have for all works of art would have abundantly sufficed. In brief, this man dying of poverty was absolutely deprived of any means of informing the public of the existence of his book and the sages concluded, as always, from the absence of advertising the non-existence of the work.

The fact is that for such resolute haters of literary beauty, Marchenoir was an uncommon opportunity. He was a leper of magnificence. Every disgusting or monstrous malady that can justify, analogically, Christians' horror for an unfortunate artist: scabies, ringworm, syphilis, lupus, plicae, pian, elephantiasis, he accumulated, in their eyes, as a writer.

It was principally in his second novel, *The Powerless*, that this flora exploded. The scandal was so great that it lasted half a century. The author was beginning to be known and the appearance of this satirical collection, already published in weekly articles in a small journal where they had been well received, unmasked in one swipe the formidable polemicist, hidden until then, for many people, under the disdained contemplative, and which a devouring thirst for justice constrained to come out finally. There was a small clamor for eight days and such was the quarter of a part of glory that Paris had seen fit to dedicate to this artist who had been dead for many years. But the book was a revelation for Marchenoir himself, who had not been aware of this sonority of the gong when indignation made it vibrate.

As a result of a quite disconcerting spiritual law, it was discovered that this enthusiast's literary form was especially consanguine with that of Rabelais. This debacle-like, unnavigable style, that always had the air of falling from an alp, rolled every which way in its furor. There were the leaping of epithets, the cries of escalation, the savage imprecations, the rubbish, the sobs or the prayers. When he fell into a chasm, it was only to jump up again into the sky. The word, whatever it might be, ignoble or sublime, he grabbed hold of like a prey and made a projectile of it in an instant, a firebrand, an engine of some sort to devastate or to massacre with. Then, all of a sudden, he became again, in a moment, a tranquil sheet of water that the gentle Radegund had azured with her regard.

Some explained it by an abject charlatanism, in the fashion of *Père Duchesne*. Others, more venomous, but not more stupid, insinuated the belief in a sort of constipated blackmail, furious at never succeeding. Nobody, among the distributors of the putrid meat of journalism, had had the equity or clairvoyance to discern the exceptional sincerity of an ardent soul, compressed to the point of explosion, by all the intolerable hackneyed expressions of mediocrity or injustice.

XXXIV

Now, he turned himself decidedly back toward history. It had always been his greatest ambition and his most fervent intellectual love. Since his childhood, he had had the impression of being much more a contemporary of the Crusades or the Exodus than of the democratic rabble. His admirable Merovingian study attested sufficiently to the anachronism of his thinking. But he had no desire to re-begin that type of effort. A monograph on a man or even a people, however dilated he could imagine it, no longer sufficed. He refused to billet himself once again in some corner of a century. He wanted, from now on, to envelope, in a single embrace, the history of the world.

As he had confided to his friend, he dreamed of being the Champollion of historic events envisaged like divine hieroglyphs of a revelation by symbols, corroborative of another Revelation. It would have been a totally new science, singularly audacious, and which genius alone could save from ridicule. Poor Leverdier had trembled in his skin from the first overture of it, then the oratory volutations of his prophet had imperceptibly involved him in this conception that he had ended up by judging sublime. It is, at least, incontestable that certain inductions that this dazzling demonstrator propped his system up with, made it appear entirely probable.

He had come up with the first idea of it in his exegetic studies that were, by perhaps an unprecedented singularity, the point of departure of his intellectual life, immediately after his conversion. Based on Saint Paul's sovereign affirmation that we see everything "as enigmas," this uncompromising spirit had firmly deduced the symbolism of the universe from the symbolism in the Scriptures, and he had come to persuade himself that all human acts, of whatever nature they might be, worked towards the infinite syntax of an unsuspected book full of mysteries that could be entitled the *Paralimpomenon* of the Gospel. From this point of view,—a point of view strongly divergent from that of Bossuet, for example, who thought, in defiance of Saint Paul, that all was clarified,—universal history appeared to him like a homogeneous text, extremely connected, vertebrate, built on a framework, dialectical, but perfectly shrouded, and that it was just a matter of transcribing it in a possibly accessible grammar.

He had conceived the hope of it and lived only for this project, which had become the center of innervation of his thoughts. Little did it matter to him that others might judge it extravagant or ridiculous. For a long time he had made up his mind to never please and to pay hardly any attention even to hostility, whose immediate effects could, after all, never very easily reach a man whose pen, tongue and muscles render redoubtable.

Ah! without doubt, the numerous enemies he had already attracted to himself in the press had the ordinary resort of generously closing off to him every outlet and, by consequence, withholding money from a poor writer who should have been able to live off his talent. That was the immediate danger and nowise insignificant. But what to do? He felt himself being dragged by the hair down a grievous path and, even though he did not want it, he had to follow his destiny. To utter, if it was possible, a great word, and then to die under the universe's slapping and spitting! For the grace of God! he often said. It is the phrase of many reckless men, but, in his mouth, it had a very high and almost holy signification.

Retired to his room at the Chartreuse, he stiffened his two arms against his own grief, both ancient and recent, in order to ward off the importunity of a foreign solicitude of his mind's work of parturition.

"The symbolism of history!" he thought, "a sure truth, a thousand times evident in my eyes, but how difficult to prove acceptable! If it was a matter of explaining, piece by piece, the symbolism of the human body or vegetal symbolism, this task, often undertaken already by mystics or philosophers, would not be too surprising. There would be opportunities for making some ideas roll on this known rail, on the condition, all the same, that they did not seem to be expressed too originally. But, here, I will bump up immediately against the bull of a skittish Liberty, impenetrable, totally misunderstood by the multitude that adores it and poorly defined by Christian doctors frightened by it. I am in departure, like Columbus, for an exploration of the *dark Sea*, with certitude of the existence of the world to be discovered and fear of outraging, midway, fifty imbecilic passions. The fragmentary history, such as I see it everywhere, is a mirror for this liberty's stupid pride, which congratulates itself without respite for having done what it wanted,—never anything else,—and the absolute synthesis, that I have a design of, confiscates, from the get-go, this toiletry, in order to constrain the old sensualist to contemplate himself in the very humble gutter water that is his homeland. Sure, I would do just fine without applause and I have never sought after it, but still I must be intelligible, so that I do not terrify all the publishers without exception, so that I can at least be as salable as a newly imported *bitter*, on zinc-covered oak counters. Religious metaphysics is no longer admissible, today, except on condition of being an aperitif and preceding a feast of rubbish. 'You write for men and not for angelic spirits,' this father told me. Must I essay to fill myself on the prose of this advice? Alas! I would earn maybe a piece of bread!"

The unchecked Marchenoir felt, nevertheless, that he was flattering himself with an impossible humility. To tease out from universal history a symbolic ensemble, that is to say, to prove that history *signifies something*, that it has its architecture and that it develops docilely with respect to anterior data of an infallible plan, that is an operation that demanded the prerequisite holocaust of Free Will, so that, at least, modern reason can conceive it. There was no getting around it. He was condemned to the uncertain experience of slapping his century in order to be heard and, on this account, the enormity of such defiance possessed for him the stew of a voluptuous temptation. His *condottiere* nature soon took hold of him and he ended up by fixing on the most imprudent of resolutions, refusing to apply, after the fact and under form of instruction, to his future book, the cowardly emollients of an apology. Maybe, also, he was right to count on the exasperation even with his thought and form, on the extraordinary excess of audacity that he foresaw clearly where his subject was going to lead him, in the hope of a scandalous or surprising success, which would be, at least, a simulacrum of that justice that contemporary vermin does not accord to a superior mind.

Moreover, the apparent sagacity of any counsel will never prevail against these torrential natures that the sudden yawning of the largest mouth of the abyss would not stop. That which prudent people call by the name of temerity, would it not be rather, in them, a heroic obedience to some superior propulsion that these martyrs would have in advance accepted the agonies of? When he was notified of a great thing, Marchenoir's breast opened like a triptych, and what was seen to appear was his heart dripping with blood, between an image of prayer and an image of extermination!

XXXV

Because he wished history were a cryptogram, it was a matter of reading the signs and penetrating the combinations thereof. But the signs had been unfolding for six thousand years, from the first man, from top to bottom of the prodigiously flared pyramid of humankind. Their combinations were innumerable like dust, infinitely complicated, contrived, weaved, braided, imbricated, folded one over the other, interlaced and tangled together at all depths.

All the hands of night had weaved this chaos. The three Concupiscences, like indefatigable spinners, had furnished the skein, and the seven Sins had unwound it, belly to earth, in all the senses, around all generations, across the inextricable whirlpool of episodes. Love, Death, Sorrow, Forgetfulness had put their parables together for an eternal commerce of *errata*, where each of them painted their own picture of all the darkness.

From time to time, an excellent historian appeared to check the balance and his gelatinous head liquified on the pans. Hypothesis said to Conjecture: Let us go amuse ourselves! and they had themselves caressed, first one then the other, by an old Lie completely naked, on the supple divan of Criticism. The surprising route of history was all at a crossroads, with the posts spinning like weather vanes, when the dates, few of them certain, indicated, in the direction of some navigable events, all the little inexistent paths, to arrive at impossible verifications. Erudition chartered Alexandrian libraries to provision innumerable rodents with glasses, whose job was to peck at fetuses in the enormous pile of documentary dung dropped by the largest animals, all the while refraining religiously from the vague desire of a conclusion. If, by chance, one among them paid any notice, it was under the express condition of insulting some great thing, while tickling with his quill the soles of the feet of Saint Scoundrel, the eventually victorious and remunerative female potentate of toadies whose boots she had cleaned the mud off of. God knows, then, the nice jobs that were performed and the abject clairvoyance of these calumniators of ancestors!

Man's floating spirit,—like that of the Lord previously,—over the inexpressible disorder, had said, "There is not yet enough like that!" and he had ordered that *darkness should be*, that is to say that the soot of the past, diluted in the ink of our printers, should become indelible and crusty on the providential mosaic. Rudimentary concepts had become so effaced, that the most enormous, the most blinding, events, henceforth orphans of their principles and widows of their consequences, deorbited, excommunicated from everything altogether, acephalous and eunuch, no longer existed in their minds but in a fantastic state of posterity by chance. And that ignorance of all laws was particularly attested, in this century, by the growing rage to philosophize on history. Obscure testimony of a conscience irremediably cut to pieces and shuddering, one last time, under the cleaver of butchers of intelligence!

To begin, Marchenoir asked for the divorce of Chance and Liberty, absurdly united under the regime of reciprocal disembowelment. He judged it monstrous this coupling that had appeared modern Reason's one resource, afflicted by the celibacy of its very dear daughter, universally decried for her incontinence and the unclean selection of her cohabitants. It was too strong an imposture to claim that something real had ever exited a faculty, already so precarious, prostituted to that bastard of nothingness, and he had the ambition,—then when dying societies pawn their children in order to obtain, while paying, that they be finished off themselves,—to affirm, once and for all, before everything collapses and in honor of the thinking man, the irreproachable solidarity of all that has been accomplished, in every place and time, to the shame of the artisans of dust who think about exterminating the unity of man while scraping old bones!

In his eyes, the word *Chance* was an intolerable blasphemy that, in spite of the experience of his contempt, he was always surprised to meet in the mouths of so-called Christians,—*Nothing happens without His order or His permission*, he told the blasphemers: "he created you, your Chance, and he became incarnate to buy you back with his blood! Is that what you are thinking? Then, I, a Catholic, spit in the face of that rival of my Christ, who does not even have the honor of existing, like an idol, in a simulacrum where, at least, he would attest to the industry of an entrepreneur of divinities."

It was evident to him that one could not be Catholic, nor even flatter oneself with the infinitesimal pinch of a religious sentiment, if one did not give absolutely everything to Providence, and, from there, the idea of an infallible plan sprang to mind. At this height, it mattered little to him the philosophical, or even theological, squabbles that one could fire off to him on the subject of Free Will, left without resources, by that invasion of the absolute, in the withered pasture of the *conditional*.

"When Providence takes all, it is to give herself over completely. Consult Love, if you do not understand, and go to the devil!" Such was all the controversy of this intellectual stylite who never came down from his column.

He had, certainly, his hands full, what with the penitential labor that he had imposed on himself, for it had to do with reducing, by such a foreshortening of formulas, the universality of evidence so that it could be taken up in a ray of thought. Since it is always God who operates, *ad nutum*, over all the earth, it was necessary, of total necessity, to prejudge a *single* act, indefinitely refracted in his creatures. If one employed the word Paternity or love, or any other suggestive vocable, the meditation always returned that simple view of a single infinite gesture, produced by an absolute Being, reflected in the innumerable apparent diversity of symbols.

At some point in time when the needle of the compass gave way, whether this was the taking of Jerusalem or the Defenestration of Prague, no matter how wide the angle had opened in the investigative gyrations, this arbitrary point became the center of the universe. The past and the future irradiated luminously from that hearth and converged, shivering, toward the umbilicus. A supernatural identity burst out everywhere at the same time. Man was denounced for having always done the same thing, in a circular translation of circumstances perpetually analogical, and the imperceptible atrocity of an Ezzelino or a Halberstadt, had just as much harmonic force and salaried just as surely the mind of synthesis as did the colossal repetitions of the despotism of men like Tiberius, Phillip II or Napoleon!

History, as Marchenoir saw it, was made of a tissue so guaranteed that one could defy any forger to try and remove the marks from it in a plausible manner. The altered characters, the lines deviated from their senses, grazed the eye and cried out for someone to reintegrate them. The symbolic text, mutilated only by an iota, no longer made sense and divulged, with its sudden mutism, the profanation. That which Providence had written in the tradition redivivus of the people, with bloodstains and mountain chains of the dead, had been written for eternity, in a way that no scraper or sacrilegious acid would ever have been capable of obliterating, of a durable solecism, this palimpsest of sorrow!

Because, such was its evocative arrangement, for this magician of exegesis, who wanted everything to appear at the same time before the tribunal in his mind: Every earthly thing is set up for Sorrow. Now, this Sorrow was, in his eyes, as much the beginning as it was the end. It was not merely the goal, the ulterior comminatory expression, it was the *logic* itself of the mysterious Scriptures, in which he supposed that the Will of God ought to be read. Genesis's terrible sentence, of the departure from Eden, he applied, in his rigor, to the ever *painful* birthing of the least peripeteia of earth's oecumenical novel.

So, on this accursed planet, condemned to *sprout* nothing but thorns, in sixteen centuries, for the fallen race, the dreadful derision of Progress was accomplished, in the sempiternal renewal of iterative prefigurations of the catastrophe which ought to explain everything and consume all on the final day of reckoning.

The angels ought to have had fear and pity of that spectacle, on which one had reason to fear lest the curtain of divine pudency should ever fall! Human generations forever devoured at the banquets of the strong, on every continent where Nimrod's children had spread their tablecloth, and the Poor, whose surprising destiny it is to represent God even, the ever vanquished poor, flouted, slapped, violated, cursed, cut into pieces, but never dying,—kicked, under the table, like a piece of garbage, from Asia to Africa and, from Europe, the entire world over,—without a single hour being accorded him to quench his own tears and to scrape off his bloody scabs! All that, for the entire duration of antique societies, sculpted in formidable foreshortening in King Balthasar's orgy.

Next, the advent of the perfect Poor, in whom are summed up the most exquisite abominations of extreme poverty and which was Itself the Balthasar of a feast of tortures, to which all the powers of suffering were invited. Such redemption as to make whoever transfigured the *poetics* of man without renewing his heart tremble, in derision of what had been announced.

A second register of formulas was simply started, and the great jubilation of goats and vultures began anew. In the immense countries unexplored by Christianity, the cuisine of peoples' pastors did not change, but, in Christianity, the poor were sometimes invited, charitably, to delight in the excrement of power, of which the poor themselves were the aliment. The burden of the feeble, from then on aggravated by spiritualism, made the bones of nine-tenths of humanity creak.

As if the apparition of the Cross had panicked nations, the universe merged together in a prodigious jostle. Onto the Roman Empire writhed by colic, gouty in the feet, rotten at heart, and become bald like its first Caesar, millions of brutes with human gobs surged. Goths, Vandals, Huns, Francs, sat down, sniggering, on their shields, and slid down in avalanches against the gates of Rome that burst open under the thrust. The Danube, swollen with savages, spread out in inundation on the latrines of the Lower Empire. From the East, the Cameleer Prophet, squatting on the dung of his flock, was already hatching, in his flea-infested bosom, the famished grasshoppers who would fill two-thirds of the known world. Men battled, men were disemboweled, men ate each other's entrails, for eight hundred years, from Persia's extremity to the Atlantic shores. Finally, the great feudal framework was installed on the mess of the slaughter.

It was believed to be the prop of a quasi-celestial Jerusalem that was going to be constructed, and it was still a scaffold. Even Chivalry, the most noble thing that man had invented, was not often merciful to the suffering members of the Lord, which it had a mission to protect. Even the Crusades, without which Europe's past would have been a little less than a pile of garbage, were not without the horrible trail of all purulences left by the responsible animal. However, it was adolescence with its heart afire, it was the time of love and enthusiasm for Christianity! The saints, they were there then, as today, a half dozen for every hundred million mediocre and abject souls,—about,—and the odious livestock that venerated them, after their deaths, was sometimes obliged to borrow mud and saliva to shout them down when it pleased them, when it had the honor of keeping them alive under their dirty feet.

Two things, barely, appeared to Marchenoir to merit that the nausea of that abominable contemplation should be surmounted: the Papacy's indestructible preeminence and France's inalienable suzerainty. Nothing had been able to prevail against these two privileges. Not the hostility of the times, or the business of Judases, or the surpassing indignity of certain titulars, or revolutions, or defeats, or renunciations, or the unconscious profanations of stupid sacrilege! . . . When one or another had threatened to become extinct, the world had appeared under Interdiction. Boniface VIII's *Unam Sanctam* bull, the famous bull of the *Two Swords*, no longer had any believers, to be honest, and France was governed by boors . . . No matter! some souls knew that there exists, in their favor, a legal prescription against all proceedings claiming restitution for the nothingness, and Marchenoir was a unit in the small number of these unfortunate souls, carried along on a melting block of ice, in the middle of a warm ocean, towards an imbecilic tropic!

But, before it sank, this millenarian wanted to summon modern Times, the most iniquitous and most stupid times that have ever been, before a Judge whose imminent Coming he anticipated, although he had the appearance of having slept deeply for the last several centuries, and whom he hoped, by dint of desperate clamors, to make, once and for all, fall from the sky! These clamors, he had gathered from everywhere, and accumulated, amalgamated, coagulated them in himself. A sublime student of his own tortures, he had syncretized, in an algebra to make minds explode, the universal totality of sorrows.

From out of this forest came roaring an unknown Symbolic system that he would have been able to name the symbolic system of Tears and which was going to become his language for speaking to God. It was like an infinite rumbling of the doleful voices of those trampled on throughout the ages, in a miraculously abbreviated formula that explicated,—by necessity in a manner of divine ransom,—the interminable adjournments of Justice and the apparent inefficacy of Redemption.

This then was what he aspired to put before the eyes, at first, of his inattentive contemporaries; subsequently, under the clear view of Him whom he called the advent, like an overwhelming testimony of the muddy apostasy of a generation that will perhaps be the last before the deluge,—if its monstrous indifference made it emissary to assume the opprobrium of its elders, who were less abominable than it, of which recorded history has so cowardly stammered the accusation!

XXXVI

Marchenoir wrote just one time to Véronique, to announce his return. By fear or by virtue, he had abstained up until then, although he was dying with desire to do so, limiting himself to mentioning her, with thinly disguised tenderness, in each of his epistles to the sempiternal Leverdier. Finally, several days before his departure, he had made a decision suddenly and what follows is his inconceivable letter:

> My dear Véronique, please add for me, to your accustomed prayers, orisons for the dying which you will find in your euchologion. My body is fine, but my mind is in the agony of death and I suppose you are particularly singled out to assist me, as it is on account of you that I endure this dreadful tribulation.
>
> I am head over heels in love with you, that is the truth of it, and I needed to get out of Paris to feel it. I am determined to write to you on this simple matter, that I need *you to know*. Women are clairvoyant in these matters, and this feeling, which I didn't notice until a few days ago, you must certainly have noticed, for a long time now, if I can judge by certain acts of caution that I recall, today, and which tended manifestly to delay the outburst. But, even if you had not understood or divined anything, I thought that it was necessary still to make myself clear, if for no other reason than to distance from our relationship the danger of such a mystery.
>
> What will become of us? There are but two issues: you save me or I lose you. As for our separating, admitting that it is possible, this would be perhaps the

most disastrous of denouements. You have infused into my life a supernatural Christianity so heady that I can no longer breathe any other atmosphere.

Now, I have lost all my courage, my soul is completely unsettled. You will need to be sentenced to an incredible reserve, for I am burning inside, after the agitation of this voyage, like a poorly extinguished torch that the wind would have lit up again. This counterfeit sister-and-brother relationship that unites us and has separated us, up to now, will no longer suffice. It would be necessary to construct some other adjoining wall that rises up to the seventh heaven and that no betrayal of the senses could cut into.

This masonry work would be for you, doubtless, possible, you, a spiritual and unsullied soul, who no longer possesses a body except for the too carnal eyes of your unfortunate friend, whose presence will stir, I sense, all the old stagnation and all the filth. Search then, dear treasurer of heroism, it is perhaps in the direction of martyrdom that you will discover what we need.

You cannot stand to be regarded as a saint, and you know whether I approve this horror. But, in the hypothesis that it would have pleased Our Lord to cast on you all the majesty of his heaven, you would continue still, nevertheless, to be a *real woman* for eternity,—as one is a priest,—for what God has fabricated by his essential Hand carries indelible *character*, as much as the Sacraments of his Church. You would be forced, by consequence, to see as clearly as any other the evil in this world, where death was introduced by the first woman.

That is why I asked you for the prayers of those in the agonies of death. I am at risk of death for my soul, because of you, my love, and I return to Paris, in one week, like someone brought back to earth. If you have not grown completely impregnable against my weakness, I will lead you into a cavern of despair.

You yourself made me understand, a long time ago, that should you become my woman or my mistress, the abomination would be equally endless. I would find in your bed and in your arms all your *past*, and this past, released from the abyss where your penitence hurled it, would snatch me from you, piece by piece, with reddened pincers, to install itself in my place. Our love would be an opprobrium and our voluptuous pleasures a vomiting. We would have lost everything that honors us and rediscovered everything that can debase us further. Instead of this luminous canton of the sky where we float while suffering, we would be squatting at the edge of a public road, in an infected corner, where the most filthy animals would have the permission to soil us while passing . . .

It is necessary then that I exorcise myself, my dearest. I do not know how, but it must be done immediately, under pain of hell or death. There you have it, my mind is full of darkness and I would not know how to offer you the shadow of an idea that might resemble an appearance of salutary expedience. Ah! my friend, my thrice loved, my beautiful Véronique of the way of the Cross! how much I suffer! my heart breaks and I weep, as I have seen you, so many times, weep yourself, on your knees, for days entire, before your large crucifix! Only, your tears were infinitely sweet and mine are infinitely bitter!

Your MARIE-JOSEPH.

146

XXXVII

The retreat at the Grande Chartreuse, however suggestive and beneficial it had been, could no longer be prolonged for this tragic soul, who had an idea of Paradise as one eternal, furious ascent toward the Absolute. The fourth week had come to an end and Marchenoir decidedly had had enough of it. The appeasement, that he had come to seek, had only been exterior and intermittent. The exquisite kindness of his hosts had been able to relax his nerves and ease the upper part of his mind, but it was unable to do anything beyond that.

It was remarkable, moreover, and quite in conformance with the irreproachable exactitude of his ironic destiny, that the worst calamity that he could fear had been revealed to him precisely on this mountain, where he had believed he would have been certain to breathe, for a few days, in perfect safety. Now, he had the most violent need to hurl himself in front of this ordeal, even if it should kill him!

He went then to take his leave of the Father General who had received him multiple times with that gentleness common among the Humble, which subdued in the past Tarasques and Emperors. Marchenoir, who belonged to neither of these two categories of monsters, expressed, as best he could, his gratitude, in supplicating the amiable old man to bless him before his departure.

"My dear child," he responded, "I will do more than that, I promise you. I know of your life and your sufferings from what your friend, Monsieur Leverdier, has written of them and what Father Athanase felt he could confide in me, and I take a profound interest in you. You have undertaken a book for the glory of God and you are poor . . . two times poor, as you renounce the glory that men give . . . Take this, I beseech you, from the Chartreuse, this feeble assistance that your Christian soul can accept without shame," he added, holding out to him a thou sand-franc bill, "and remember, in your battles, the old *useless servant*, but full of tenderness, who will pray for you."

The unfortunate man, overcome with emotion, fell to his knees and received benediction from this head of the greatest souls on earth. The General helped him up and, having embraced him in his arms, escorted him to the door while exhorting him to manly virtues that Christian society appears to have taken a strong dislike to, but the tradition of which perseveres, in spite of everything, in these solitudes,—without which, so far as it seems, heaven, having grown tired of vaulting, after so many centuries, over such a disgusting race, would collapse, wholeheartedly, in order to annihilate it.

Father Athanase waited for him anxiously. He had spoken warmly, but his superior's intentions were unknown to him. The good monk was transported by the naïve joy of his friend, who this money delivered from hideous anguishes, over and above his more intimate torments.

"I see you leaving without too many anxieties," he said to him. "At least, I am assured that dark poverty will not immediately seize you again and I am persuaded that a little later, God will send you some other assistance. You must not be permitted to believe that this good Master would have showered upon you the most rare gifts, merely to make you suffer. Besides, the Church Militant has need of writers of your sort and I hope that you will overcome, in the end, all obstacles, by virtue of your talent alone.

"But, I have other subjects to be anxious about and it is precisely the excess of your strength that terrifies me," he added, with a melancholy smile, while touching his finger to his forehead and to his breast. "It is here and there where your most redoubtable persecutors are located. I have thought a lot about you, my dear friend. It is a grievous mystery that a man such as yourself should have been born in the nineteenth century. You would have been a Leaguer, a Crusader, a Martyr. You have the soul of one of these ancient apologists of the Faith, who found

148

the means to catechize virgins and executioners even in the jaws of beasts. Today, you are delivered into the gums of cowards and mediocre men, and I understand that it appears to you an intolerable torture. You have passed forty years and you have not yet been able to acclimate nor even to orient yourself toward modern society. This is terrible . . .

"I am not accusing you, nor judging you, poor friend. I feel sorry for you with all my soul. Render me justice. I do not reproach you for not having known how to *make yourself a position*. I am not one of those bourgeois whose name alone causes your retina to turn black. I am a Carthusian, simply, and I believe that the best position is to do the will of God, whatever that might be. If it is your lot to write beautiful books, without consolation and without salary, in the midst of continual sufferings, your situation is cut and dried and fifty times more brilliant, I imagine, than that of a prime minister who will be, tomorrow morning or tomorrow evening, kicked down the stairs of forgetfulness. Only, I am afraid lest this gift of strength, which will turn you, perhaps, into a great man of action by the sword or by words, if you should make use of it,—lest it turns against you in the end and hurls you into despair."

"You are right, my father, and I also am not without terror," responded Marchenoir. "Hope is the only one of the three theological virtues that I can accuse myself, in all sincerity, of having knowingly and gravely sinned against. There is in me an instinct of revolt so savage that nothing is able to dominate it. I have ended by giving up on the idea of the expulsion of this ferocious beast and I am arranging things so as not be devoured by it. What more can I do? Each man is, at birth, matched up with a monster. Some wage war with it and others make love with it. It appears that I am very strong, as you say, because I have been honored by the habitual company of the king of masters: Despair. If God loves me, may he defend me, when I no longer have the courage to defend myself! What is reassuring is that I can no longer be surprised by it, for I do not believe in happiness. It has been said several times that I am a superior man and I do not deny it. I would be a sot and an ingrate to disavow this largesse that I did nothing to merit. Ah well! if happiness is already nearly unrealizable for the most mediocre of beings, for the easiest to content among the reasonable pachyderms, how could this diapason of sorrows that one calls a man of genius demand it? Happiness, my dear father, is made for beasts . . . or saints. I have then renounced it, for a long time now. But, for want of happiness, I would like, at least, peace, that inaccessible peace, that the angels of Noel have, however, announced, *on earth*, for men of goodwill!"

The father hesitated for a moment. Whatever could be inspired by the most ardent sacerdotal charity, he had already said to this disconsolate man. He had attempted everything to solidify a little hope in this broken vessel, out of which flowed the cordial, as soon as it had been poured in. He could no longer accuse his penitent of being indocile or self-acclaiming. The suspicion of pride,—of such a convenient resource for confessors and directors lacking clairvoyance or zeal!—he had put it aside, from the first day, with defiance, estimating that it is more apostolic to penetrate hearts than to seal them, from the first, implacably, under seminary formulas.

No-Love is one of the names of the Father of Pride and, certainly, in his life he had not known many beings who loved as much the poor as Marchenoir did! He felt himself in the presence of an exceptional man of misfortune whom nothing could save, a witness for Love and for Justice,—lamentable holocaust of a society struck by madness who thought that Genius sullied it and that the aristocracy of a single soul is a danger for its pastors' kennels.

"You ask for peace at the very moment you are leaving for war," he said finally. "So be it. You believe yourself called to protest solitarily, in the name of justice, against all contemporary society, with the preliminary certitude of being absolutely vanquished, whatever might turn out to be the consequences for you,—in contempt of your security and the judgments of your peers, with a complete disinterestedness in all that determines, ordinarily, human actions. You believe yourself unfree to choose another route of death . . . It is God who knows this. It is easier to condemn you than to understand you. All that can be done for you is to raise one's arms towards heaven. But your corsair is too loaded . . . You are not alone, you have taken on the responsibility of another soul. What will you do with her? Have you calculated the horrifying obstacle of a passion stronger than you and distinctly legible, for me, in the least movements of your physiognomy? And if you are allowed to triumph over it, will you still not hesitate to drag this poor creature into unequal quarrels, which I foresee too well you will immediately engage yourself in? . . ."

Marchenoir, having grown pale, had appeared to stagger and sat down, with such a poignant expression of grief, that Father Athanase was deeply distressed. There was a painful silence of several instants, at the end of which the miserable man began in a voice so low that the father was obliged to strain his ears to hear him.

XXXVIII

"What would you want me to respond? It will be what God wills and I hope to bless his holy will at the hour of my last agony. If I were rich, I could arrange my existence in such a way that the dangers you fear for me would disappear almost entirely. On my knees I would write my books, in some solitary place where I would not even hear the world's clamors or its maledictions; it is not like this, unfortunately, and I have no idea where the loathsome combat for life will drag me.

"You speak of this passion . . . It is true that I am a little bit powerless to resist it. For many years, I have been chaste, like the 'desire of hills,'[1]—with a plethora of the heart. You are

_____
1 A phrase from the Catholic Litany of the Sacred Heart of Jesus.

a practitioner of souls, you know how much this circumstance aggravates the peril. But the noble girl will invent something to save me from herself . . . I do not know what . . . however, I am sure that she will succeed. As for quarrels, I will probably have them, and all sorts. I must expect them.

"But that is nothing," he said in a stronger voice, while getting up all of a sudden. "If I profane the stinking ciboria that are the sacred vases of democratic religion, I must expect that they will redound to me, and the rare spirits that will take delight in my audacity will be armed, assuredly not, to defend me. I will combat alone, I will succumb alone, and my beautiful saint will pray for my soul's repose, that is all . . . Perhaps, also, I will not succumb. The temerarious have been, sometimes, the victorious.

"I leave your house in absolute ignorance of what I will do, but with the most inflexible resolution of not leaving truth without a witness. It is written that the starving and those dying of thirst for justice will be saturated. I can then hope for an unmeasured drunkenness. Never will I be able to make do or console myself with what I see. I do not intend to reform an irreformable world, nor to abort Babylon. I am one of those who cry out in the desert and who devour the roots of the burning bush, when the crows forget to carry the nourishment away for themselves. Whether someone listens to me or does not listen to me, whether someone applauds me or insults me, as long as I do not kill myself, I will be the consignee of Vengeance and the very obedient domestic of a *foreign* Fury that commands me to speak. I am absolutely powerless to resign this office, and it is with the bitterest desolation that I declare it. I suffer an infinite violence and the fits of rage that emerge from me are but echoes, singularly enfeebled, of a superior Imprecation that I have the surprising disgrace to reiterate.

"It is for that reason, doubtless, that poverty was accorded to me with such munificence. Wealth would have made of me one of those ambulant rotting carcasses, duly propped up, that men of

152

high society sniff at with sympathy in their salons and which the gourmand vanity of women lick their lips at. I would have made a feast of the poor, like the others and, maybe, exhaling, in the fashion of a glorious man of my acquaintance, several moaning phrases on the subject of pity. Happily, Providence with hands of thorns has watched over me and preserved me from becoming a charming fellow, ripping me to shreds with its caresses . . .

"Now, that it might be fulfilled, my frightful destiny! Contempt, ridicule, calumny, universal execration, it is all the same to me. Whatever sorrow that comes to me will no longer pierce me, surely, like the inexplicable death of my child . . . I could be starved to death, but I cannot be prevented from barking under the leather straps of indignation!

"Obedient son of the Church, I am, however, in a communion of impatience with all the rebels, all the disappointed, all the unfulfilled, all the damned in this world. When I remember this multitude, a hand grabs me by the hair and pulls me, beyond the relative exigencies of social order, into the absoluteness of a vision of injustice to make even the pride of philosophies weep. I have read Bonald and the other theoreticians of equilibrium. I know all the rational things that one can say to find consolation, among virtuous people, in the temporal reprobation of three quarters of humanity . . .

"Saint Paul did not find consolation, he who recommended *waiting*, while bemoaning with *all* creatures, the adoption and the Redemption, affirming that we were not redeemed but 'in hope,' and that in this way nothing was accomplished. Me, the most recent arrival, I think that an agony of six thousand years gives us perhaps the right to be impatient, as never before, and, given that we must *lift up our hearts*, we should tear them, once and for all, out of our breasts, these desperate organs, to stone the sky with! It is the *sursum corda* and the *lamma sabacthani* of those who have been abandoned by this last century.

"When the Word incarnate bled and cried for this *unaccomplished* redemption and when his Mother, the only creature who has truly given birth, became, under the dying regard of the divine Lamb, that fountain of tears that overflowed all oceans, the inanimate creatures, innocent witnesses to this double agony, preserved forever the compassion and trembling for Him. The *Master's* last breath, carried by the winds, went off to fatten the hidden treasure of tempests, and the earth, penetrated by these tears and by this blood, began again to germinate more grievously than ever, the symbols of mortification and repentance. A curtain of darkness extended over the already somber veil of the first malediction. The thorns of the royal diadem of Jesus-Christ became interlaced around every human heart and attached themselves, for tens of centuries, like the spikes of an agonizing cilice, onto the flanks of the terrified world!

"On this day was inaugurated the perfect penitence of Adam's children. Until then, veritable Man had not suffered and torture had not received divine sanction. Humanity, moreover, was too young for the Cross. When the executioners descended from Calvary, they brought back to all peoples, in their bloody gobs, the great news of the Majority of humankind. Grief passed beyond, with a bound, the infinite abyss that separates the accident of substance and became NECESSARY.

"At which moment, the promises of joy and triumph that the Scriptures are saturated with, inscribed in the new law under the abbreviated vocable of Beatitudes, traveled across generations, rushing headlong like a whirlwind of swords. In a word, humanity began to suffer *with hope* and this is what is called the Christian Era!

"Will we soon come to the end of this exodus? God's people can no longer take a step and will, shortly, expire in the desert. All the great souls, Christian or not, beg for a denouement. Are we not at the end of everything, and is not the palpable disarray of modern times the prodrome of some immense supernatural perturbation that will finally deliver us? The centuries-old notions of aristocracy and sovereignty, which were the pillars of the world, cover, today, with their dust, the impure alleys of three-quarters of the royal Races in deliquescence, which contaminate them by their emunctories. To hell with respect, resignation, obedience, and the old honor! All is misshapen, polluted, defamed, mutilated, irreparably made destitute and fricasseed, by what has served as a tabernacle over the intelligence. The deafness of the rich and the hunger of the poor, those are the only treasures that have not been dilapidated! . . . Ah! God's word of honor, this sacred promise to 'not leave you orphans' and to come back, this advent of the renewing Spirit from which we have received merely the premises,—I summon it with all the violent voices that are in me, I lust for it with all the burning concupiscences, I am famished for it, dying of thirst, I can no longer wait and my heart is breaking, in the end, however hard one might suppose it, when the evidence of universal distress has broken out too much, over and above my own distress! . . . O my God Savior, have pity on me!"

The lamenter's voice that sounded, for several minutes, like a whelk, in that pacific residence unaccustomed to such cries, faded away in a shower of tears. Father Athanase, much more moved than he would have wished to appear, placed his hand on Marchenoir's head and, constraining him to get down on his knees, pronounced over him that efficacious sacerdotal benediction that partakes of absolution and exorcism.

"Go, my dear child," he then said, "and may the peace of God be with you. Maybe you have been destined for some great thing. I do not know. You are so removed from the common ways that an extreme reserve is naturally imposed on me and paralyzes me up to the point of expressing my fears. You have acquired the prayers of the Carthusians and they will follow you even to the scaffold, considering, in the worst case, that you are in danger of death. That is all there is to tell you. Go then in peace, dear unfortunate man, and remember that if all the doors of the earth should close themselves before you with maledictions, there is one, wide-open, on the threshold of which you will always find us, arms extended, to receive you . . ."

XXXIX

The return voyage seemed interminable to Marchenoir. It was mid February and the night train he had chosen with plans to arrive in Paris in the morning gave him the impression of rolling through a polar country, in harmony with the desolation of his soul. A moon, in its last quarter, hung funereally over the flat landscapes, where its miserable brightness succeeded in naturalizing phantoms. This residue of a cold face, nibbled at by weasels and screech owls, would have sufficed to wean from lunar illusions an imagination tinted gray by the ewe milk of old romantic elegies. Small glacial shadows circulated around the chipped celestial body, in the grooves lined with clouds, and came to sink like needles into the ears and along the loins of the voyagers, who tried in vain to make their mucous membranes draft proof. Those dear rugs of delectation were abominably permeated and became sponges, in all the compartments of this *omnibus* train, which endlessly crawled from one station deprived of genius to another station lacking originality.

From one quarter of the hour to the next, bellowing or lamentable voices indistinctly uttered the names of places that made every ounce of courage turn pale. Then, in the conflict of pads and the prolonged whinnying of brakes, exploded a squall of doors clacking brusquely, cries of distress, yells of victory, as if this gouty convoy had been assailed by a party of cannibals. From the nocturnal grayness emerged hybrid mammifers who rushed into the cars, vociferating prognostications or irrefutable observations, and deboarded again, one hour later, without any conjecture, even kindly, that would have been capable of justifying sufficiently their apparition.

Marchenoir, installed in a corner and having remained almost alone until it was nearly the end of the night, by an unexpected stroke of good luck that he attributed to the grace of

God, stretched out his legs on the implacable third-class bench seat, put his sacks under his head and tried to sleep. He was cold to the bone and cold in his heart. The wagon lamp vacillated sadly in its porthole and poured its raw, dismal light on him. At the other extremity of this cell, or cabin on wheels, a poor being, apparently belonging to the human species, a young idiot almost bald, agitating without cease, with chuckles of joy, a kind of milk bottle in which he listened to hazelnuts or little stones jingle, while a very old woman, who shivered no less, endeavored, weeping, to temper his exhilaration the moment it threatened to become too shrill.

The miserable artist closed his eyes to avoid seeing any longer this group, who appeared to him a foreshortening of all misery and who gripped him with a horrible sadness. But he was dying of cold and sleep did not obey. Things of the past came back to him, more lugubrious than ever. That hideous innocent represented to him the son that he had lost and, by a monstrous association of images and memories, he saw himself as the grandmother, whose old visage streaming with tears recalled so many tears of his own, without which he would have been dead a long time ago. Truly, a fine misfortune! His reflections grew so atrocious that he let a groan escape, instantly echoed by the idiot with a burst of jubilation that his guardian had some trouble to calm down.

At that moment, Marchenoir engrossed himself in the memory of his Véronique as if before an altar of refuge. He wanted to hypnotize himself with this unique thought. He commanded the dear face to appear to him and to fortify him. But he saw her so grievous and so pale that the assistance he waited for from her, was, in reality, nothing but a mutation of his anguish. The imperceptible facts, of their life in common, immense for him alone, and which had been his presentiment of heaven; their very pure chats in the evenings, when he poured out into this simple soul the best of his spirit; the long prayers they made together, before an image lit up by a naïve sanctuary lamp, and which she prolonged, quite a long time after he had retired to his room and fallen asleep, saturated with joy; finally, the singular pilgrimages to unknown churches in the neighborhood: all that charming flower in its true spring, seemed to him, that night, discolored, without scent, livid and bruised, having the air of floating on a basin of darkness . . .

He recalled, above all, a trip to Saint Denis, last October, on a delicious day. After a rather long stop before the apostle's relics, whose history Marchenoir recounted, they had descended into the crypt to visit the empty tombs of France's princes. The majesty appeared to sound quite empty to them in this cave musty with Death's best vintages, and the epitaphs of these absent personages *judged* over many centuries, whose dust had been eaten by the dogs of the Revolution, they read emotionlessly like the inanimate text of some register of nothingness. Emotion had come, however, like an eagle, and it had scratched them with its claws, those two, those strange dreamers, to the very depths of their entrails.

At the center of the obituary hemicycle, under the choir even of the basilica, a kind of black and savagely bricked dungeon was permitted to be explored to its interior, through narrow barbicans from which exhaled a catacombal stench. They apperceived, in this cave lit up by sordid lamps, a row of twenty or thirty coffins, aligned on boards, bound with strips of silver, riddled by worms, made over with molds, ripped open for the most part. That is all that remains of the Three Christian Kings' sepulture.

This scene had been for Marchenoir of infinite suggestion and, now, he found it, with precision, in the lucid reminiscence of a half-sleep where his pain grew numb. His very sweet friend was next to him, totally shaken with her distress, and he explained in a sovereign fashion the transmutation of royal furniture, the example of which was before their eyes. The red brightness of the lamps struggled trembling against the abysmal mist that rose up in black volutes from the gaping cracks in the biers. All that one wanted to call the honor of France and of Christian name lay there under that fetid arch. The sarcophagi, it is true, had been emptied of their treasures, that the ditches and the sewers had been battered to obtain, and it would certainly not have been possible to find, in their cracks, the wherewithal to nourish a family of centipedes, for a single day,—but the cases of oak and cedar, penetrated and unctuous by the liquid potentates who lived there, no longer appertained to any ligneous essence and could very well claim, in turn, in the quality of royal putridness, the peoples' veneration. One could have even hoisted them, with respectful grapnels, onto the throne of the Sun King, where they would have done as much as he, for the glory of God and the protection of the poor.

By dint of looking into this tissue of darkness torn by impure light, Marchenoir finished by no longer being able to discern anything with certitude. A vile lamp in front of him appeared to become enormous and dropped down, as if by unction, toward the coffins. There was, below, a frightening movement of black staved-in forms, while a glacial gust blew above, and Véronique struggled in the middle of a riot of specters, with strident cries, without his being able to understand what was happening, nor how to help her, nor even how to call out to her . . .

A supreme effort woke him up. The idiot, seized by a violent crisis, having lowered the window on the door, vociferated with rage and the poor old woman, in distress, implored assistance. The dreamer had had lots of experience with idiots and he knew how to control them. He approached then, took the two hands of the poor being in one of his strong hands and, with the other, he held his head, constraining him to look at him. He did not have to say a word even, he had the kind of eyes that were needed and he would have made an exquisite guardian for lunatics. The exasperated boy went slack like a rag and fell asleep immediately on the shoulder of his companion.

He himself, alas! really could have used someone to relax him and to appease him. He needed several minutes to recover completely from the agitation of his nightmare. Fortunately, dawn was arising and he was sure to arrive before an hour. In vain, he proposed to become extremely strong, to practice the most sublime heroism, whatever negative might come of it. Nothing could act against the dreadful presentiments that tortured him. He told himself he would have perhaps done better to travel second class. He would have been less cold, and the cold ripped out his heart, he had often felt . . . In the end, he had done what he could do, God would do the rest . . . He had not notified his two faithful friends of his time of arrival. He was too sure that they would have passed the night waiting for him at the station. He felt a relief at the thought that he was going to have to traverse Paris before seeing them again, and that this delay, this taking in of new air, would dissipate, assuredly, his irrational disquietude. It was the letter to Véronique that was poniarding him. He felt atrocious and insane to have written it. And, nevertheless, what could he have done or not done, without seeming, in his own eyes, a total madman or a veritable traitor?

"I am a sot, all that happens is for the best," he concluded, this surprising optimist; "God permits with his left hand and orders with his right hand and everything works itself out within the ellipse with its two foci of his Providence!"

XL

Marchenoir exited the station in Paris at the break of day, his light bag in hand. He needed to walk, to wear himself down on the paving stones and the bitumen of this city of damnation, where each road reminded him of a stopping place on the pilgrimage to hell that had been his life.

He felt, with all the renewed vigor of his sense faculties, the despotism of this *fatherland*. It is necessary to have lived by the soul and by the spirit in this umbilicus of human intellectuality, to have flayed alive one's illusions and hopes, and then, to have found the means to preserve a little piece of heart in order to understand the voluptuousness of the inhalation of this atmosphere empoisoned by two million chests, after a somewhat prolonged absence. Man, naturally a slave, reimmerses himself then, with delight, in a cesspool one hundred times cursed and licks over again, with a canine emotion, the hobnailed soles that are placed so often on his face . . .

Marchenoir disdained, hated Paris, and yet he conceived no other terrestrial city habitable. The multitude's indifference is a surer desert than the desert itself, for those haughty hearts that the soiling sympathy of mediocre people offend. Then, his affective and intellectual double life had really debuted in this pile of peelings where dogs,—probably dead, today,—had been surprised, previously, to see him peck out his subsistence. His moral genesis had commenced in the midst of these matutinal sweepers and market-gardener carts that descended in a mad dash toward Les Halles, to reach the opening of the great Gob. Before, when one of those transpierced nights had ended which seemed to last three hundred sixty hours, to the vagabond without linen and without asylum; he remembered, now, to have had hope, all the same, and to have dilated his imprecise dream in the shiver of similar auroras.

Here, on this bench on the boulevard Saint-Germain, in front of Cluny, he had sat down, once before, in the early morning, twenty years ago! He had had no more strength to walk and, besides, he had *arrived*, going nowhere. He had subpoenaed the sun to appear, if for no other reason than pity, and made believe he was not sleeping, to avoid the beat cops' attention, when a still sadder being came to sit down beside him. It was a wandering girl, worn out by a vain pursuit and on the point of going home. The noctambulist's physiognomy had stirred, to a certain extent, the deplorable stemless heart of this faded flower, who wanted to know who he was and what he was doing there.

"Poor sir," she had said to him, "come home with me, I'm just a poor person, but I can certainly give you my bed for several hours, I sleep with anyone for money, it's true, but I'm not a disgusting person and I don't want to leave you on this bench."

This love affair of mud and misery had lasted half a day and he was never able to see his Samaritan again. It was one of the memories that most moved Marchenoir.

From Cluny to the Observatory, climbing the boulevard Saint-Michel, he found again thus, with each step, indelible impressions, because this was the quarter he had most often walked through in the sinister nocturnal cruisings of his adolescence. When he had arrived at the crossroad and nearly at the entrance to the rue Denfert-Rochereau, where Leverdier lived, whom he had, not without some struggle, resolved to see first, before returning home,—a palpitation shook him when he saw the banal restaurant, the theater of his first encounter with the Suction Cup, having become, by him, the sublime Véronique wiping the Face of the Savior. He was, instantly, seized anew by all his troubles and by a fear greater than the unknown. His friend seemed to him an infinitely redoubtable man who was going to pronounce definitive things and he climbed the stairs trembling.

After the first cries and the first embrace, these two so singular beings, each in his own way, sat down face to face, hands inside the other's, panting, gasping for breath, shedding tears, stammering: "My dear friend!"—"My good Georges!" both of them, already! sensing the rise, from the very depths of their joy, of the impossibility of expressing it,—as if the bourgeois were right and there did exist a jealous prohibition of the Infinite against all absolute sentiments!

"But I think," cried Leverdier, getting up hurriedly, "you must have need of something to eat. I have just made some coffee and I possess some excellent juniper. You will be served in an instant."

Marchenoir, silent, shivering, not daring to interrogate, noticed that the name Véronique had not even been pronounced. He observed, also, that his friend's assiduity was somewhat less febrile and tumultuous and, that in sum, it would have taken ten times less time to serve the largest cup of the best coffee in the world.

All of a sudden, he went towards him and put his two hands on his shoulders: "Georges," he said, "there is something, I want to know."

Leverdier was about his age. He was one of these blond negroes, washed in the saffron of stars and rubbed with a pastel of blood, who pleased women much more than men, who are ordinarily better armed against the surprises of the human face. The dominant trait of his vibratile physiognomy was the eyes, like Marchenoir's. But unlike those clear mirrors of ecstasy, illuminable only at the hearth of some deep emotion, his eyes were perpetually darting and scrutinizing, like those of an eagle in chase or of a lynx. No flash of ferocity, however. From this entire face transuded, on the contrary, a joyous and active kindness, whose expression was of equal value to a miracle, and the very intensity of his regard was a simple effect of the marvelous attention of his heart. A vague irony turned up just barely, sometimes, at the corners of his mouth and went up to crease the corner of his right eye. Visibly, this soul's palette was quite complete, with the exception of one color, black, which a deluge of darkness could not repair the absence of. This man had evidently received the vocation of being the great public consoler, all by himself, and for the single virtuoso who could do without the vulgar applause.

The contrast was striking when one saw them together, each one appearing to have precisely everything that the other lacked. Of medium height both of them, Marchenoir had the aspect of a big guard dog, whose approach made people tremble, but whom the first flight of anger could carry off into a chasm if he missed his prey. Leverdier, on the other hand, frail in appearance, but slightly feline under the crest of his curly hair, and practiced, since his childhood, in every sport, had artful resources that would have made him a most feared auxiliary light infantryman before a common enemy, if one had been advised to attack them. And one divined that he must also act similarly in their moral coalition.

The poor lynx, seeing himself cornered, tried at first to lower his eyes, but no sooner had he done so than his loyal and valiant soul made him open them again and the two friends locked eyes for several moments.

"Well, yes!" he responded, nervously, "there is one thing . . . unmentionable. You wrote an insensate letter to Véronique and the poor girl *disfigured* herself to make you disgusted with her."

At that unexpected announcement, Marchenoir turned around on his heels and distanced himself obliquely, in the manner of an insane person, his arms crossed on his head, and he began to exhale horrible raucous sounds that were neither sobs nor cries. Waves of pain escaped him, that spread out over the room and came back to weigh like a mountain on Leverdier. Transpierced with compassion, but powerless, this true friend bent over, and pressed his face on the marble fireplace to hide his tears.

This scene lasted nearly a quarter of an hour. Then, the enormous groaning stopped. Marchenoir approached the table and, taking the bottle of gin, filled a glass halfway with it and emptied it in one shot.

"Georges," he said next, in an extraordinarily gentle voice, "dry your tears and give me some coffee . . . Very well . . . Sit down here, now and tell me all the details. From now on, I can listen to it all."

XLI

Leverdier cherished Véronique in his own way, in the most brotherly way in the world, because he saw in her something appertaining to Marchenoir. This being, so singularly organized for the exclusive passion of friendship, had never found the need to struggle in order to distance from himself other feelings. He filled his life well enough, having enough amplitude to reach multitudes, should his great artist ever become popular. He had devoted a sort of gratitude, exalted to the point of cult, to the simple creature in whom Marchenoir had found consolation and comfort. Mediocrely open to this sacred Mysticism, which Marie-Joseph had made a study of and which Véronique assumed in her person, it was enough for him that his friends found their joy there or their alimentation. He asked for nothing else, being rejoiced or afflicted sympathetically, without ever understanding, but confessing with candor his mind's ineptitude.

For the two years that the seraphic concubinage had lasted, a very intimate mutual penetration had formed among these three souls, living among themselves and separated from the rest of the world. Although Leverdier did not live on the rue des Fourneaux, he was seen there nearly every day. He had even resolved to move there in the near term. In the last six weeks, he had regularly to receive news of Véronique, read with her the letters from the absent person, and could testify to a perfect uniformity of life,—up to the day when that girl of prayer and spontaneous holocaust, having received the message from the Grand Chartreuse, had executed, without alerting him, the unheard of act that he now had to recount to this unfortunate man, for whom he would have voluntarily suffered and who was now commanding him to cut his friend's throat.

He recounted then what he knew, and what he had seen or understood. His emotion was so great, that he stammered and sobbed almost, this rapid and precise dialectician. He was suffering for three people, as God would like to suffer, going into a panic and fainting for grief under the open wound of these two souls, who could not bleed except through him!

As for Marchenoir, it was all he could do to not expire under the rod that was breaking him, like a vulgar assassin that he accused himself of being. With each detail, he let out a cavernous "oof!", clenching his fists, and grinding his teeth like a man suffering from tetanus. Only, he saw further into it than Leverdier and he knew his Véronique better. He discerned, through the mist of his agony, by himself, an immense beauty of martyrdom, that this man of *little faith* could not perceive in his supernatural plan, and he came to connect thus with a principle of future consolation in the very paroxysm of his despair.

Now, here is what had happened. Véronique had received the letter, about eight days before. Leverdier having come to see her almost right after, found her, according to his expression, in a dark mood and agitated, wearing on her beautiful face an "autumn sky," the stigmata of a recent deluge. He had not conceived from this any suspicion nor any alarm, having gotten in the habit of attributing everything about her to the exigencies of a hyperesthetic mysticism, and knowing with what luxury one wept in that house. Véronique, besides, had not spoken to him about the letter. They had spoken, as always, about Marchenoir, expressing the ordinary wish of his near return and of a calming in his destiny . . .

Left alone, the saint began to pray. It was one of her endless and boundless entreaties, the duration and fervor of which surprised even Marchenoir,—the assumption of a rigid flame, white, sharp like a sword, without vacillation, without exterior vibration, in this magnetic silence of contemplation, that gathered around her all the murmurs and all the shivers in order to assimilate them. Unformulated prayer and impossible to transpose on the clavier of any language whatsoever, the sensual desire of which is, perhaps, a distant symbol, degraded, but intelligible.

Night fell slowly around that pilaster of ecstasy. When Véronique could no longer distinguish the pendant face of her crucifix, she revived a small prayer lamp, always lit in a rose crystal glass, and she got back down on her knees again. The amorous objurgation started again, more inflamed, more vehement, more extortive . . . It would have been a spectacle of terror and of heart-rending pity, to see that supplicant on her knees on the ground, her arms crossed, two streams of tears running from her eyes to the floor, absolutely immobile, with the exception of her superb throat, lifted up and palpitating by the surge of a prodigious hope!

The hours passed like this, their distant tolling coming to expire in vain in this room immersed in delectation, where atoms had the appearance of collecting so as not to trouble the great work of charity.

Towards morning, she got up again finally, broken, shivering, for a long time kissed the plaster feet of the image, curled up in a wool blanket, stretched out on the bed without getting inside, as she was wont to do, and fell asleep immediately murmuring: "Sweet Savior, have pity on my poor Joseph, just as he's had pity on me! . . ."

When a pale ray of sunlight came to awaken the penitent, the first thing she saw, as always, was her crucifix and her first thought translated into an outburst of joy.

"Ah! Monsieur Marchenoir," she cried out, jumping to the edge of the bed, "you permit yourself to fall in love with Madeleine. Wait a bit. I'll make myself pretty to receive you. You don't know yet what a pretty woman can think up to please the man she loves. You'll find out soon enough."

Then, undoing with one gesture her magnificent hair, the color of the setting sun, which fell to her knees, and in which forty lovers had been bathed, as if in a river of flames where their desires are reborn, she gathered it together with her fist on her head, with a single hand, and with the other, made a gesture to pick up a pair of scissors. Then all at once, changing her mind:

"No," she said, "I'd cut it badly, the merchant wouldn't want it and I've need of the money for *something else.*"

She got dressed rapidly, said her morning prayer and left the house.

When she returned, she was shorn like a golden ewe, and carrying sixty francs. The despicable hairdresser, who had robbed her besides, had restored, for better or for worse, with bands and tow, her head's harmony, but the massacre was evident and horrible. She had been able to escape, under the thick headscarf, the examination by people of the house, but if Leverdier had come! . . . He had very good eyes and it would be impossible to hide it from him. He would surely be opposed to what she wanted to do next. That fear put her to flight. "Better get it over with immediately," she thought, going out again like a thief.

XLII

She remembered having known before, on the rue de l'Arbalète, an industrious little Jew who lived off twenty, more or less suspect livelihoods. The peculiar old man ostensibly made a dirty business of pawn tickets and she had let herself be ransomed by him a good number of times. He was precisely the man she needed, that guy! He was certainly not encumbered by scruples! For two francs, one could make him clean a tile in the Morgue, with his tongue! Besides, he knew her and knew she would never denounce him to anyone.

"Monsieur Nathan," she said, arriving at his place, "do you need some money?"

This Monsieur Nathan was a little judaic putridity, as one will have sight of, it appears, until our planet's abrogation. The Middle Ages, at least, had the good sense of confining them in reserved kennels and imposing on them a special second-hand frock that allowed people to avoid them. When one absolutely had to deal with these foul-smelling people, one did it in hiding, as if from an infamy, and one purified himself afterwards as best one could. The shame and the peril of coming into contact with them was the Christian antidote of their pestilence, since God depended in perpetuity on such vermin.

Today when Christianity has the air of groaning under the heel of its own believers and when the Church has lost all credit, one grows indignant stupidly to see in them the masters of the world, and the enraged contradictors of apostolic tradition are the first to be surprised by it. One prohibits the disinfectant but one complains about having bugs. Such is the idiocy characteristic of modern times.

Monsieur Nathan had had diverse fortunes. He had lost millions and, although he was quite clever, he was considered, among his brothers, as a little gullible. His real name was Judas Nathan, but he wanted to be called Arthur, and such was his principle of death. This Jew was eaten away by the Christian vice of vanity. Successively tailor, dentist, merchant of paintings, seller of women and crooked capitalist, but always given over to *dandyism*, he had sacrificed everything, compromised everything for this ambition. A glorious hour, however, had sounded in his life. He had become the director of a legitimist journal, toward the last days of the second empire. But precisely this elevation had been his downfall. The grace of Israel had left him and he had made some stupid business decisions. His discomfiture, although sensational, had been too ridiculous for him to ever recover from. Now, God alone could know what he was dealing in.

But, growing older, this little swell, who was met with wherever ruin struck, had become positively sinister. In the midst of unspeakable jiggery-pokery, this grotesque swindler had abdicated not one of his ancient pretensions, and he was always found to be the same hilarious crafty devil who had offered, one day, to the Count de Chambord, to *be converted* publicly to Catholicism, if he could be made a marquis. He always had the politeness of a public baths attendant or that of a gambling den bouncer, and the same famous gesture, to tap the two lateral cauliflowers that made the corbel construction of his otherwise bald cranium. He above all had the same attentiveness to women, whom he enriched gratuitously by his counsels or his prophecies, while divesting them of their jewels and their money. Because he was well-liked by the girls on the left bank, where he had come to establish himself, being at once their banker, their courtier, their merchant of toilette, their consoler and their oracle,—sometimes, also, their *doctor*, it was said. But this last thing floated in a salubrious mystery . . .

"Ah! so . . . it's you, dear child! Good God! it's been so long since I've seen you! I thought you were lost forever. Your disappearance had made all of us desperate, and, on account of you, I give you my word of honor that I was inconsolable . . . But you've found pity on your victims and you've come back to us, for sure. Poor lamb, he's left you, I hope, that savage beast you were living with?"

These words tantamount to nothing and proffered with a distant, *defunct* voice, seeming to come out of a verdigris phonograph, where they had been inscribed for sixty years, were intended above all to hide the surprise of this old brigand.

Fifteen or eighteen months earlier, he had had the audacity to show up at Marchenoir's residence, whose address he had discovered, under the pretext of offering an occasion to buy lace, but in reality to negotiate a luxurious debauchery, the extraordinary conditions of which, whispered in the ear of his former client, seemed to him would win her over. But, from the first word, Véronique had gone to look for her friend who was working in the neighboring room, and this person had simply opened the window, manifesting with his eyebrows in a very clear fashion, when the ambassador, abandoning, for several moments, his dignity, had believed it necessary to disappear immediately down the stairs.

"Monsieur Nathan," responded the visitor firmly, but without anger, "I've not come to confide in you and I ask you to speak with me properly, without familiarity, if possible. It's a very simple business matter. You know how to extract teeth, right? How much would you charge me to take out *all* my teeth?"

For once in his life, Nathan did not even try to dissimulate his stupefaction. Mechanically, he verified with a gesture his two diarrhea-blond painted tufts, which garnished his temples, tightened, around his coleopteran torso, the bell cord of his dressing gown, which had a pissy firmament color to it, and returning with a forced march from the end of the room, where the first commotion had been launched:

"Take out all your teeth!" he cried,—immediately animated, bursting out, almost human, "ev-er-y tooth! Ah, young lady, I must've misheard you, or am I so overwhelmed with disgrace that you should plan to come here and mock me?"

Véronique showed him her head:

"And that, sir, what do you think of it? Is this a joke? I repeat, I want you to remove all my teeth just as I've had all my hair, this morning, removed. It's absolutely necessary, for reasons I don't need to tell you. I've approached you, because I fear an ordinary dentist would not want to do it. You must know me, I suppose. Nobody'll ever know that I came here. I've three louis to offer you for an operation that won't take two hours, and I'll make you a gift of my teeth to throw into the bargain. It seems to me that you won't have made a bad day of it. If that doesn't suit you, good evening, I'll go elsewhere. Is it yes or no?"

The dispute was long, however. Never had this miserable Nathan been shaken in such a rude manner. He saw clearly that Véronique was not crazy, but he could not conceive why a pretty girl would want to become ugly. That turned all his ideas upside down. Then, there was, in this male putridity, a phosphorous angle that was not perhaps altogether execrable. He stepped back from the thought of destroying this pretty face, in the same way he would have hesitated, for at least a minute, if not a million minutes, to burn a painting by Leonardo or Gustave Moreau. The pure and simple annihilation of riches of this type confounded him.

This scruple, besides, involved several fears. He had received blows before in his life, but Marchenoir's hand, not yet experienced, seemed to him more redoubtable than that of the Lord,—not to mention the grappling iron of human justice that could intervene as well and stick its nose curiously into his little affairs.

Véronique, discerning with surprise what was happening in this muddy soul, decided, despite her repugnance, to conclude the matter with intimidation. "You didn't hesitate so much," she told him, "when it was a question of little Sarah. I know by heart that whole story, and many others still. Pay careful attention. Let's go, be reasonable and don't let me languish any longer. Once again, nothing bad'll happen to you because of me, I promise, and it's always good to earn three louis."

171

She was referring to an abominable affair of an abortion, in which the mother had nearly perished, and which had caused untold solicitude to the handsome Arthur. He agreed immediately, went to look for his tool of torture, arranged everything with small nervous movements and, finally, installed Véronique into a deep leather armchair, in full light.

She put back her head and displayed a double row of luminous teeth,—teeth to bite the hardest human metals. The abject torturer, with a last impulse of vague compassion, declared to her that she was going to suffer atrociously.

"I'm prepared," responded the saint. "I hope to have enough courage. I'll try to remember I deserve even much greater suffering."

Then, the horror began. With each tooth that was pulled, poor Véronique, against her will, let out a light cry and her eyes filled with tears, while streams of frothy blood ran down the thick cloth of the kitchen apron that Nathan had tied about her neck.

When the upper jaw had been completely emptied, the executioner had to stop. The ill-fated girl had lost consciousness and writhed spasmodically. He had to reanimate her, staunch the blood that was leaving in torrents, stop the hemorrhaging, calm his nerves, all in a day's work for this person omniscient in vile surgical practices. He expressed his advice to put off the second part of the operation for a few days, in the secret hope that he would never see her again and thus escape a chore that displeased him, having, moreover, carefully pocketed the money. But, at the end of a quarter of an hour, the surprising martyr energetically indicated to him, without saying a word, that she wanted it to continue.

Nothing was more horrible. The operator earned his salary. Ordinary anesthetics were without effect on this bundle of routed nerves, horribly shaken already, in spite of the patient's heroism. The syncope recurred five or six times, each time more disquieting. One minute, Nathan, terrified, believed she had tetanus.

Finally, the torture was completed, and little by little, equilibrium returned. Véronique drank a cordial prepared in advance and, suffering still from atrocious pain, but having become empress of herself again, she looked sadly at the table, at the treasure laid out from the casket of her mouth, empty forever; then, approaching a mirror, she let out a scream, one funereal scream only, for her devastated beauty, a type of groaning that she could not suppress.

The sordid Nathan, surprised by his own agitation, stammered some empty phrases, citing the species of violence that he had undergone. That is when the Christian, with a nobility of humility eternally unintelligible to base souls, obeying that fury of self-debasement that is one of the characteristics of mystical love, took up the hand of the foul bandit, that waxy, podgy hand, which had held all sorts of scum, and kissed it,—like the instrument of her martyrdom!—with her bloody and deformed lips.

"Goodbye, Monsieur Nathan," she then said, in a voice she no longer recognized. "Thank you. Don't be upset. You often do nasty things in your profession, but I'll pray to my Savior for you . . ."

XLIII

Leverdier hardly needed to recount to his friend the deeply distressing emotion that he had felt, the next day, on seeing Véronique. The poor fellow had received a terrible blow which left him stunned. That charming face, which had brightened for him the drabness in life and which poured hope into the both of them, no longer existed. It was horribly, irremediably changed. There was no beauty left at all. Such was, at any rate, his impression. It is true that he had seen her deformed by the swelling, beaten by the suffering and that, now, after a week, these incidentals had disappeared. But he could no longer recognize that completely toothless mouth, and the memory of what she had been made her appear dreadful to him.

The first day, he found himself speechless, deprived of intelligence, asphyxiated by sorrow, half crazy. It was necessary for Véronique herself to re-animate him, telling him something like this: "I'm the only one who wanted this. Had I any other means to obey the letter than this?" And she had given him Marchenoir's letter, which he was unable to read in her presence, but which he carried back to his place, taking leave of her, dumbfounded by astonishment, drunk with dejection and remorse. For he accused himself of being a depositary without vigilance, odiously unfaithful. He should have divined it, prevented it. But also, that letter was from a madman. How could Marchenoir, knowing this excessive soul, capable of any resolution, how could he have written it?

Leverdier was prey to a mixture of despair and rage that made his heart leap, so to speak, out of his chest. Whatever experience he believed he had had with these two friends, there were, in spite of everything, certain things that he could not come to grips with. If Marchenoir had consulted him, he would have certainly responded with the counsel of marrying, *in any case*, Véronique, and he would have, with all the power he possessed, worked to demonstrate to Véronique the absolute necessity of becoming Marchenoir's wife.

Not a disbeliever, but shaky in practice and in no way organized for the contemplative life, he had sometimes disbelieved in the purity of their relationship. He needed reiterated affirmations by his friend, whom he knew incapable of hypocrisy, and the irrecusable evidence of certain facts, to persuade him. In the last months, he had noticed Marchenoir's enthusiasm for his companion, but lacking the psychological diagnostic of Father Athanase, he had not concluded as the other had as to the amorous passion, only reading into it a new period of common religious transport that he was prevented from judging. The letter to Véronique had been for him like a flame without reflector, in one of those subterranean passages where the shadows, accumulated and piled on top of one another for long periods of time, only get thicker as they recoil, three paces away from the insufficient light that they threaten to snuff out.

What did it mean, for example, this retrospective jealousy in a man whose acts and words set him apart from the common ways of men and whom the world's opinion could not touch? Did the carnal act touch then the very essence of the woman, for whom the sullying must have been ineffaceable forever? Without doubt, this past was an irreparable evil, but since one had been so terribly bitten, was it necessary, after all, to sacrifice one's life for phantoms, and to rush headlong into hell, to escape a purgatory that would have been the paradise of many less unfortunate people?

Repentance, penitence, sanctity even, did they no longer have that much-celebrated virtue of making sinners new again? What was there in common between the Véronique of today and the Suction Cup of before? Ah! He had known a ton of virgins who were not worthy, certainly, to clean the mud off her shoes! And, supposing that there remained something to suffer, could this something enter into the balance with the unheard of torments of a passion without issue, that would eat the brain of this great artist, after having devoured his heart? Finally, he was in love with the idea of the fireman, and thought, in general, that he needed to put out fires, as soon as they started, at whatever price, and because concubinage revolted these two devotees, he concluded, without hesitation, in the sacrament of marriage.

Leverdier forced back these thoughts he had, henceforth pointless to express, not applicable to his friends whose principal affair consisted in triumphing in their own wisdom, by loading on the already-broken shoulders of castaways the leaden treasure of their onerous recriminations. Besides, he had told himself, for many days in a row, that, doubtless, this time, love's rage would be finished! Marchenoir would suffer, for some time, all that can be suffered, then that passion would die out, for lack of alimentation. A supportable melancholy would be installed in its place and his mind would resume its equilibrium. Véronique, made irreparably ugly, would become that very sweet friend, that beneficent companion of his hours of intellectual lassitude and sadness, that quasi-sister one had dreamed of and that the pretty woman could never be.

She would discover then that she had been right, at the last reckoning, to accomplish this thing that made them, at the present hour, suffer so acutely. Nothing else would remain, in the end, of all these heart-rending emotions, but a souvenir of heroism on the inoffensive ruins of that beauty, that the most astonishing miracle of charity had sacrificed . . .

The two friends were silent for several instants. Marchenoir rose like a hundred-year-old man, trembling, pale, hoary, weary of living and, in a suffocated voice, declared that that was enough discourse, that he would see for himself distinctly all that he had to see: the cruelty of his imprudence and the horrible fruit of remorse that he had harvested, but that it was time to go and console the poor girl.

"She suffers for me," he said, "and not for herself. Her person, she does not care a bit for it, you must have noticed. If my peace is restored, she will judge that all is very well and her joy will be perfect. You do not know, Georges, this creature's quality of the sublime. What she has just done for me, she would have done for you as well, I am persuaded of it, or for some other person, if she had believed it necessary . . . But the remedy, will it be efficacious? That is the question, it is my life that depends on it and the answer is not certain . . ."

They were in the street. A fiacre picked them up and carried them together, neither one saying a word, to the boulevard Montparnasse. Having arrived at the avenue du Maine and on the point of entering the rue de Vaugirard, which leads into the rue des Fourneaux, Leverdier felt that Marchenoir wanted to be alone for the first tête-à-tête. He left him then, and, standing on the sidewalk, watched the coach move away, until it disappeared. Only then did he go on his way, overcome with sadness, his soul drowned in frightening presentiments.

XLIV

When Marchenoir got out of the coach parked before the house, he could have been taken for one of those men in the agony of death with a calculable number of days to live, that numbered cars vomited on the Dantesque doorstep of hospitals at the hour of consultations. He trembled so much when searching for his money, that the cabman offered to accompany him up to his door. That reanimated him. He made haste to enter, did not even see the concierge, whom his aspect seemed to have disconcerted, and climbed the staircase.

Before his door, he was surprised that his courage had brought him this far and realized, at the same time, that he had none at all, that he would never make up his mind to enter, and that there was nothing to do but sit on the step, waiting until the end of time. He began to turn with muffled paces, like a feline, on the narrow landing, absolutely incapable of coming to a resolution, his fingers burning on the key that he had drawn from his pocket, in the coach, and that he held in his hand for a quarter of an hour, bitterly deploring the absence of Leverdier, and he cursed himself for having let him depart.

All of the sudden, he heard climbing beneath him and recognized, with certitude, Véronique's step. Terrified by the idea of a repatriation in this public place, where twenty unknown renters could appear, he brusquely opened the door and threw himself into the apartment as if it were a citadel. The young woman was returning, in fact, from the Lazarists' chapel on the rue de Sèvres, where she went, every morning, to listen to mass, at seven o'clock, no matter the weather. Marchenoir, who accompanied her, ordinarily, nevertheless had forgotten this circumstance.

When she appeared, this man, normally so strong, had weak legs. He fell down on the tiled floor, and stretched towards her his two hands, moving his lips, without being able to articulate a word. Véronique ran to him, enveloped him in her arms and, pulling him up, constrained him to sit down. She herself got down on her knees at his feet,—by an impulse of humility and tenderness that recalled their first interview,—and looked at him, her elbows resting on him.

"Dear victim," he said with the sweetness of infinite commiseration, "what have you done?"

"Pardon me, my love," she responded, "I wanted to obey you and to save you. Ah! I'd have suffered much more still, if it'd been necessary . . . Weep at your leisure, poor heart, God will console you."

Then, hearing her voice so modified by the torture, which became loving by charity, he became less tense and broke down. He pulled her onto his knees and hiding his face in her arms and in her chest, he sobbed unrestrainedly. It was one of those bursts of tears, as he had had so often, and which, already, so many times, had delivered him from suggestions of despair. For a long time, his tears, enlarged by all the internal storms that had preceded this instant, fell in streams on the mutilated head of the martyr, who melted, herself, with compassion, huddled, like a swallow, against the wall of this moving breast.

In the end, seeing that the crisis was abating and that a bit of calm was going to return, she gently disengaged herself, went to moisten her handkerchief in fresh water and, with maternal movements, came to bathe and dry the eyes of her friend.

"Now, dear unwell man," she said to him, kissing his forehead, "I'll lead you to your room. You'll lay down on your bed and you'll sleep for some hours. You must need to . . . Don't look at me with this sorry attitude. You'll get used to my new face, and you'll finish by finding it very agreeable. I assure you I find myself as beautiful as before. It's a habit to form. Come on, Monsieur weeping willow, stretch out your legs, here are two blankets, a pillow for your head and I'll draw the curtains. When you get up again, your servant will have made you a good fire, a good breakfast, and your guardian angel will have chased away your heavy sorrow."

Marchenoir, completely exhausted, permitted himself act like a baby and was sleeping already.

Véronique, retired to the other room, went to prostrate herself before the immense crucifix that she had purchased, on order, from the rue Saint-Sulpice, on a day of riches, the reproduction of an abject art that that thaumaturge's piety had transfigured into a masterpiece.

"My sweet Savior," she murmured, "don't be upset with me. You see well I've done what I could. My confessor has blamed me very severely for what he calls a rash zeal and I must believe you inspired him in this blame. He told me I'd misunderstood your precept of tearing out one's members, when they became an occasion of scandal, and that could very well be, for I'm a girl full of ignorance. But, my Jesus, if I've made a mistake, judge only my intention and have pity on this unfortunate man who has risked his life in order to give me to you. If I must be an obstacle for him, destroy me instead, make me die, I beg you by your divine Agony and the merits of all your saints! I've nothing but my life to offer you, you know, for I don't have innocence and I'm the poorest woman in the world! . . ."

XLV

It was the hour when the worst of brutes, assuaged by his repose, exits his lair and pours out through the streets of Paris. The needy beasts with a million feet, in pursuit of money or lust, bellowed around the outlying areas, in this eccentric quarter. The sovereign proletariat, with a *hangover*, dashed from his kennel toward hypothetical workshops; the subaltern employee, less august, but more correct in the rigging, sped away with exactitude towards the imbecilic administrations; businessmen, their souls muddied from the night before and the night before that, ran, without ablution, to new scams; the army of little women workers sauntered to conquer the world, with empty heads, chemical taints, black eyes from dubious nights, joggling proudly with their autoclave hind-quarters, where the rudimentary operations of their intellect were performed as in their true brain. All the Parisian vermin swarmed while stinking to high heaven and surged, in the horrible clamor of base transactions on sidewalks or in roadways. Who would have known, then, to suspect there, behind one of those connecting walls, from which backs away, while lamenting, the angel at the cutoff corners of the architecture, a veritable mystic, a repented Thais, a fury of mercy and prayer, such as has not been seen for many centuries? And who, then, having found out about her, would not have burst out with that rich laughter that pulls good people's pants down, when they are about to be spanked?

The act that she had just performed, this simple Christian, was as perfectly unintelligible to her contemporaries as the Transfiguration of the Lord could be in the eyes of a hippopotamus wallowing in a pool of mud. Such a high temperature of enthusiasm is invincibly repugnant to the vanishing mackerel tail of this end of the century. Never, without doubt, for six thousand years, in any society, has heroism been so generally cuckolded by human nature as this rare pilgrim of love is, who has been forced to cohabit with it.

Christianity, what remains of it, is nothing but an escalation of stupidity or cowardice. Jesus Christ is not even sold any more, he is *sold off* at a discount, and the craven children of the Church stand humbly at the door of the Synagogue, begging for a little piece of the rope of Judas that one awards them, finally, tired of fighting, accompanied by an infinite number of kicks.

If the poor girl had to be judged, it was not, assuredly, by the heretics nor by the atheists that she would have been the most rigorously condemned. They would have been content to gratify her, while passing, with several shovelfuls of filth. But the Catholics would have carved her up into pieces to fatten their pigs,—anything, with the exception of genius, not being as ferociously detested as heroism by the current titulars of the most heroic of doctrines.

What they name *spiritual life*, by a strange abuse of the dictionary, is a seriously complicated program of study diligently muddled up by captious merchants of ascetic soup, with a view to working toward the abolition of human nature. The culminating watchword of masters and tutors appears to be the word *discretion*, as in matrimonial agencies. Every action, every thought not anticipated by the program, that is to say every natural and spontaneous impulse, however magnanimous it might be, is regarded as *indiscreet* and capable of leading to a reprobative blacklisting.

To give one's wallet to a man dying of hunger, for example, or to jump into the water to save a poor devil, without having first consulted one's spiritual director and completed at least a nine-day retreat, these are the most dangerous indiscretions that pride can inspire. The devout *scruple*, on its own, would demand a second Redemption.

Modern Catholics, monstrously engendered by Manrèze and Port-Royal, have become, in France, so fetid a group that, by comparison, the masonic or anticlerical mofette nearly gives the impression of a paradisiacal condensation of perfumes, and God knows, however, that, in this respect, their minds and their hearts no longer have much to receive, now, for their porcine reintegration, from the materialist animal Circe!

To be honest, not all crosses have been pulled down yet, nor the ceremonies of cult replaced by antique spectacles of prostitution. Nor have public latrines and urinals quite yet been installed in the cathedrals transformed into dives or into café-concert halls. Evidently, not enough priests are dragged through the gutters, not enough young nuns are entrusted with the maternal solicitude of *proprietresses* of unregulated brothels. Childhood is not corrupted soon enough, a large number of poor people are not beaten down enough, fathers' faces have not yet been used as spittoons or doormats enough . . . Without a doubt. But all these things are upon us and can already be considered as having arrived, for they arrive like the tide and no dyke can be built to contain them.

Evil is more universal and appears greater, at this hour, than ever before, because never before has civilization hung so close to the earth, have souls been so depraved, or the arms of masters so feeble. It will get even worse. The Republic of the Vanquished has not given birth to its full belly of malediction.

We have been descending spirally, for fifteen years now, in a vortex of infamy, and our descent accelerates to the point of losing our respiration. We go now, like a tempest, with no chance of return, and every hour makes us a bit more stupid, a bit more cowardly, a bit more abominable before the Lord God, who regards us from the recesses of heaven! . . .

Joseph de Maistre said, over nearly a century ago, that man is too evil to merit being free.

This Seer was a contemporary of the Revolution whose grandiose horror he contemplated as a prophet, and he spoke to it face to face.

He died in fear and contempt of this colloquy, pronouncing the funereal orison of European civilization.

He would have nothing more to say then today, and the final pigsties of our last childhood would add absolutely nothing to the terrifying security of his diagnostic.

Well! when all the menaces of the anti-religious scum have finally let loose on us, like the clouds of a dirty deluge, when the so-called Christian society, irreparably disintegrated, takes off, like a fleet of sulfurous jetsam on the phosphorous liquid that will have submerged the earth, what will that be like compared to the monster already formed, the reason for which is terrifying, and which reigns as a squatting despot on the sterile dung of our hearts?

There are only two sorts of filth: the filth of beasts and the filth of spirits.

Now, it is a stench quite subaltern to the revolutionary and anticlerical mud. It is fabulously outdated and older still than Christianity. It has flowed from the nether parts of humanity for six thousand years now and has used shovels and brooms to pay the ransom of a king of cesspool emptiers.

It is an inconvenience of this sad world, a simple affair of garbage collection and purification for the diligent authorities who have public sanitation at heart. The brute must follow its law and evil is nearly nonexistent, as long as these authorities do not up and leave. And, even then when they have up and left, evil leaks into persecution to be transformed into glory.

Bestial insults, goitrous defiances, stupid sacrileges, idiotic atrocities of negroes escaped from the rod and trembling to return, all that is small potatoes and does not essentially contaminate either truth nor justice.

Since Calvary and the Mount of Olives, there is nothing that has not been attempted by the internal swine of man's heart, against this excessive magnificence of Sorrow.

Invention is no longer possible and the Galileos or the Edisons of democratic roguery lost their genius there. Constant rehashing of secular refrains, sempiternal recopying of immemorially decrepit farces, rumination of filthy jokes puked out by innumerable generations of identical mugs, hackneyed parodies for two thousand years now; one imagines nothing more.

It is probable that the Jews were stronger, at first, for having been the initiators and, perhaps also, because having caused suffering to the Man who was supposed to assume all expiation, they knew things that the thick ignorance of blasphemers of today do not even suspect.

What is really appalling is the filth of minds.

The Feet of Christ cannot be sullied, but only his Head, and this need for ideal iniquity is the unconscious or perverse choice for the multitude of his *friends*.

Christ, no longer able to give any additional grandeur to those he called his brothers, leaves them at least the terrible majesty of perfect outrage that they exercise on Him. They abandon themselves that far and let themselves be dragged into the dumping ground.

The imbecilic rage of enemies conscious of the Church inspires pity. The legendary patter of subterranean Jesuit conspiracies, romantically organized by nauseous cockroaches, but full of genius, can still act on the *populo*, but begin to lose credit everywhere else, which is surprising for such enormous foolishness. Stupid calumnies ordinarily have a harder life. Dejected, cobbled, worn out, uncleansable and unmarriageable, they subsist, immortally juicy.

To be honest, the Catholics themselves have taken their own ignominy at a fixed rate settled on in advance, and that is exactly what supplants an infinite number of venomous traps. It is Voltairian childishness to accuse these cravens of *wickedness*. The surpassing horror is that they are MEDIOCRE.

A man covered in crimes is always interesting. He is a target for Mercy. He is a unit in the immense flock of pardonable goats, capable of being absolved for salutary immolations.

He forms an integral part of the redeemable material, for which he is instructed that the Son of God suffered death. Far from breaking the divine plan, he demonstrates it, on the contrary, and verifies it experimentally by ostentation of his appalling misery.

But the innocent *mediocre man* turns everything upside down.

It had been *foreseen*, doubtless, but only just, like the worst torture of the Passion, like the most insupportable of agonies on Calvary.

He slaps Christ in the face, in such a supreme fashion and erases his divinity of Sacrifice so absolutely, that it is impossible to conceive a more beautiful proof of Christianity than the miracle of its duration, in spite of the monstrous inanity of the greatest number of its faithful!

Ah! one comprehends the terror, the frantic flight of the nineteenth century before the ridiculous Face of God that is offered to him and one comprehends also his fury!

It is really low, however, this lowlife of a century, and it has hardly got the right to show itself as difficult! But precisely because it is ignoble, it would be necessary that the monstrance of the Faith were arch-sublime and fulgurated like the sun . . .

Want to know how it would fulgurate? Listen.

XLVI

It was noticed one day, three hundred years ago, that the bleeding Cross had too long covered the earth in its shadow. The unpacking of lust that one wanted to call the Renaissance had just been inaugurated, several Germanic or cisalpine pawns having divulged that it was no longer necessary to suffer. The thousand years of the Middle Ages' resigned ecstasy stepped back before Galatea's croup.

The sixteenth century was a historic equinox, where the Ideal held up for ridicule by the sudden showers of sensualism came crashing down finally, roots in the air. Christian spiritualism, scuttled in the meninges, bled at the trunk of the carotids, emptied of its most intimate substance, did not die, alas! It became idiotic and deliquescent in its pierced glory.

It was a terrible convulsion for one hundred years, accompanied by an infinitely useless and lamentable recall of souls. Our circulating sphere appeared to roll past the other planets like a watering can of blood. But the martyrdom itself having lost its virtue, the old original mud was reintegrated triumphantly, all the doors of the stables were torn off their hinges and the universal modern pigsty began its fecal exodus.

Christianity, which never knew how to vanquish nor how to die, did then like all conquered things do. It accepted the law and paid the tax. In order to subsist, it made itself agreeable, oily and tepid. Silently, it slipped through the key holes, infiltrated the wainscoting, managed to be utilized like some unctuous essence given as a plaything to institutions and became in this way a subaltern condiment, that any political cook could employ or reject as convenient. One had the spectacle, unexpected and delicious, of a Christianity *converted* into pagan idolatry, respectful slave of oppressors of the Poor, and smiling acolyte of phallic cults.

Miraculously sweetened, the ancient asceticism assimilated all sugars and unguents in order to have itself pardoned for not being precisely voluptuousness and became, in a religion of tolerance, that plausible thing that one could call the harlotry of piety. Saint Francis of Sales appeared, at that time, just at the right moment, to coat everything in a smooth finish. From head to toes, the Church was pasted with his honey, aromatized with his seraphic pomades. The Society of Jesus, run dry of its three or four first great men and not producing anything more than a vomitive rehash of its apostolic debuts, received with joy this theological perfumery, where the Glory of God, definitively, was well stocked. The spiritual bouquets of the prince of Geneva were proffered with caressing sacerdotal hands to the explorers of the Tender, who immediately dilated their geography in order to induct so charming a Catholicism . . . And the heroic Middle Ages were buried then ten thousand feet under . . .

One is quite forced to avow that Christian spiritualism is completely finished, now, as, after three centuries, nothing has been able to restore a semblance of verdure to the calcined stock of old beliefs. Some sentimental formulas still give the illusion of life, but it is dead, in reality, really dead. Jansenism, that infamous back-ooze of the Calvinist emunctory, had it not finished by licking its lips, with a Jesuit tongue selectively obtained, and had not the philosophical riff-raff espoused its progenitor at the highest niches of Gallicanism? The Terror itself, which should have, it seems, had the magnifying efficacy of antique persecutions, served only to make appear smaller the Christians that it *cut short.*

For the trouble of cutting the throat of the Dove that floated in the golden skies of legends, Art lost its own wings and became the companion of reptiles and quadrupeds. The extra-corporeal Transfixions of the Primitives descended, in the carnal drunkenness of form and color, until coming to Raphael's troubled virgins. Having arrived at this brute of stupid suavity and false faith, religious esthetic made a last prodigious bound and disappeared in the irrevocable liquid that senile Catholic generations had secreted.

Today the crucified Savior of the world calls to him all the people in the display window of the glaziers of devotion, between a mischievous Evangelist and a too-promoted sorrowful Mother. He writhes correctly on delicate crosses, in a nudity of pale hydrangea and creamy lilies, decorticated, from his knees to his shoulders, with identical vinous wounds executed on the uniform type of a worn out panel.—Italian style, affirm the merchants of mastic.

The French style is a glorious Jesus, in purple brocaded robe, half-exposing, with a celestial modesty, his chest, and revealing, at the end of his fingers, to a Visitandine beaming with ecstasy, an enormous heart of gold crowned with thorns and shining like a cuirass.

It is still the same wounded Jesus, opening his arms for the hypothetical embrasure of an inattentive multitude; it is the eternal sebaceous Virgin, prey to the same formula of secular desolation, holding on her knees, not only the head, but the entire body of a pitiable Son, taken down off the nails following art school entrance exam formulas. Then, the innumerable Immaculate Conceptions of Lourdes, with first communicants azured with a large ribbon, offering to heaven, with hands joined, the indubitable innocence of their enamel and of their carmine.

Finally, the polychromatic mob of subaltern elect: St. Josephs, nursing and frizzy-haired, generally clothed in a tartan striped with slug smudges, offering a potato flower to a little baby that gives blessings; St. Vincent de Pauls in licorice, gathering, with a refrained joy, little monsters made of stearin, full of gratitude; the ingenuous St. Louis de Frances, bearers of crowns of thorns on small plush cushions; St. Louis Gonzagas, kneeling like cherubim and waxed with the greatest care; hands crossed on virginal surplices, mouth in the shape of a hen's arse and eyes drowned in tears; St. Francis d'Assisis, glaucous or cerulean, by force of love and continence, in the spiced bread of their poverty; St. Peter with his keys, St. Paul with his sword, St. Mary Magdalene with her death's head, St. John the Baptist with his little sheep, palmated martyrs, mitered confessors, virgins decked out in flowers, popes with spatulate fingers of infallible benedictions, and the infinite cohort of Way of the Cross firemen.

All that wisely, comfortably, commercially, economically packaged and priced. Rich or poor, all the interior walls can be provisioned with pious simulacra of these throw-aways, where the ineradicable Raphaelic tradition perpetuates itself, for the chaste assuagements of the eyes of the faithful. These purgative images derive, in effect, from the great detersive infusion of ultramontane *madonistes*. The Italian debasers of great mystical Art were the incontestable ancestors of this roughcast. Whether they were or not the divine talent that was so credulously exalted in refrains plucked on lyres, they were nonetheless the mattress makers of the bed of prostitution where fornicating paganism came to deflower Christian Beauty. And there you have their progeny.

The Disputation of the Holy Sacrament[1] had ineluctably to lead, in less than three centuries, to the fraternal emulation done by the plasterers of Saint-Sulpice,—which today would make the sanguinary iconoclasm appear orthodox and holy!

And literature is in keeping. Ah! Catholic literature! It is in Catholic literature, above all, that the incomparable depravity of decadence is verified, to the point of bedazzlement. Its history is, moreover, infinitely simple. After a pile of centuries full of freedom and genius, Bossuet[2] appears finally, who confiscates and locks up forever, for the glory of his caliph, in a penitentiary dependence on the monarchy's seraglio, all genital forces of French intellectuality. It was a political operation analogous enough to the precedent prunings by Louis XI and Richelieu. That which had been done for the Very Christian King's redoubted vassals, the domesticated eagle of the Meaux diocese accomplished for

---

1 A fresco by Raphael in the Vatican.
2 Bossuet: presumably Jacques-Bénigne Bossuet

the even more menacing feudality of thought. After that, from the time of this cutter, absolute silence, miraculous infecundity.

Every religious philosophy must be configured like his and this inconceivable sacrilege of the immense clergy has been seen, ass to the ground on the holy Host and head lost in the low small valley of his soutane, adorably prostrated before a spoilt peruke, in posthumous obedience to the episcopal instructions of a court valet. That for two hundred years, from 1682 up until our imbecilic days.

The abortive culture of seminaries did not attain, however, at first, its solstice of impotency. It was necessary that the growing hostility of modern times should make this militia comprehend, little by little, the need for being a coward, and the sublime wisdom of throwing one's weapons at the feet of the enemy when decamping. Each time that impiety would show itself more insolent or philosophical antagonism better equipped, religious instruction grew narrower by the same amount and the priests retracted their horns. The theological telescope swallowed its tubes while collapsing, in the unassailable hope of having no more stars to discover.

Then, in the penumbra of apostolic warrens, under the limiting wingspan of a Gallican goose, the mold of old, arch-deceased schisms would be grazed on voluptuously. The entire Christian tradition being reputed to fit into the paired tomes of the sublime bishop, and he himself summarizing the universal Church in his umbilicus,—as it was necessary that he make a floor rug of it for his royal master,—what other authority would one need and what could the demonetized human spirit try after that?

The deletion became infinite. All that was accomplished after the seventeenth century was stuck right there. Catholic pedagogy, in order to chastise itself for having formerly accorded an exuberant esteem for God's creature, decided to confine itself desperately and forever in the "great century's" catafalque. Consequently, absolute prohibition from writing anything else than imitations of this hearse, and fulminating anathema against the most obscure wish to be free of him.

The most unprecedented literature resulted from this blockade. It is to be asked, really, if Sodom and Gomorrah, which Jesus, in his Gospel, had declared "tolerable," were not holy and of divine odor in comparison with this cesspit of innocence.

The Great Day Approaches!—*Life is no Longer Life,*—*The Lord is My Lot,*—*Where are we Now?*—*Lightning Before the Thunderbolt,*—*The Clock of the Passion,*—*The Gnawing Worm,*—*Drops of Dew,*—*Think About It!*—*The Beautiful Evening of Life,*—*The Happy Morning of Life,*—*In Heaven We'll See Each Other Again!*—*The Stairway to Heaven,*—*Follow Me and I will Guide You,*—*Manna of the Soul,*—*Kind Jesus,*—*That Religion is therefore Kind!*—*Plaints and COMPLAICENCES of the Savior,*—*Virtue Adorned with all its Charms,*—*Mary, I Love You,*—*Mary Better Known,*—*The Catholic in all Positions in Life*, etc. Such are the titles that leap out at you, as soon as you regard a boutique of devotional books.

And one should not believe that we are talking about small volumes. *Kind Jesus* alone is in three volumes. The stupidity of these works corresponds exactly with the stupidity of their titles. Horrible stupidity, swollen and *white*! It is the snow-white leper of religious sentimentalism, the cutaneous eruption of internal purulence, accumulated in a dozen of putrid generations who have infected us with their farcy!

An unqualifiable library on the rue de Sevres sells this, for example: *Timetable of the Line of Heaven*. A very small paper about the size of a prayer book, to be inserted therein like a pious image. The first page offers precisely the consoling view of a railway train, on the point of rushing into a tunnel, through a little mountain planted with tombstones. It is the "tunnel of death," beyond which is found "Heaven, blessed Eternity, the Feast of Paradise." These things are explained, in three miniscule pages of this cloyingly jovial writing, that *The Pilgrim* journal has propagated to the last confines of the planet, and which appears to be the last literary juice of Christianity's salivary caducity. One takes his one-way ticket, at the window of Penitence, one pays in good works, which serve at the same time as baggage, there are no sleeping cars and the most rapid trains are precisely those that are the worst. Finally, two locomotives, *love* at the head, and *fear* at the tail. "All aboard, gentlemen, all aboard!" The benevolent opuscule unfortunately leaves us in the dark as to whether women are admitted, if they are allowed to strut their stuff a little, or if it is permissible to organize three-card tricks, as in the suburb trains. This ingenuous jokoscope seems like nothing, right? It is the last dying breath for the Christian Faith, first, and then, for all spirituality in this world that it has engendered, of which it is the unique substratum, and which will not survive it a quarter of an hour.

But what to think of a clergy that tolerates or encourages this pollution of the flock that it has been entrusted with, that takes the childishness of the most abject cretinism for humility, and which the most timidly conjectural hypothesis of the existence of a modern art transports with indignation?

Entrenched in the infertile glaciers of the century of Louis XIV, the highest contemporary heads have passed before it, without producing anything better than an outrage or a contemptuous observation. Writers of the most curative magnitude have volunteered to infuse a little young blood into the desiccated carcass of their forbears. They have been denied, cursed, placarded with filth: "It is you who are the centenaries and the decrepits!" it cries to them with an empty mouth, and the only great artist who honored its boutique for thirty years now, Jules Barbey d'Aurevilly, is put on the rubbish heap by formal order of the Archbishop of Paris.

The truth is that it has its great writers, this Gallican Church fallen into senility! It harbors, for example, on the highest place of its cornice, no less a bishop than the schismatic Dupanloup, whose sickening grisailles on *Education* make it blink, as if they were torrents of purple. This miter bearer, who was the disgrace of the most mediocre episcopacy that has ever been seen, is considered something of an intellectual lightning rod by those very same people who scorn the astonishing baseness of his character. *De Pavone Lupus factus[1]*, as they used to say in Rome, during the Council, while decomposing the name of Mademoiselle his mother. One really has to know this pastor's tyrannical insolence and his pompous negligence with respect to the *twelve* vicar-generals, who could never reside in his diocese; one has to be familiar with the turpitude of his political intrigues and his filthy hypocrisy of revolt that betrayed the universal Church, while protesting his filial desire to "not expose the Pope to the humiliation of an uncertain vote," no matter! he is venerated like a master, and the literary dysentery of this violet Trissotin[2], whose books the most lowly journalist would hesitate to sign, passes, in the Catholic world, for the overflow of genius.

Infinitely below this prelate, shining, as best they can, inferior amethysts and subaltern croziers: the Landriots, the Gerbets, the Ségurs, the Mermillods, the La Bouilleries, the Freppels, infertile spouses of their particular churches and glairy lovers of a muse in a ruff collar, who divides her favors among them.

Then the uncountable ecclesiastics: the Gaumes, the Gratrys, the Pereyves, the Chocarnes, the Martins, the Bautains, the Huguets, the Noirleius, the Doucets, the Perdraus, the Crampons, all a black swarming on the decomposed rhetoric of defunct centuries. Do the addition: fifty thousand of these brains can be piled up but the total will not furnish enough cloth to complete one poor idea.

As for the laymen, one exhibits for the admiration of the good faithful a considerable assortment of prigs as stiff as the hanged and as arid as mountains on the moon, such as Poujoulat, Montalembert, Ozanam, Falloux, Cochin, Nettement, Nicolas, Aubineau, Léon Gautier, historians or philosophers, politicians

---

1 Latin for "The wolf was made from the peacock."
2 Trissotin is a character in Molière's *Femmes Savantes*

or simple lecturers. It is the literary firmament's milky way. These donkeys of religious esthetics have confiscated human thought and coffered it in the obscure jail of little conventions and solemn refrains of the grand century. Nothing is allowed to subsist without their permission, and the greatest art that ever was, the modern Novel, which resorbs all conceptions, is judged as nothing at all, when they appear.

But the phoenix among the fowl, that is Henri Lasserre, the Benjamin of success. It becomes pointless to look at the others, as soon as this virtuoso enters the scene, as he epitomizes in his person the hypocrisy of pundits, the hoary pedantry of high critics and the greasy volubility of hagiographers. He adds to these exceptionally rare gifts the totally personal superabundance of a Gascon self-importance that would discourage a person from Garonne. He is an adjutant-traveler in pity, a Gaudissart of miracles who, better than anyone, arranges his small virginal garlands made of azure-colored paper. Also, the most incontinent fortune has hastened to rush towards this audacious monopolizer, who retailed the Virgin Mary in boutiques and in markets. Nothing less was needed than the near divine triumph of Louis Veuillot to counterbalance such a credit,—and the pure contemplative, Ernest Hello, is dead, ignored, in the resplendencies of their two glories.

It is still true that the same remunerative hand retains, on the fossilized heart of this Church haunted by the void, the dilapidated Pontmartin, a catacombal nightingale, whose role as a eunuch opportunely refrigerates prehistoric ardors. It is no less true that one gathers at the mouth of the collector, where he manipulates the guano, a Léo Taxil, henceforth God's adjutant and announced prophet.

Finally, the pastors of souls fertilize with their benedictions the *good press,* instituted by Louis Veuillot for the inexorable discomfiture of public bathhouses of thought. After that, the door closed. Hate, malediction, excommunication and damnation on all that deviates from the traditional paradigms . . .

"The holy clergy makes the people virtuous," said a man powerful in formulas, "the virtuous clergy makes the people honest, *the honest clergy* makes the people IMPIOUS." We are at the honest clergy and we have preachers such as Father Monsabré.

This miserable man has been given the reputation of a great orator. Now, this mediocre Thomist, this exasperating school teacher, systematically hostile to any spontaneous illumination of the spirit, has neither an idea, nor a gesture, nor a palpitation of the heart, nor an expression, nor an emotion. It is a faucet of warm water when it comes out, frozen when it falls. And he needs all of a year to draw us these baths!

There are naïve people whom this vacuity stupefies. But that is how they have all been manufactured, for a long time now, these heralds of the Word of God!

A Sulpician glair that is passed from mouth to mouth for two hundred years, formed of all the mucous of tradition and mixed with Gallican bile baked over the driftwood of liberalism; a scholastic arrogance to pay the expenses of a million prigs; an infinite certitude to have inhaled all the exhalations of the Holy Spirit and to have in this way circumscribed the Word such that God himself, after them, has nothing else to say. With that, the formal intention, albeit unavowed, to not endure any martyr and to evangelize but only a very few of the poor; but a condescending esteem for earthly goods, that curbs in these apostles the chagrined zeal of remonstrance and restrains them from grieving over the opulent bourgeoisie who strut about at the foot of their pulpit. Quite right the congruous dose,—almost imponderable,—of bitter slaver on the delicate flowers of the Great Book, for whom the laxative distinction of the *precept* of *council* was invented. Finally, eternal regenerative politics, irremovable moaning on the spoliations of Free Thought and the incommutable anxiety of peroration on the presumed future of the *dear* fatherland . . . If anything else is heard, one is either enjoying being deaf or has the irreverential consolation of sleeping.

Father Monsabré is incontestably the most successful subject, and reputable commercial enterprises where the article is packaged work hard, presently, to manufacture innumerable imitations of him. There is also another trend that would need to be called Didonian, wherein the soul's mediocrity is not less, nor genius more, absent. For they are made of diverse straw packings, the tumblers of the Dominican Order, such as the adulator of liberty, Lacordaire, confectioned it. They all have, more or less, the nostalgia of meaningless patter. But Didon, who is not satisfied to be a mouthpiece for emptiness, and who goes about prostituting his monk's robe on the stage of international comedy, would have us leave the *honest* clergy behind and lead us directly to apostate ecclesiastics or schismatics,—which would evidently be less decisive, like spitting into the enduring Face of Christ!

As for the altar's other servants and the entire mass of the faithful, it is inexpressible and confounding.

Everyone sticks close together, elbow to elbow, each one piles on top of the other in the manure of imbecility and cowardice. One hastens to the Absence of thought, to escape the contamination of *libertinage* or incredulity.

At the same time, by a totally orthodox about-face, one carefully turns a profit from the century's impiety to elongate the cord of ecclesiastical prescriptions just a bit. The Church having reduced to almost nothing the rigor of its penitences, in the ever disappointed hope of a prompter return of the frolicsome sheep that were lost, the sheep who remained faithful, bellowing from the back of the fold, make use of their pastors' *regrettable* concessions. And every practice leads down the same slope, the epoch not at all being up to the supererogative works of heroism.

Never, moreover, was there so much talk of *works*. To be occupied with works, to be *in* the works, are acclimatized locutions, significative of every good, although they have the air, in their imprecision, to implicate, morally, something bordering on the most imminent Protestantism. Catholics, in effect, understand and practice charity, love for their indigent brothers, in the Protestant manner, that is to say with an usurious pomp that demands the prerequisite abandonment of the Poor's dignity, in exchange for the most derisive aid. It is almost without example that one of these Christians rich to the gills, should have picked up in his arms his brother, tears streaming down his face, to save him once and for all, by paying his ransom with a part of his own superfluity.

That even resembles politics. "You will always have the poor among you," says the Gospel, and this fearsome phrase, that condemns the possessors of wealth, is precisely the occasion for the sophism of cannibals who procure their security. God has ruled that there would always be the poor, so that the rich should piously find comfort in not being poor, while resigning themselves to the *providential* necessity of not diminishing their number.

The rich need the poor in order to prove to themselves, at the cheapest price possible, the sensibility of their tender hearts, to prepare in a short period of time for Paradise, to amuse themselves, finally, to dance, to cut the neckline of their women down to the navel, to be moved over Champagne by those dying of famine, to wash in a bowl of broth their perfumed fornications where the highest virtues can be allowed to sink.

One would be forced to do these things for them, if there were not any, because they need them for all circumstances in life, for joy and for sadness, for celebrations and for mournings, for the city and for the country, for all emotional attitudes that poets have allowed. They need them absolutely, so that they can respond to Poverty: *We have OUR poor,* and by a weary gesture, to turn back from this lamentable kneeling, that the Savior of men has chosen for his Bride and whose escort is ten thousand angels!

Maybe one day the terrible God, *Vomiter of Luke Warm Christians,* will accomplish the miracle of giving some moral sapidity to this revolting flock that reminds one, analogically, of the frightening symbolic mixture of acidity and bitterness that the tormented genius of the Jews forced him to drink in his agony.

But there will be need of, it is much to be feared, strange flames and the seasoning of no small amount of blood to render digestible, in this day and time, these repellent Christians of the butcher shop.

There will be need of despair and tears like the human eye has never shed before, and it will be precisely these same *impious* people so scorned by them, from the top of their disgusting virtues,—but justly designated for their chastisement, holily elected for their perfect confusion,—which will force them to shed them! . . .

In the meantime, Christ is indubitably dragged to the dumping ground.

That bloody Face of the Crucified that had beamed for nineteen centuries, they rebathed Him in a nauseating ignominy, so that the most filthy souls are afraid of coming into contact with Him and are forced to turn away screaming.

He had defied human Opprobrium, this Son of man, and human Opprobrium vanquished Him.

Vainly, He triumphed over the abominations of the Praetorium and of Golgotha, and of the sempiternal recommencement of these abominations of *Contempt*. Now, He succumbs to the abomination of RESPECT!

His ministers and His believers, overcome with zeal for the fetid Idol rising from their hearts onto His altar, have splashed Him with such a destructive ridicule, we do not say adoration, but the most embryonic will of religious emotion, that the miracle of miracles would be, at this hour, to resuscitate a cult to Him.

The tragic dream of Jean-Paul is no longer in season. It is no longer the Christ weeping who would say to men exited from their tombs:

"I had promised you a Father in heaven and I do not know where he is. Remembering my promise, I have sought Him for two thousand years across the universe, and I cannot find Him and here I am, now, an orphan like you."

It is the Father who would respond to the doleful souls who lack asylum:

"I had permitted My Word, engendered by Myself, to make Himself in your image, to deliver you from suffering. You others, My faithful worshipers, whom he guaranteed by His Sacrifice, you come to ask Me for this Redeemer whose furnace of tortures you have contemned and whom you have so disfigured with your love, that today, Myself, His Consubstantial and His Father, I could no longer recognize Him . . ."

"I suppose that He inhabits the tabernacle that was made for Him by His last disciples, a thousand times more cowardly and more atrocious than the executioners who had covered Him with insults and bloodied . . .

"IF YOU HAVE NEED OF MY SON, LOOK FOR HIM IN THE GARBAGE CAN."

XLVII

Véronique had experienced infinite misery from this clergy, with a rigor proportional to the supereminence of its own mystical vocation. She had endured, from the beginning and for the entire first year, a continual interior torment, defying the flames and racks of martyrology.

Just after having moved in with Marchenoir, she had been resolved to present herself at the window of any confessional whatsoever and, thirsty for scorn, anxious to be tread underfoot, she had begun immediately by declaring this: "My father, I'm a dirty whore." The effect of this word, although not unheard of in these vestibules of hope where so many wrecked souls show up, had been immediate and confounding. The window was slammed shut in her face, with a sudden gesture of unbelievable violence.

She never learned which ecclesiastic had performed this virtuous act, and she did not want to know. It was, perhaps, one of those young priests caramelized in the white confiture of little "inviolable" purities, who conceive of life as a very long path lined with innocent linden trees in the seminary, with a small statue of an unblemished Mary at the end of it, under an edifying phylactery deployed by two cherubim, while the immaculate soft and asexual surplices go and come, with syrupy chastity. Maybe, also, she had fallen in with some mature ecclesiastic, admirer of Fénelon and Nicole, and bitter enemy of penitential naturalism, by consequence, a pitiless expeller of any repentance that disconcerted the litotes and hypotyposes of his formulary. These two varieties of sacerdotal vermin replace often enough, in the most effective manner, the fishing nets of the Prince of Apostles with the net of the morgue where certain wretches end up, to whose despair all that they lacked, until that moment, was the suggestive disgust of encountering them.

The valiant girl found the thing a bit rough, but absolutely normal and went away, with a heavy heart, in search of an intendant less parsimonious of apostolic provender. She had the good fortune of finding almost immediately, at Notre-Dame des Victoires, an old Jesuit practitioner, now passed away, whom his special dexterity as confessor of libertines and prostitutes had made famous. This curious old man of eighty years, whose psychological penetration partook of a miracle, had healed hundreds of abandoned souls. "I cast my line for the big fish only," he said, with his derisive bonhomie, an ancient, converted pandour himself, "let the small fry go elsewhere. I am the cesspool emptier of consciences and I remove the strong filth, but I declare myself inept in beauty shops and perfume parlors."

Discerning apostle and full judicial moralist, he thought that the habitual sin of the flesh is principally an infantile neurosis, in truth terrible and mortal, but untreatable, in the largest number of cases, without the attractive benignity of a sort of prophylactic lactation. The energy, sometimes surprising, implied by the pure and simple act of the penitential vow, he decreed it eminently satisfactory and, taking gallantly everything upon himself, reintegrated immediately the repentant sheep,—without demanding the prerequisite and discouraging chores that Jansenism invented to put them to flight. Véronique was then received by him as a prodigal daughter, with a boundless joy. He killed for her the fat calf of absolutions . . .

But this feast could not last. When he perceived that his new client was good for her word and did not relapse, like the others, he declared to her his insufficiency to guide her usefully toward whatever summits might be in store for her and encouraged her to search for a spiritual director.

That was the dawn of tribulations. Nobody understands anything of this burning love that grows more diaphanous as it rises towards the light. The most tenacious and hardest of her trials was the unclairvoyant obstinacy of a ton of priests, fattened on identical formulas, who endeavored to throw her into discouragement by their advice, uniformly comminatory, to leave Marchenoir. The simple creature held in the vice of dilemma between her obedience and the absolute impossibility of living alone, would have lost her mind twenty times over, without the precedent good fortune of the absolutions given, *all the same*, by the fellow who had accepted the compromise of this inevitable situation, which she was quite certain to have never abused.

And then, she exasperated them, all these vacillating ecclesiastics, by her adorable simplicity that must have moved them to tears. Confession, which takes the grandiose name of Sacrament of Penance, has become, in the present casting and watering down of Christianity, a vulnerary so perfectly colorless and neutral that its therapeutic strength on souls ought, in general, to be practically nothing. It is almost always a small predictable mechanical act, of the most infantile functioning. The penitent gives his formula of contrition and the confessor hands him in exchange his formula of exhortation. It is a negotiation of hackneyed expressions learned by heart, where the heart, precisely, has nothing more to do on the one side, and which the Lord God puts up with as he hears it on the other. Véronique was profoundly ignorant of this behavior of foolish words in two parts. She had learned another,—a little different,—and since she had forgotten it, she no longer knew anything at all in the world, if not the sublime feeling of divine love and human love blended together in one flame as candid as all lilies. But that is something that could not be understood.

As much as they wanted, they twisted the heart in their dirty and clumsy hands of this very submissive ewe who did not ask for anything better than to suffer. Interpreting the naïveties of her tenderness for the indiscreet zeal of satanic pride, these consecrated beasts saw nothing better to do than to oppress her ceaselessly with her past, some with vehemence, others with irony, and these latter were by far the cruelest.

Irony is, for sure, the most dangerous weapon that exists in the hand of man. A writer, redoubtable himself for irony, named this instrument of torture "the gaiety of indignation," much superior to the other gaiety that it makes look like a shepherdess of turkeys. But, what to think of the irony of a prig foolishly indignant at the inobservation of an etiquette or a rudiment, and rendered all-powerful by the humility of a repentance that his stupidity makes him mistake for abjection?—for the evangelical precedence of the *unique* penitent over a multitude of just men without blemish is, in the eyes of any true Sulpician, merely a funny joke without practical application. Many priests use then successfully this happy means of disgusting them with their persons and with the sacrament that they debase. The poor girl, resigned to everything, was by this, however, crucified to the bottom of her heart. In silence, she experienced this humiliation, like the saint that she was, and Marchenoir knew absolutely nothing about it from her.

In the end, however, she was put into contact with a good missionary man who had accepted her for the most part just as she was. The experience of fraternal cohabitation was in its eighteenth month of the most conclusive innocence. The red-hot grief, that had irritated so many prudish bulls, was dying down finally, and peace had begun to settle in, when the devastating letter from Marchenoir arrived. To tell the truth, a mystic of this caliber found herself disoriented for having nothing else to suffer.

The surprising holocaustic mischief that followed had appeared enormous to her confessor, who did not hesitate to blame her energetically for her excessive zeal, all the while acknowledging, in the privacy of his counsels, to have been singularly edified by this Christian, whom he had the pretension of acting as the tugboat of. Even still, he could not prevent himself from expressing doubts on the efficacy of the expedient, alleging, not without profoundness, the instinct of mendicant resignation particular to sensual love, which makes desirous people, the most haughty among them, covet the smallest crumbs from the feast they were deprived of. He thought, above all, but did not express it, that in the eyes of an easily transported spiritualist such as Marchenoir, the moral splendor of immolation ought infinitely to surpass with its enticing vertigo—the carnal, sacrificed beauty . . .

XLVIII

In fact, what was left, exactly, of that almost famous beauty that had formerly made men go mad—austere men, men full of prudence, like camels,—and which, even, it is said, had cost two men their lives! Were the ruins of this Palmyra decidedly repulsive to every enthusiasm? A profound artist, contemplating Véronique in prayer, would assuredly not have settled the matter in the affirmative.

Without a doubt, she had ruined, forever, the facial harmony of that sparrowhawk of love, who, after all, after she had become devout, had only spiritualized its rabbits and renounced, in favor of the *Dove*, its indigestive woodpigeons. Hygienic substitution of prey, which could not change essentially her physiognomy. What was needed, for that, was mutilation, a violent fall from the high place of the aquiline rostrum onto the dismantled substratum, and the labial depression of a mouth whose terrible arc,—which had emptied so many quivers in its day,—finally distended, elongated, in a pallid rictus, from one commissure to the other. Bizarre and sad disfigurement, that made one think of the phantasmic juxtaposition of a portion of the old face at the inferior crack of some sublime human capital. But her physical traits, remaining intact, seemed to have become more beautiful, in the same way as the remaining body members become stronger, it appears, after an amputation.

Above all, there were her eyes, immense and unlimited eyes, that nobody ever was able to get around. Blue, doubtless, as was befitting, but an occult blue, out of this world, which covetousness, with a horn-rimmed telescope, had absurdly reputed to be clear gray. It was actually a full palette of unknown skies, even in the West, and just beneath the frozen paws of Ursa Major where, at least, the ignoble azure intensity of Eastern skies held no sway.

Taking their cue from the diverse states of her soul, her incredulous girl's eyes, starting, sometimes, with a sort of blue consternated by lactescent iris, shined, one minute, with the pure cobalt of generous illusions, was injected passionately with scarlet, brass red, dots of gold, then changed to a hopeful reseda, to only then be attenuated immediately in a resignation of gray lavender, and finally to be extinguished, for good, in the safety of slate.

But they were most affective during the hours of ecstasy, remaining motionless, the hours of absolute inagitation familiar to contemplatives, at the lunar twilight diamonded with tears, inexpressible and divine, that rose all of a sudden, from the bottom of these foreign eyes, and which no chemistry of painting would have been able to capture the most distant impression of. A pale and translucent double gulf, an insurrection of clarity in the depths, above the waves, speckled with forgetfulness, with an inaccessible contemplation! . . .

An alienist, a profaner of sepultures, any human brute what-soever who wanted to constrain Véronique to look at him, at certain moments, by forcibly taking her head into his hands, would have been stupefied to the point of fright by the infinite *inattention* of this landscape of simultaneous sky and ocean, which he would have discovered instead of a gaze, and in his coarse soul he would have become obsessed. "They were," said Marchenoir, "the eyes of a blind person groping his way through Paradise . . ."

It took those unprecedented eyes, formed like lakes, and which appeared to grow larger every day, to excuse the paradoxi-cal absence, nearly complete, of her forehead, admirably wider at the temples, but inundated, almost to her eyebrows, by the overflowing of her hair. Previously, during her time as the *Suction Cup*, this sublime fleece, which could have, it seemed, offset fifty setting suns, overhung her eyes with its heavy mass and it was something to make one go stark crazy over seeing the conflict of these elements. A conflagration in the Pacific! . . .

When the Suction Cup no longer existed, this blazing swell of hair surged back every which way that it could, pressed and packed in headbands, braids, rollers, packages, dislocating the pins, pushing the combs out on their teeth, falling onerously on her shoulders and sometimes to the small of her back, until, twisted into a despotic and monstrous chignon, she could finally remain tranquil, for the love of God.

Then there was a precarious forehead, a narrow band of forehead, which appeared incommensurable in length from one temple to the other, and this was a new sort of beauty, almost as redoubtable as the first . . . Now, there was a third distressing and inexplicable aspect. Her eyes appeared to have grown, her head, reduced by half, withdrew shamefacedly, and her forehead, bare, was terrible and seemed to carry the mark of some infamous punishment . . .

Her nose, by good fortune, had escaped all harm. Slightly aquiline and of plausible dimensions, a little too fine, perhaps, at the extremity, that one would not have dared to hope for from this irresponsible organ of sensuality, it was flanked by nostrils surprisingly mobile, significative, for certain women, of an immeasurable cupidity,—providentially established in a manner to counterbalance masculine heroism, of which this physiological particularity is equally a prognostic.

As for her mouth, there was nothing more to say, alas! It had been as dangerous as all traps and all suckers of the abyss. It had been the *profound pit* that Solomon affirmed that those whom the Lord is angry with should fall into. A kiss from those thick lips, bestially exquisite, shattered nerves, withered marrows, derailed brains, unscrewed all cuirasses, unhinged to the point of avaricious lust, transformed alienists into idiots and simple imbeciles into energumens. A bankruptcy syndicate was hiding under her tongue, and thirty-two bureaus of undertakers tied up their dossiers in the canicular shadow of her teeth. When she spat, the earth was desirous of abounding in fish like the sea, and the Ocean itself would have barely been able to respond, swelling with pride: The foam of my shipwrecked victims is no less bitter!

The demon of Debauchery, for a long time expropriated from this ancient patrimony, was finally coming to distance himself irrevocably from these ruins, in the middle of which, from now forward, nothing remained, not even a humble stump where he could sit down. Her lips, returned by force, had lost form and color, and that was really the most notable loss of this brothel caryatid, transformed into a striking Ivory Tower pilaster. However, the tint of the whole of her face had remained intact. It was ever the same pigmentary combination of chamois, nasturtium, vermillion, bistre, and gold, imperceptibly attenuated by a fortieth part of lunar reflection.

In sum, Véronique had somewhat missed the mark and had not become less beautiful than before,—the squander of a part of her riches having proportionally accrued value from the fertile garden of love, that the unfortunate Marchenoir had so inopportunely sown with the indivisible concupiscence of heaven.

XLIX

Events have this in common with geese, that they go in groups. Anyone not absolutely deprived of observation could have noticed it. The truth is that curiosity stops there, ordinarily. No one asks for an explanation of this law, the non-existent fountain of Chance having to suffice for the satisfaction of all this thinking flock's thirsts. The proverb: "Misfortunes never comes singly," is the unique monument of man's attention or sagacity with respect to one of the least negligible particularities of his history. It is, however, well assured that good or bad events, whatever might be the illusion of their size, seem both to be called, as soon as they are born, by irresistible clamors. They pop up everywhere, emerging from holes in the ground or falling from mountains on the moon, for the eternal stupefaction of a race extracted from nothingness, which never knew what to expect and which never expects anything.

One finished by observing, in a fairly certain manner, that the physical union of two individuals of different sex have for probable effect the apparition of a third of the same nature, in rudimentary state. This quasi-certitude is one of the most savory fruits of the experience of sixty centuries. But who then is occupied with the otherwise profound mystery of the metaphysical sexuality of events of this world, of their rigorously matched alliances, of their faithful lineages, of their perfect solidarity? The whole family hastens toward the first wail of a newborn baby, and God only knows if it is innumerable, because these events never stop and because they continue forever to make babies! The first imbecile to come along, to whom something happens, is, for an instant, the well of truth where a formidable people all descend to drink from. All the Norms lean over him, all the Rules, all the Laws, all the occult Wills rest on their elbows like so many Polymnies,[1] on the unconscious edge of stupidity that does not doubt even of their presence . . .

Leverdier was no imbecile and he knew too well that something had happened! However, he was amazed to stumble, immediately after having quit Marchenoir, into an individual whom he had had the pleasure of not running into for several months: Alcide Lerat, "French historian and literate," as he liked to call himself. This was, for the saddened guest of so many heady rites of grief, a nearly physical commotion, in the manner of a funereal presentiment, to see again all of a sudden, in such a moment as this, this sordid puppet who trotted, his nose to the wind, like a polecat looking to track a rotting carcass.

This Alcide Lerat, well-known in the world of newspapers, is a sort of literary Benoît Labre, without the saintliness, whose posthumous panegyric would be a work to make the most audacious mud cleaners of aureoles tremble. Living exclusively on alms gathered from men of letters, whom he amuses with his calumnies or with his pieces of scandal and who receive him in drafty places, the funny fetid man, luckily incapable of catching a cold, indefatigably takes his carcass out for a walk, from one twilight to the other,—peddling in this way, in the pants of a romantic that he had defamed the day before, at an editor-in-chief's whom he had just plied with filth and who will give him perhaps twenty sous, the base conjectures of his dishonorable mind on the private life of a poet all of whose hats he has *worn out.*

He avenges himself in this way for having been deprived of first place among writers, which he has never ceased to claim since the success of his famous pamphlet: *Diderot's Household and Finances.* This lampoon, which lacked talent but contained an exasperating erudition of detail like vermin on the hides of the philosopher's worshipers, produced, in effect, a lively riot of

---

1 Polymnies, or Polyhymnias, are Greek mythological muses of sacred music and poetry.

opinions in the public sheets, thirty years ago. Alcide Lerat's later works are, truth be told, not worth the drop of ink that would be dispensed to write their titles. No matter. Assured of being the greatest genius of the centuries, he thinks in good faith that all is owed to him and that his mere presence is an honor, an occasion of rapture that nothing could sufficiently recompense.

"I say too much," he said, and one takes note of it. In consequence, he exacts ransoms, as much as possible, from his *disciples*, whose largesses, somewhat larger than what one would suppose them to be, could never have, by reason of the cataracts of joy spilled on them, anything but the false weight of ingratitude.

"All yours, *except the socks*," he wrote, one day, to one of them who had forgotten this one article in the filial abandon of a complete defrocking. Admirable and definitive words which the addressee, a species of barefoot intellectual, did not catch the profound irony of.

The name of this dangerous critic is so suited to his physiognomy, that is impossible to present the usufructuary without being exposed to the inconvenience of appearing a *farceur* at the host's table. The *rat* is evidently his animal, unless it is the other way around and he is the rat's animal, which could be sustained as a probable opinion. His nose, sharply pointed like a beet, drawing to it a thin face with insect specks, planted with an arid copse of graying hairs, is straddled by a pair of small, brilliant and restless eyes, to incite a mastiff's fury. This last trait determines and fixes instantly the analogy. The perpetual trotting, the vestral incurvature of the superior vertebrae and the customary folding of the arms onto his often menaced midribs, adds but very little to the depiction.

Leverdier had known the animal for a long time now. He was even inexplicably honored by him with a sort of consideration or esteem. Lerat, whom he had nearly thrown out the door two or three times and who had renounced it as pointless to present himself again, did not see, however, the need to deprive him, when he encountered him, with several nutritive minutes of conversation, which Leverdier could have admirably done without, on that day in particular. He had the best reasons in the world for moving away from this bore, whom he strongly suspected of having spread dirty calumnies about his friend, into whose indigent hand he had often dropped the acorn of a small ecu. Once he had even given him the placid counsel to profit from his excellent sight as a rodent to avoid carefully all roads that Marchenoir frequented. "He is not too patient, you see, my dear Monsieur Alcide, and would be very capable of making a gift to you of your own ears. I warn you as a brother. *Think on it well.*"

In his actual state of mind, such an encounter, so sudden, had the effect on Leverdier of a presage of the most ill-fated kind. He was on the verge of awarding him with a complete thrashing, the memory of which would have been extremely durable. But it would have been like beating an old woman and, what is more, he feared the ridicule of taking flight.

He was not slow to recognize that, in effect, the encounter was not absolutely vain and could have serious enough consequences.

L

"Oh! what a *serious* attitude you have this morning, Monsieur Count of Pylades; would we have anxieties regarding the dear health of Monsieur Marquis of Orestes?"

Such were the first words of Alcide Lerat, the most disappointing imitation of an imbecile that one had ever seen. He had retained from his failed seminarist's education a complete stock of this type of facetiousness, insupportably crooned in a minor soprano, with the ordinary accompaniment of a mocking reverence.

"Monsieur Lerat," responded Leverdier, who felt himself running out of patience, "I am very much in a hurry and incapable, for the moment, of savoring your delicious pleasantries. I beg you to excuse me and to go to the devil, if you please."

"We're all there, with the devil," said the bore in repartee, "insofar as he's the Prince of this world, but you receive me so poorly that I'm quite of the mind to keep for myself an interesting communication that I was wanting to entrust you with for your friend Marchenoir."

At the mention of this name, Leverdier became attentive. To be sure, he was not expecting, in general, anything good to come from his interlocutor, but he knew him to be a cistern of often surprising information, and it is said that a very pure water can fall sometimes from the most hideous gargoyles, in a time of storm.

"You have," he said, "something of interest relating to Marchenoir?"

The other, leaning then with both hands on the handle of his cane, which was as lamentable as he was, and bending forward toward his auditor, like a crooked old tree,—without stopping for a second his sempiternally smacking smile,—began to lisp like an altar boy who a calamitous circumstance had invested with some important secret for the prosperity of the vestry.

"Your friend likes to make himself desired as much as a pretty woman. He hides like a bear and all the world complains. I encountered, this week, Beauvivier who'd like to see him. I believe that his intention is to entrust him with the leading article in the *Basile*, in order to harass the imbeciles at the *Universe* a bit. If your friend Marchenoir doesn't profit from the occasion, he'll deserve to wander, like his biblical homonym, 'over the face of the earth,' because they've need of him over at the *Basile*. You who are a practical man, you ought to counsel him to file his nails down and prevent him from doing anything stupid. Beauvivier deigned to tell me that he was counting on me to bring him to him. He seems to believe that I'm close to this riparian of the Danube. Speaking of which, he's returned, hasn't he, from his edifying voyage?"

"Yes," affirmed dreamily Leverdier, "but do not visit him, I will take it upon myself to talk with him."

This communication got him thinking a lot. The all-powerful *Basile*, the universal journal of well-bred people, must have been feeling terribly anemic to wish to invoke the reagent of such a moxa! In this case . . .

At this moment, he realized that the seductive Alcide had taken on a familiar pose. Having, as prerequisite, inspected, while whistling, the state of the sky and brought back onto his temples, with the tips of the tweezer-like fingers of his left hand, several undisciplined locks of hair, he had finally lowered this hand to the presumed height of the organ of general sentiments and held it there, now, open and thrust against the breast of his adversary.

"Oh, right," he said, "I forgot!" And taking out from his wallet, he let fall a fifty-centime piece into that wind-up begging bowl, which dishonors, with the most horologic exactitude, Christian mendicity.

Lerat did not want to move away, however, without having completed his role as benefactor with a last piece of advice. In consequence, he exhaled these prototypical admonitions:

"If your friend wants to succeed at the *Basile*, you should recommend that he stop acting so much like a wild beast. If he knows how to please Beauvivier, his fortune is made. He doesn't lack talent when he wants to moderate himself and not to continually employ his abominable scatological expressions. That's what that boor Veuillot lost out on, who always repulsed my reprimands and who finds himself pretty well off now, don't you agree, now that he's died of his own venom! Look at Labruyère and Massillon. They say more in a single decent phrase than all your epileptics do in two hundred lines. Persuade him then to read my book on *Everyone's Table*, which you should have in your library. He'll learn what it means to have true strength united with distinction."

The odious character had stopped smiling. He was floating adrift on his own river, with God's majesty. After having executed, with the tips of his exorable fingers, a very small merciful gesture, he moved away, full of his power, cane under arm, his two arms clerically crossed at the interior of his sleeves and his chest thrown out in advance, towed by his muzzle, having the air of traitorously jolting his lamentable derrière.

"In this case," thought Leverdier to himself, for whom this skillful retreat had been a lost beauty, "Marchenoir could, in an instant, regain widespread publicity. He has not succeeded in launching more than a small number of articles; he would immediately reclaim, by means of such a resounding journal, the intellectual group collected previously by his audacity and which his silence, for so many months now, has dispersed. And then, what a revenge against all the cowards who believe he has been vanquished! This vermin Lerat should have told the truth. He has all the lowliest reasons in the world to desire with all his power that a formidable firebrand be launched, by no matter whose hand, onto the kitchens of the Catholic press. He must have even worked intensely on Beauvivier in this sense and made him swallow the necessity of being Marchenoir's *discoverer*. Properce, in any case, an artful devil, has carefully protected himself by not writing, and has been contented to dispatch this scout who could, by fortune's good graces, receive the kicks of a presumable indignation and who was on his way, evidently, to the rue des Fourneaux, when I met him."

Leverdier resolved to see, that very same day, Properce Beauvivier, the sadistic poet-novelist, who had become, not long ago, director and editor-in-chief of the *Basile*. He barely knew him, but he wanted, as much as possible, to understand his game and to prepare, with extreme care, the negotiations,— Marchenoir having many times expressed very loudly his disdain for this arrogant swamp dweller, the which must have had the devil of a need to stir up his alluvium by determining to broach the subject by means of this cormorant. There was also the fear that he was offering a ladder to this desperate man only to induce him to break his neck definitively on a rotten rung. Doubtless, it would have been highly imprudent to try and sound out this infamous Jew on the vital question of money. His practices, in this regard, should have resembled those of his predecessor, the famous Magnus Conrart, whose repugnant suicide caused such a stir, and who put an enormous tax of prelibation on the emoluments of guest authors, who he knew were dying of hunger and reduced to contenting themselves with any salary whatsoever.

But, in the absence of an immediate budgetary security, it was absolutely indispensable to assure, at least, the writer's independence. Marchenoir no longer at all being the happy young man to purchase the insertion of his patronymic vocable in a great journal, at the price of any pork-butcher emasculation of thought.

LI

The next day, Marchenoir and Leverdier got together, at five in the morning at the Café Caron, at the corner of the rue des Saint Pere and the rue de l'Université, in front of one of the forty thousand branches of Calman-Levy's literary pawnshop. It is a café for virtuous old men, who seem to want to replace, in this quarter, the old Café Tabouret, unknown to the new generation, where, formerly, so many illustrious writers and quill pushers drank and whose names, for over ten years now, have been totally forgotten. The two friends sometimes made a rendezvous in this café, which they preferred above all others, because of the perfect silence observed by the three or four centenarian journalists that one is always assured to find there, and who form incomprehensibly the essential basis of the establishment's commercial operations.

Leverdier, being the first to come, saw Marchenoir arrive, just as he had quit him some hours earlier, pale and melancholic, but visibly relaxed. The *real* presence of Véronique, as changed as she was, the saintly girl, had sufficed to pacify the unfortunate man.

"I am getting used to that new face," he said after a moment. "She is still beautiful, *our* Véronique. Soon you will see her with the same eye as I do, my friend. The first impression was terrible, I thought I was going to die. Then, I do not know what virtue came out of her, but it seemed like a dome of peace descended on us. In an instant, all anguish disappeared and I think my tears have carried away in one sitting all my sorrows, while I sobbed over her, yesterday morning, holding her in my arms. Soon after, you already know, I slept for twenty hours, for the first time in my life. Long enough to believe that I would never rise again . . . And what a sleep of Paradise, refreshing, beatific, without precise dreams, without distinct visions, lucid, however, in the manner of a vermillion twilight refracted in the limpid waters of a lake, at the bottom of which the ravished eyes of the diver opened! I had something of a confused sensation, deliciously inexpressible, spiritual and physical at the same time, of being immersed in a lunar creek filled with my tears . . . On awakening, I immediately encountered the magnificent face of my sacrificial sweetheart, who was overjoyed to see me sleeping like this, and her appearance did not cause me surprise, nor grief, but, on the contrary, a sort of very sweet tenderness, composed, I imagine, of fraternal compassion, and of religious enthusiasm melted together in one internal, absolutely chaste transport! . . . You remember, Georges, those mysterious birds that made us dream so much, one day, in the Jardin d'Acclimatation, and which are named accurately *stabbed* doves, because of the blood mark that they carry in the middle of their white throat? We were very astonished, you remember, by that unexpected pleonasm of symbolism, in the exceptional creature that, not content to signify Love, wished to flaunt the stigma. Well! Véronique will be my wounded dove, just as I saw her this morning, in the supernatural light of my renewed soul by virtue of her sacrifice . . . But that is just me yammering on and you have, doubtless, much to tell me. Did you uncover, finally, that trafficker of human milt?"

"Beauvivier! yes, I just left him," responded Leverdier smiling. "Your last word reassures me more than all the rest, my dear Caïn. If you find your nasty verve again, we are not near to losing you. Extremely upset to have missed him yesterday and not caring to wait indefinitely in his shop, I mentioned on my card that I came on your behalf. I was received immediately. My friend, it is a sure thing. The *Basile* has need of you. Beauvivier did not even bother to hide it from me. Basically, I believe I understood that above all you were needed, at this moment, to oust someone, Loriot, perhaps, whom he spoke to me about, incidentally, like one of the most encumbering pieces of filth, but quite difficult to be rid of in one instantaneous sweep, having been defecated by the too copious deceased,[1] with particular attention. But that augurs well also.

"Personally, I know very little about Beauvivier, whom I saw today for the third time. But I have my sources of information. He is the most loathsome of men and, to be completely frank, his benevolence is more to be feared than his declared enmity. He is a kind of Judas-don-Juan, crossed with Alphonse and Tartuffe. His life is a fabric of abominations and betrayals. One is forced to disinfect oneself with phenol, like a cadaver, after having been seen by him. Ah, well! it appears that this being has, nevertheless, a quality, the most rare of qualities these days. He loves literature, and bingo, that's what redeems him. Maybe he really does have a project of elevating a bit the editorship of the *Basile* which Magnus had brought down to himself, that is to say, beneath everything. 'I've read everything that Monsieur Marchenoir's written,' he told me, 'and I'm aware of nobody better than him, at the present moment, and I consider him nearly as an equal. He's a great writer, of disconcerting originality. Please repeat my words to him. I consider that the *Basile* would be honored by his collaboration and I solicit it. I certainly would've run myself to his domicile, if I'd thought I could've returned. I know that

---

1 Deceased, viz. the previous managing editor.

he was badly treated at the journal, when I wasn't in control of it. I want to repair this injustice by giving to your friend carte blanche, etc., etc.' Let us consider that even if only a quarter of all these wonders are true, that would still be excellent and, whatever he is hiding, all the same, he must have had a hell of a need of your services to let such talk escape from his prudent mug! . . .'

"How did this conversation end?" asked Marchenoir.

"As neatly as possible. 'Marchenoir,' I told him, 'is extremely tired from his travels and would be much obliged to you to allow him a few days to recover. Do you authorize me, however, to gain some time, to tell him to prepare, starting from today, without his having to see you beforehand, any article whatsoever? In this case, it is necessary that I can assure him of the insertion, because he has ceased, for many years now, being a debutant, and he does not want to work in vain. After what I have just understood, the preliminary accord, between you and him, of choice of subject, appears to me to be a most useless formality.' 'And one of the most injurious for a writer of talent, you might add, Sir.' That was his immediate response. 'Let the author of the *Powerless*, send or bring to me whatever he judges appropriate to write. I will give his article immediately to the typesetters and, as for the rest, he should believe it, we will see eye to eye forever. All that I ask is that he takes aim outward and does not gun down our own troops.'"

"Oh!" said Marchenoir. "This last bit ruins everything that went before. Since you began talking, I was expecting it. This supererogatory recommendation, which has the air of nothing important to it, resembles those insignificant clauses thrown offhandedly at the bottom of a contract, in the guise of a paragraph intended to empty one's pen, but which suffice to annul everything that went before it. You should have known it, old Georges. Those people there are the vermin of the earth and it is impossible to target anyone without touching them. Now, I am incapable, this is well-known, of conceiving of journalism other than as a form of pamphlet. What the devil do they want me to do, then? I cannot however set myself to writing optimistic pastorals or inspired schoolboy psychologies, in the style of Dulaurier!"

"But, for God's sake!" replied Leverdier, "everyone knows perfectly well what you are capable of, and Beauvivier knows it better than anyone. If he's soliciting you, it is apparently because he has need of your virility or even your violence. I found in him a man of exquisite politeness, irreproachable,—a slice of rotted galantine, glazed on top,—but determined, vibrant with I do not know what. He is clear that he wants to astonish someone or upset something and he is moving your catapult into position, in view of producing a demolition effect or a simple intimidation that we have no means of conjecturing. What difference does it make? That rogue has too much spirit to ever ask you to be his accomplice. But your known hatreds can serve him without you knowing it. It will happen, for the millionth time, that an honest man's indignation will have favored a villain's schemes. And what difference does that even make? The Truth is always good to tell, even if it were only God listening, for then one would address Him by one of his names!"

The outcome of this conversation was what it had to be. The two friends sought together a subject for the article. Marchenoir, without peremptory objection, but highly suspicious of these energetic crises that sometimes shake the sterile fig tree of journalism,—for the invariable deception of knights errant who wait half-starved under its shade for the falling of fruits,—decided, despite the representations by Leverdier, who would have preferred that they go slower, to offer, at the start, an article of unprecedented vehemence.

"If it goes well," he said, "echoing his friend's own words, I will have the honor of having written *all* the truth on one of the most complete ignominies of our time. I will be glorified for my courage and cowardly sorts who would never fail to accuse me of cynicism, in case of failure, will then come to pluck a laudative guitar under my gargoyles. If it goes badly, my situation remains exactly as it was before and I will still not have missed the occasion to become a happy scamp, because it would be in any case inept of me to prostitute myself. I would disgust the client without giving him the least pleasure. Beauvivier knows it marvelously well, as you have just remarked. He wants me just as I am or not at all.

"Do we not know that it is always useless to make concessions? I have sometimes tried to tone myself down a little, in the hope of earning a few miserable sous. I dishonored myself without succeeding in getting myself any more accepted. I have no hopes of succeeding in the least at the *Basile*. Supposing for one minute that Beauvivier really wanted to go to great lengths for me, he would be immediately surmounted by a united front of all the publishing house scum. It would be the same adventure all over again as with that old bastard Magnus, who wanted to launch me himself last year, for dirty reasons I am not privy to, and who, suddenly, coming to discover that I was decidedly a 'hateful fellow,' informed me of it, right then and there, with a severance letter. I do not want to swallow those garter snakes again. My first and probably last article will give the measure, the form, and the color of all the others. It will be take it or leave it."

Leverdier knew quite well that Marchenoir was right. This corsair would have needed an independent literary press, which does not exist any more in France, where the vile republican tyranny is on the verge of asphyxiating everything. But it was important to seize the occasion all the same, even if just once and for the honor of justice itself. Besides, Marchenoir had just found a subject that he was already ablaze about. The artist and the Christian, which he was the most powerful combination of, simultaneously exulted.

"Why," he exclaimed, "would I not take advantage of this first article, in all likelihood the only one, to execute a terrifying charge on pornographic literature and publicity, on the occasion, for example, of the recent bills posted by anticlerical publishers.

You have, doubtless, noticed the monstrous poster, announcing the *Secret Loves of Pope Pius IX*, accompanied by the pontiff's portrait and a series of medallions, representing heroines, notably supposed, by this villainous libel. The man putting filth on the walls whom I would beg pardon for mentioning his name, the stinking idiot Taxil, is a sub-abject person whom I know very well that it is not worth the pain to talk about or even think about. But when the garbage is at its peak, when that which should remain shamefully at the bottom of the walls climbs and exposes itself on the facades; when the manure, previously immobile, becomes a violent enemy, helmeted, cuirassed, venting its feelings openly, lying in ambush, for the lithographic aggression of innocence, at every turn in the streets, one is finally forced to ask for an explanation from every repressive authority of this intolerable sedition of excrement!

"It is true that this is nothing more than a spit in the tear-streaming face of a so-called Christian society, which has already received and endured so much. The peoples, as well as the governments, have received only the humiliations that they merited, in exact proportion to their cowardice or their crimes, and perhaps it is too fine even, in the eyes of a rigorous justice, to be trampled on by this little runt.

"What could break anger's legs,—admitting the unoriginal metaphor of these ineffectual bronze limbs, that are always invisible,—is the multitude's indifference. One passes before the obscene exhibition without revolt, without murmur, without astonishment. Fathers do not lead their progeny away and find it plain and simple that the august face of the Father of Fathers should be decried like this for the joy of some matutinal emptiers of cesspools whom this puts into a bawdy mood. Two or three generations ago, if that, the bourgeoisie was inflamed for or against these eruptions from the sewer. Today, the same bourgeoisie, having become a little dumber and a little more ignoble, contemplates them with the stupidity of disinterestedness. Tomorrow, without a doubt, its filthy idiocy having no bottom anymore, it will become completely softened to it. It will tell itself that the heroic independence of a heart burning for justice is attested to by the spurting of this pus and that it is necessary to water young flowers just bloomed on its fertile lap. We will witness, on that day, the apotheosis of Tartuffe expected for two hundred years!

"Ah! that will be all we need, then, and Moliere's hypocrite will cut a poor figure! To appear a man of property distributing, with saintly gestures, ostensible acts of grace at the foot of altars, what could be easier, even in a century where religious faith is almost extinguished? One would always have man's supernatural uneasiness of heart and his unconscious veneration for naïve or haughty bearers of relics. But to obtain a similar triumph by spreading absolute ignominy, by contaminating those same altars, by prostituting children's glances, irreparably deflowered by contact with this repulsiveness, is a little too much, and the seventeenth century is buried terribly deep in the ground.

"To be Léo Taxil or any other hooligan of the pen, Francisque Sarcey, for example,—because the Barnum of anticlericalism should only be a pretext here,—and not to die under the always imminent adventitious thrashing, many times administered already, without the recoiling disgust of the feared bat at such an approach, must be devilishly beautiful, doubtless! What would it be like to be worshiped under this form, to appear a confessor of the true faith and to vanish into thin air like that, with mackerel scales and golden wings, into the fecal paradise of the elect so admired by republicans? . . . Such, however, is the future presaged by universal indifference for the unspeakable assassination attempt represented by this bill posting, as perfectly criminal as a public spectacle of prostitution could be.

"Ah, well! I want to evoke it once and for all, this future and to put it in view of the herd of stinking scribes who are preparing it for us and who I will summon to appear. My Catholicism will appear but very vaguely in this study wherein I have only to proclaim it. One will have neither the consolation nor the possibility to throw sacristies into my face. The circumstance of the outraged Pope will have only occasion to warn, quite in vain, I know, of the necessity of disencumbering the public ways of this filth that strikes with the plague. I will call them by their names, these pieces of filth,—as the Lord called the stars,—I will make them visible with the most indisputable clarity, I will say that a bloody cleansing becomes necessary when administration of the refuse dump neglects, at this point, its primary duty and that everything becomes preferable to this boorish cholera and irremediable imbecility, that menaces to precipitate, tomorrow, what is left of poor France into the most sinister corruption of the people that a Dantesque pessimism could only dream of! . . ."

Leverdier would have been, perhaps, a *practical* man, had he not met that reckless fellow who orbited him, like a satellite, from day one. In general, he exhibited at first some prudent objections,—some objections of little worth, always dismissed, that he returned to the substratum of his mind as soon as Marchenoir began to inveigh against the universe. When that happened, he willingly installed himself at the intersection of the abysses and offered to pilot the delirium. On this occasion, he watched with wonder how the maneuver decided upon by the incorrigible daredevil was going to sink him indubitably. To begin with, he had to renounce that collaborative nutritive, momentarily dreamed about, of him working at the *Basile*. Beauvivier would publish, maybe, the hammering circular and then it would be over. But how to confront so eloquent a maniac? For Marchenoir, it was a matter of pride to burn his bridges when someone tried to contain him. Consequently, Leverdier took his side, as always, an inconstant temporizer who ended up an extremist.

"The subject is superb," he said, in effect, after some silence. "As it is decidedly impossible to find a steady job in the press for a man of your character, do not hold back, knock them out, disembowel them, exterminate whatever you can of these cowardly scoundrels who always know how to take it out, by their silence, on talented writers whose solitary height frightens them and whom they can surely starve, by closing off all publicity to them. It certainly will not be me who will plead on their behalves. But, just now, did you not discover your article's title? *The Sedition of Excrement!* Ha! it is not too bad, it seems to me. Your reputation as a scatologist has left nothing more to be desired for a long time now. Everyone is perfectly certain that only smells please you and that you are incapable of taking your images from anywhere else than the latrines or the garbage dumps,—where it is generally suspected that you keep your napkin and your rolling pin. This title, by consequence, will surprise nobody. As for me, I confess that it fills me with rapture."

"You may be right," responded Marchenoir smiling. "But it is time to leave. Véronique has gone out of her way, I believe, to make us a meal this evening. She is fond of a meal with the *family*, as she likes to call our reunion, the dear creature. Vaugirard is far away, and the hour is near. Let us not keep her waiting."

The two friends rose that very instant and left.

LII

Back out on the street, they decided to walk. It was February and the night's commencing dry coldness pleased them. Walking through Paris in the company of a person with whom one may say anything is a rare enough pleasure, allotted to some artists who are gloriless, whose hours are not easily monetizable. They returned to the eternal object of their intimate thoughts, to Véronique, inasmuch as they were just about to see her again and pass several hours together with her. Marchenoir was the first to speak. God knows with what tranquility and discernment!

Certainly, it was miraculous that this agonizing man of the day before could have been able to establish, in less than thirty hours, so impregnable a line of defense between himself and his own troubles! But finally, he explained, *as best he could*, the marvel. He was analyzing himself now, and dissecting himself with the greatest care, causing his friend to admire the sudden healing of enormous wounds, which it seemed would have been the end of many men's lives, and telling him: "She is an admirable girl who did that. What will I do for her, my God?" The ordinary lyricism of his language became more exasperating as he spoke, and Leverdier, in tow, thanked God with all his heart for the incomprehensible recovery from intolerable agonies which he himself had suffered indirectly.

"Do you see, Georges," said the exorcised lover, "it is not the changed traits that have restored my heart,—once more, I do not find her any less beautiful than before,—it is the mysterious beauty of the *interior action* by which this immolation was determined. The prerequisite intention of sacrifice sufficed to establish the spiritual current that has just brought our two souls a little closer together, while driving back all my senses fifty thousand leagues from my flesh. It is her prayer that saves me, her prayer alone,—that she had *pulled out her teeth* and *shaved off her hair* to make her seem pitiable beyond the farthest reaches of heaven,— in the heroic illusion of mutilating merely her body! . . ."

Thus they arrived at the distant rue des Fourneaux where cobblestone merchants procure for powerful dreamers the mirage of the Pyramids, in the melancholic aridity of their incommensurable quarries.

Marchenoir lived, not far from these quarries, in an almost isolated house with a humble enough aspect, the second floor of which he occupied, where above him were just two mansards rented out to impeccable omnibus employees, absent during the day and who slept there, at night, for only a few hours. He loved this quarter and this house for having spent there, ten years now, the best part of his moral and intellectual life. The street's relative calm refreshed him, outside the center of Paris which had the effect on him, by comparison, of being the most uninhabitable of hell-holes.

The apartment, made up of three rooms and, with a kitchen, was the kind of artist's flat no longer seen. It would have been useless to look there for crockery, copperware, ironwork, paintings or curious medallions. Not a single Japanese bronze, not a single impressionistic watercolor, not the shadow of one of those old pieces of wood, scaled, vermiculated, friable, that represent as best they can, according to received attitudes, the crackled devotion of ancient ages. Marchenoir's contempt for this bric-a-brac almost had no bounds. In all, a seventeenth-century enamel from Limoges, a family souvenir, offering the vision of a St. Peter in an azure robe and an orange-colored mantle, kneeling on a freshly washed landscape, under the spindly foliage in asparagus-green and gold brocade, flanked by a white porcelain cock that crows in a corner of the most impenetrably ultramarine firmament. At his feet, a red book, gamboge-colored keys and a gigantic chocolate burdock. This image, of contestable naïvety, sufficed, such as it was, the antiquarian appetites of its possessor.

The furniture, in vituperatable walnut and even pine, acquired piece by piece and second-hand at the cheapest price, would have made a concierge of the Faubourg Saint-Antoine indignant. In this regard, the misanthrope was absolute,—"There are only," he said, "two sorts of tables that an artist can write on: a fifty-thousand-franc table and a fifty-sou table." But, even if he became a millionnaire, he would probably have kept the second one, for fear of making himself look stupid, at the expense of the poor, by buying the first.

The books themselves were few: a gigantic synoptic Bible, the most costly of his follies, several tomes from abbé Migne's *Patrologia*, a dozen Greek or Latin Elzevirs,[1] a few history books, a few modern novels and a horde of dictionaries in diverse languages, at most a hundred volumes. When he needed a book he did not have, he borrowed it from his friend, who was better provisioned, or went to the library.

---

1 Elzevirs were the esteemed Dutch seventeenth- and eighteenth-century publisher.

Only Véronique's room had a semblance of comfort of the twentieth order, which three or four dozen good working girls, favored by heaven, still put up with, who have figured out the means of reconciling the precepts of virtue with the exigencies of their stomachs. In the case of the penitent, this moderation was all the more extraordinary in that she had had to renounce all the luxury of lucrative dissipation, certain sums of which excited previously the envy of a crowd of prostitutes. As soon as it was decided that they would live together in the desert, Véronique had accomplished, without ostentation and without speaking about it, the legendary act of sending her furniture off to the auction room, retaining only some indispensable old clothes, and bringing by herself her money to diverse charitable establishments that Marchenoir had designated,—not wanting to *keep* anything, she said, of what she had eaten out of the Devil's hand.

Her room, where the least shabby engines of their domestic felicity had been brought together, even though she would have been content with nothing, recalled well enough the interiors of pious izbas, illuminated by perpetual lamps lit up in front of the propitious figures on the iconostases. A little nightlight, with a rose-colored glimmer, was suspended in front of a great pale crucifix, and another just like it, but a little larger, cast its tint, with a vague rosy pink hue, a hateful lithographic reproduction of the Holy Face of Jesus, such as it was venerated by Monsieur Dupont, "the saintly man of Tours," who had propagated this devotion in France,—unfortunately coupled with the contradictory imbecility of a profaning art.

Ah! They were not too fine, these two images, and Marchenoir had more than once groaned in secret. But Véronique carried within herself the esthetic of all imaginable situations, she would have made her own proper sublimity stand out like a platitude and breathed spirituality even into imbeciles. She had spent days, and entire nights, in the twilight of that room with the shutters always closed,—like the shutters of a bad place,—conversing with God and with his saints, taking the attitude of supposing that they were really present, invested with joy and with certitude, crying more tears than the hydraulics of all ordinary sentiments would have been capable of obtaining, and it seemed, in the end, that these indigent simulacra were impregnated with this double current of physical and moral beauty that came to converge on them!

Her housekeeping, moreover, suffered so little because of it that it would have been difficult to find a better kept house, a more strict propriety, a more exact economy, a cuisine, in fact, more ingenious in multiplying the patriarchal delights of mutton stew and pot-au-feu. One might say that she had not even the need to act. She passed as if in a dream, brushing by things and forcing them to clean themselves, to arrange for themselves, to cook themselves even, by the irresistible virtue of her glance alone.

Charming and imperturbable dominatrix, that only her friend's sadness could trouble but who would not be disconcerted by either deluges, or conflagrations, or tremors, or the dismantling of the universe, for she carried in herself a permanent catastrophe of love to defy all accidents! Marchenoir was everything to her. He floated in her sky and sat on her circular horizons, he walked on the ocean, the mountains, the clouds, the abysses, all of creation,—the only thing visible everywhere and triumphant! Her savior! . . . The poor devil was *her Savior*, just as she called him sometimes, with a simplicity of enthusiasm that many theologians would have reproved as blasphemy. The two feelings, natural and supernatural, were, in her, so perfectly amalgamated and melted into the single thought of a Savior, that there was no longer any means of separating them, for this naïve soul, who did not believe it was too much to pay for the recovery of her innocence, while pouring all the glory of the heavens over the sorrowful human *resemblance* of her Redeemer!

LIII

"Let's go, misters, to table!" said Véronique to the two friends who were in the midst of contemplating the Pyramids through the window of Marchenoir's room. For Leverdier this was already an old habit to eat at the table of his friends. They got together like this two or three times a week, not counting the unexpected sudden arrivals of this good man, whose presence was always considered to be like a benefaction.

In this circumstance, the homemaker was anxious to surpass herself, offering to her guests a menu far superior to the ordinary, almost frugal, fare of their feasts. She wanted this dinner be a veritable welcoming feast for each of them, whom emotions and diverse feelings had, for a moment, appeared to separate.

The fact is that one would have thought all three of them had returned from some devilishly distant place, and the beginning of the meal did not start off without a strong sense of embarrassment. However much Véronique tried to distract the attention of her guests, her new and awkward fashion of eating, for example, could not escape them, and, however much they were vigilant to not let anything of their grievous impressions escape, it was impossible to brush aside, at first, a visible uncomfortableness which Leverdier hastened to break by announcing to the simple girl Marchenoir's newly hatched resolution.

"You know," he said, "that our friend has arrived from Chartreuse a more redoubtable dispenser of justice than ever. He wants to start off at the *Basile* with a general massacre of poisoners and by a mass hanging of arsonists."

"Oh! my God!" she cried, "always the violence? And it's you, I don't doubt, Monsieur Leverdier, who has embarked him on this new adventure? Do you know, bad man, you'll end up being a friend of the most tragic sort? Surely, I'm incapable of judging either one of you, and I'm convinced my Joseph has nothing in mind but justice. But how can you expect me not to tremble, when I see him alone against everyone?"

Marchenoir, who had been chosen to shell, laboriously and silently, a lobster claw, intervened with this:

"My dear Véronique, spare, I beg you, poor Georges here who does not merit, I assure you, any reproach. He found the occasion to render me a service, once again, by negotiating, in my place, with a rather contemptible, but all-powerful, man, my re-entry into the *Basile*, and he has given himself, as always, a lot of trouble. I would have been, I admit it, quite incapable myself of setting up this arrangement which can, in sum, have happy consequences, from the point of view of our material well-being, but which will most importantly give me the means, so much desired, of accomplishing what I regard to be a writer's strict duty: to tell the truth, whatever it might be and whatever dangers might result from it."

It was curious to watch this beautiful creature listening to the man who she cherished barely less than her God and infinitely more than any earthly thing. She listened to him with vast, wide-open eyes, even more than with her ears, as if the words that he made her hear were light!

"Dear friend," she responded, with a sweetness of the most charming humility, "I believe you're always right, but I don't know much of anything and I'm often in need of instruction. My director spoke to me about you one day. He told me your way was dangerous from the Christian point of view; you have no mission to judge your brothers, no more than to punish them, and in this way, holy charity has run a great risk of being injured by your writings. I didn't think he was completely right himself to judge you so severely. However, I remained without responding and, sometimes, his words come back to me and afflict me a little. I've kept it to myself for quite a while now, but today, I feel moved to open this corner of my heart to you. My confidence in you is without limits. Tell me, please, what I ought to think exactly."

Marchenoir was, perhaps, of all his contemporaries, the most exposed to ridicule. To be admired and honored at home, when he could reasonably expect, outside, hotpots of maledictions, is, for an unfortunate man's brain, the smoke of revenge heady enough to make him drunk with most foolish pride. One can always offer up one's vanity, like a host, under the consecrated species of an unjust proscription that one is a victim of. A simple-minded woman with a burning heart gobbles down devotedly this eucharist. But in the case of Véronique, the lineamental psychology of a trusting tenderness complicated matters, in regards to the man who had been her apostle, with a sort of mystical reverberation, very like the feeling a priest's servant has for the bishop of the diocese on pastoral visit to the presbytery. Happily for Marchenoir, he had a horror of being *cultivated*, like a fetish, and did not accept any formula of anthropomorphism. Besides, he sincerely considered himself inferior to that titan of love whose scalings had long ago overshot his poor heaven!

Apparently, the interrogation that had just been addressed to him had nothing surprising in it for him, because he responded at once in a tranquil voice, at first, and almost grave, but which soon grew animated, resounding and clear like a brass musical instrument, as was his habit, when he ascended, while speaking, the mountains and volcanic peaks of his thought.

"Your spiritual director, Véronique, has expressed the opinion of the masses, your own, perhaps, unperceived by yourself even until this instant. I would quite like to see him in my place, this minister of clemency, who believes that one can wage war without offending or wounding anyone. Did he also tell you that one must never fight? At least, that is how it would be in the logic of his cowardly conciliations. I have been accused of this often enough, this reproach of lacking charity, because I thrashed some aggressive dogs,—under the pretext that these animals belonged to the human pack! . . .

"I want to believe that your spiritual father is an excellent ecclesiastic paved and built with the bricks of the most evangelical intentions. But I doubt that his clairvoyance equals his zeal. You could, my close-sheared ewe, make an observation to him gently that the inculpation of intolerance is a hoary tactic, renewed by the Pharisees, by the modern enemies of the Church, against all those who wish to expose themselves in order to defend this old mother. You have become indignant over some of the numerous articles launched against me by the entire press. Atheists or Catholics, liberators or authoritarians, all have accused me of spitefulness, hate and envy. For one instant unanimous on this one point, the columns from every provenance have designated me as a reptile of enormous grandeur, whose rampant ferocity menaces cities and countrysides. Do you not see how much this universal accord dishonors sad Christians who transform themselves into beasts and fraternize with wild animals, in a vilified arena, to tear apart one of their witnesses? . . ."

"Just at the moment," said Leverdier, "when that witness became powerful, as Veuillot did, the same Christians, without shedding their skins, came to lick his feet and even something else . . ."

"Louis Veuillot," responded Marchenoir immediately, "arrived at the right moment. France, at that time, had not traded the wings of Empire for the fins of the Republic and the man's profession had not yet become completely impossible. If the man had had as much grandeur as strength, Christianity would be shining forth everywhere perhaps, for there was an hour of supreme anxiety when the century's errant soul could as well have run into God as 'into itself.' Such was the power left to this condottiere whose boorish and mediocre vanity would have vilified to the point of martyrdom. No other layperson has had nor will have, without doubt, ever, his resources and his immense Catholic credit, which have been to the utter exhaustion of the liberality of the faithful. What profit did Catholicism draw from it? Nothing more than the gleaming from this *animal of glory* that has always wanted to be unique and has never suffered an equal. It is therefore to him above all that we owe the opprobrium of Catholic journalism, whose narrowness and contagious abjection has infinitely surpassed the secret hopes of the most utopian impiety.

"No depository has ever had the occasion of being so disastrously unfaithful nor so sinisterly abused. You know, Georges, with what eunuch vigilance the editor-in-chief of the *Universe* removed from his seraglio talented writers who could have been admired at his expense, and how paternally wide his arms opened to the puny runts imposed by his good pleasure on all of a so-called Christian society, so very idiotic to accept them. It was not enough for the funny old man that one abased oneself before him and before his dog of a sister—Pius IX, himself, had the misfortune of misfortunes of tolerating her intrusion *into the Church's government,*—one also had to idolize the most slappable of his Mamelukes. Did we not see, one day, with our own eyes dilated by terror, at the top of the stairs at the journal, that sacristy ointment, that geriatric hairdresser whom one calls Auguste Roussel, dismissing, face in the air, two retrograding bishops who were bent before him and shying away while moving backwards in their violet robes, well done and juicy with happiness for having been received by that plenipotentiary? . . .

"Today, they are finished, the dictatorships of talented men, and Veuillot's shoes cannot be filled by anyone anymore. That jealous posthumous has left such a filth on the sill of the religious press that it is no longer possible to penetrate the house. Christians, whom he has made bow their heads, will continue to graze on the sainfoin of the most sheeplike stupidity, until they become fat enough to be eaten. But the greatest genius of the world would not obtain going forward the credit of this singular shepherd of journalism, who changed his subscribers into beasts to better protect them."

LIV

"May God help us!" said Véronique. "But, dear friend, you know the Church has promises, and that it'll never die."

"I know it as well as you do, which is to say by Faith, which is 'the substance of things to hope for.' But experience has taught me nothing except the immense misery of every miscreant whose infidelity condemns to go without hope. I am very assured that the Church must surmount everything in the end of days and that nothing will prevail on it, not even the predatory imbecility of its children, which is, in my eyes, is its greatest peril. I will expose, as much as one wants, my sad life for this belief, outside of which there is nothing for me but darkness and putrefaction. But It can fall, tomorrow, into absolute contempt, in the most excessive ignominy. It can be shouted down, whipped, crucified, like Him whom She is named the Spouse of. It can happen that, definitively, one prefers a filthy bandit, that all its friends take flight, that It cries of thirst and nobody gives it anything to drink. It can happen finally that It expires, for a perfect arrangement with its Christ, and that It is locked up, two nights and one day, in the best guarded of all sepulchers. All that would remain then is to explode, in an apotheosis of resurrection, the mountain chains or bedrocks of wicked people who form the walls of its derisive tomb,—because it is capable, as God is himself, who confers his power on it, of defying extermination right up to the ensnarement of the most effective of deaths.

"It seems to me even that this *Easter* of the Holy Spirit must appear singularly near to any individual able to think and to see. What is happening, at the end of the century where we find ourselves, is in no way an ordinary *persecution*,—to make use of this word which has been so abused by the rhetoric of cowards. Leverdier ought to remember what I attempted, at the time of expulsions, in order to inspire in them a little courage. For eight days, I ran to all the religious houses, menaced by the decrees and jam-packed with grotesque cravens, waiting with constancy,—

martyr's palm frond in hand,—for the legal opportunity to *gun down*, with their inoffensive protestations, the commissary of police, who kicked them out without anger, by the extremity of his Diocletian boot. I tasked myself stupidly with instilling virile resolutions into their cretinous guts. I demonstrated to them twenty times the evident insolidarity of this government of scoundrels who lacked energy, that the *armed* resistance of several audacious men would have toppled,—God knows with what tones of voice!—that it was either then or never, to redeem itself for having been for so long a time, so expensively, renegade or lukewarm; that honor, reason, strict justice, *charity* even, vociferated with one voice, for them to run to arms, because it was probably the last time they could do it! . . .

"I found souls with greasy dishtowels who showed me their consultation with a lawyer, whose advice they had needed to seek while someone violated their mother. They accused me of being a fool of the most dangerous kind. One of them, even, insinuated that I could well have been a provoker sent by the police. 'Sir,' I told him, 'I advise you to count your teeth, because I warn you I have a loose fist.' This procession dog had the presence of mind to render himself invisible immediately, and such was, in totality, the result of my efforts. It would be therefore ridiculous to pronounce the word persecution with respect to this clique of diddling cockroaches, who go to suck, after leaving the Holy Altar, the syphilitic bubo of Legality, and who hand over their own wives, their younger sisters, and even the sacred Body of the living God to the blackest swine, to conserve the integrity of their skin and their ecus!

"Nonetheless, one can say that the Church is oppressed in a most unprecedented fashion, as the children that it suckles dishonor it, while strangers beat it to a pulp, and thus it no longer has a soul to comfort it or to plead for it. It is the agony of Gethsemane, it is the supreme dereliction! 'The assembly of the unfaithful,' the catechism says. I know, by God!, that it is the Church. But how many are there, at this hour, the true faithful?

233

Several hundreds, at most, who compose, barely, an imperceptible group of heroic and humble poor folk, scattered to the most distant corners of the universe, where they wait, weeping, until it please the Father, who is in heaven, finally to inaugurate his kingdom expected for eighteen centuries now . . .

"The Church is locked up in a madhouse," whispered the strange visionary all of a sudden, "as punishment for having espoused a beggar on the cross who called himself Jesus-Christ. It has endured unspeakable torments, in neighborhoods that would frighten demons. The doctors who are charged with watching over it and who declare that all they want is its greatest good, are full of smiles and full of pity, when one asks them about its recovery. 'Poor child,' they say, 'what will become of it without us?'—And the mendicant that it had dreamed about worshipping is, at a distance, mutilated by malicious eagles and honest crows, on its solitary gibbet! . . ."

By virtue of a certain mysterious conformity that united these two beings, Véronique had become as extraordinary by her concern as Marchenoir had by his words. From her large eyes that were cut out from the seventh heaven, two heavy tears had emerged, rolling slowly down her pale cheeks; her hands, at first resting on the table, had joined together and now she had the air of imploring silently the invisible spirit that seemed to her, without any doubt in her mind, to be inspiring her *master*.

Her physiognomy was so surprising that Leverdier, himself already strongly affected by the last words he had just heard, could not help but point it out to Marchenoir. "Look," he murmured.

The interrupted man retracted the wings of his lyricism and looked at her.

"What is going on, my Véronique?" he asked her, visibly moved.

"But . . . nothing, my friend," she responded, quivering. "I'm listening to you, not understanding much. Your words are true, I think, but so terrible! Truthfully, I thought for a moment someone else was speaking in your place. I didn't recognize your voice any more or your thoughts."

"Is that then what made you cry, my sad one? You also, Georges, seem troubled. Is it possible that I said such strange things?"

"To tell you the truth," he said, "your last phrase about the Church surprised me a little, perhaps by reflexive virtue of our friend's emotion. But your voice, even more than your words, was extraordinary. I suppose that you saw, I do not know what . . ."

"I see very certainly," responded Marchenoir, "the horrible evil of this world expropriated by the Christian faith, and I am not familiar with any other thoughts, whatever the words that I choose to express this with, that I carry like a knife in the sheath of my bosom. It is a passion so true, so poignant, that I will finish by becoming incapable of fixing my attention on any other object whatsoever. But this incident reminds me that I have not entirely responded to you, Véronique. I brought your attention to the revolting coalition of Christians and their adversaries, each time it is a question of combating a common enemy, that is to say a man such as myself, temerarious by force of love and veracious without fear. Then I spoke of Louis Veuillot and the Church's misfortune. Connected things. Let us leave it at that.

"Someone said to you, am I right, that my violent writings offended charity. I have only one word to say in response to your theologian. And that is that Justice and Mercy are *identical* and consubstantial in their absoluteness. There you have it, something neither sentimentalists nor fanatics want to hear. A doctrine that proposes Love of God as the supreme goal, has principally a need to be virile, for fear of sanctioning all illusions of self-love or carnal love. It is too easy to emasculate souls by teaching them only the precept of loving their brothers, in contempt of all the other precepts that one hides from them. One obtains, in this way, a sluggish and sticky religion, more redoubtable for its effects than even nihilism.

"Now, the Gospel has menaces and terrible conclusions. Jesus, in twenty places, hurls anathema, not on things, but on *men* whom he designates with fearful precision. He still gives his life for everyone, but afterwards we have abandoned the orders to speak 'from the rooftops,' as he spoke himself. It is the unique model and Christians have nothing better to do than to practice it according to his examples. What would you think of the *charity* of a man who would let his brothers be poisoned for fear of ruining the consideration of the poisoner, if he warned them? Me, I say that from this point of view, charity consists in vociferating and that true love should be implacable. But that supposes a virility, so defunct today, that one cannot even pronounce its name without affronting decency.

"I have not got the authority to judge, he said, nor to punish. Must I infer from this base sophism, whose perfidy I am familiar with, that I am also not qualified to see, and that it is forbidden for me to put a hand on the arsonist who, full of confidence in my fraternal inertia, goes, under my very eyes, to ignite the mine that blows up an entire city? If Christians had not listened so much to the lessons of their mortal enemies, they would know that nothing is more just than mercy, *because* nothing is more merciful than justice, and their thoughts would get adjusted to these elemental notions.

"Christ declared 'blessed' those who are hungry and thirsty for justice, and the world, which wants to amuse itself, but which detests beatitude, has rejected this affirmation. Who then will speak for the mutes, for the oppressed and for the feeble, if they who were invested with the Word keep silent? A writer, who does not keep Justice in plain sight, is a robber of the poor and as cruel as the nasty rich. One and the other, they squander their depots and are accountable, by the same title, of desertions of faith. I do not want that crown of burning coals on my head, and, for a long time now, I have chosen which side I am on.

"We are dying perhaps of hunger, my Véronique, and it serves us right, doubtless, because all the world, except you and Leverdier, condemn me. Whatever the cost, I will guard the virginity of my testimony, while preserving myself from the crime of leaving inactive any of the energies that God gave me. Irony, injuries, defiances, imprecations, reprobations, maledictions, lyricism of mud or flames, whatever my rage can use to offend is all good to me. What other means remain at my disposal to avoid being the least of men? A judge has but one way to sink beneath his criminal, and that is to become a prevaricator, and every true writer is certainly a judge.

"Some have said to me: 'What is the point? The world is in agony and nothing will affect it anymore.' Maybe, but in the furthest recesses of the desert, even still, to render testimony, is this not for the honor of Truth and for the edification of wild animals, just as the solitary anchorites did formerly? Besides, is it credible that such an opulence of rage was bestowed upon me for nothing? Certain words of the Holy Book are quite strange . . . Who knows, after all, if the most active form of adoration is not blasphemy *by love*, which would be the prayer of the forsaken? . . . I will live then by my vocation until I die, in some orgy of poverty. I will be Marchenoir the contemptible, the vociferator and the desperate,—joyous to skim off the scum, and satisfied to displease, but difficult to intimidate and willfully crushing the fingers that attempt to gag him."

"Poor dear friend, poor dear sufferer!" said the mutilated woman in a half voice, as if speaking to herself, "why is this burden on your shoulders?" She looked at him with a tenderness so pure, so deep, that the executioner felt he was going to cry and began to speak of diverse things. The dinner ended almost joyously. Véronique served a divine coffee and the inevitable literature made its return. Marchenoir, in brilliant form, eructated comical apothegms and inexpiable similitudes that made the good Leverdier break out in laughter. Toward midnight, finally, they separated in the effusion of a tender joy that these three suffering hearts hardly recognized and that they were probably condemned never again to feel.

LV

Properce Beauvivier is Jewish by birth and named Abraham. Abraham-Properce Beauvivier. Cosmopolitan Jew, of Portuguese origin, met and baptized, it is said, by a passing monk, in the water of the first stream, in route to Germany; a little later, breast-fed by Deutz, the famous kike who *sold out* the duchess de Berry, and growing up in Bordeaux with this patriarch. It may be that the secret of his moral destiny is held in the circumstance of his conjectural baptism, given by an unknown, on the symbolically muddy edge of a ditch off the main highway. One is assured that his parents conceived an unprecedented rage over it, which they continue to gnash their teeth over, and that he was never able to take his part in the occasional sacrament which appears to act on him like an evil spell.

As devoid of genius as a person could be, for instance, like a copyist in the Office of Public Assistance, but surprisingly filled with every faculty of assimilation and imitation, he lifted himself up, with a bound, in the already worn-out casket of Romanticism, with a vigor in the loins which earned him, at twenty years old, literary adoption by old Hugo.

From this happy instant, his life was a dream. He became the reservoir of his Father's blessings. "Look at my son Properce," he said to some avid debutants, "and go in peace!" Properce, for his part, dipped both hands into the drawer on the shelves and ransacked the strongbox of aureoles, piled them by the dozens on his own head, like crowns of a twenty-times-elected college laureate. In this way he became glorious by his poetry, novels, stories, the theater pieces and even by profound politics, having been sagely impetuous against the Communards, when they were shooting, and surpassing them later, when they were no longer shooting. He above all became the lyricist of proxenetism and of betrayal, and it is from there that he entered into an original hermeticism, which the hooks and the crowbars of his other lyricisms would have been unable to break the lock of.

To imitate Victor Hugo as perfectly as Beauvivier did is not forbidden to all other mortals, but no one can claim to reflect only the umbilicus of this Retiarius of Innocence. That is all one can say about it. He who will sing, in tune to the cithara or the dulcimer, this man's hatred of innocence, will be certainly a moralist with a robust wing and a proud fellow. It is not necessary to expect better than to take note of certain effects. It appears that the old Jewish filth burned like limestone sediment, when touched by baptismal water.

Beauvivier is the author of an infinite number of books of diverse sorts, a perverse and complicated mosaic, where an intimate obsession to dishonor and sully shows through, relentlessly. His last novel, *Incest*, one of the most shameless copies of Hugo that one could get it into one's head to write, is a monstrous dose of snow, phosphorous and cantharides, calculated to corrode the bowels of an adolescent, twenty-four hours at least after absorption,—the cowardice in his heart being equal to the timidity in his thought. The object of this book is, in effect, the *glorification* of incest, not by a vulgar mania to make it more sophisticated, but by this primordial, sovereign and peremptory reason that the Lord God has *forbidden* it. Because he cannot prevent himself from believing in God and his manifest vocation is to play "Ancient Serpents." Only, he runs off at the concluding moment and finishes with an equivocal triumph of virtue, leaving the desire for evil to insidiously hover over the curiosity that he has excited. This poisoner has dared to put into circulation, under the form of *Stories* for young girls, dissolving and inexorable toxicants. It is said that he is preparing other books, even for children below the age of ten.

A sickly hysteria, of a frightening nature, is the insufficient explanation of this fury that would aim no less than to contaminate the light. One must ask oneself whether the physical execration of whiteness is not somehow involved in the inconceivable excess of his body of writings.

He passes for having been handsome before. He declares it himself in these simple terms: "I was so handsome." He has felt the need to compare his own face with that of Christ's. As a ladies man, by consequence, he put, early on, his person up for tender and even sold it in *shares*. One has seen families pay very dearly for *coupons* of intimacy.—Doubly fatal pimp, it was not enough for him to ruin women in order to make himself their master, he took pleasure afterwards in locking them up in a tribadic Tower of Hunger,—unforeseen by Dante,—where the wretches, deprived of the nutritive testicles of man, are reduced to devouring themselves . . . He is married, however, this conqueror, and he married the most beautiful woman that one could find, in the hope, not disappointed, of conquering more easily the others.

He has a particular characteristic of being defenseless against shoemaker boutiques, before which he forgets himself in incontinent ecstasies. It is necessary to have heard him pronouncing the word "boots" to fully understand the history of England, where the *ham* of a woman has prevailed for five hundred years, as opposed to the dorsal spine of the highest aristocracy of all globes. It is true that the good Deutz's pupil is reduced to being content with the one aristocracy of his dung of origin, but he does not lack the whorish haughtiness of a certain dandyism.

From the point of view of a soul's baseness pure and simple, without psychological complications of any sort, Beauvivier's originality does not appear humanly surpassable. With the exception of Renan, who discourages disdain, and whose spherical abjectness appears like a mystery of Faith, the author of *Incest* is, probably, the only man of his century in the mood to sympathize with Iscariot's destiny. "Jesus had *perhaps* humiliated him!" he said, and it is not intended to be a witty remark. It is reflective of his most intimate substance. He does not breathe but to cheat, and betrayal is his only after-thought, his constant preoccupation. Judas was content to hand over his Master, Properce would have undertaken to sully him probably. His soul is a condensation of lackluster and fetid smoke, as capable of hiding the abyss of hell from which it came as it is of obfuscating the chasms of light towards which it does not permit one to soar.

Jesus pardons the adulterous woman. The sacristans themselves have also absolved her. Properce blames him, objecting that this pardon is an attempt on the husband's authority, who had probably *bought* his woman and, by consequence, has the right to punish her. Such is his conception of justice. In all honesty, the Man of God, gathering the stones to help the cuckold husband stone this unfortunate woman, would not any less excite his indignation, but, an indignation, then, that is tempered by the subterranean joy of finding Mercy at fault and of supposing plausible flaws in Beauty itself. It is an ancient procedure,—in no wise invented by the abominable Ernest,—to not deny God precisely, but to amputate his Providence, by not permitting him any intrusion into our sublunary stories.

"You will cry, Emmanuel, for *not* being God!" he wrote, addressing himself to this same Christ whose sovereign Tears are an outrage to the infernal aridity of his impure eyes. Ah! if he could have been in the comforting angel's place! How he would have cleverly, *lovingly*, ridiculed this Agony! The terrible chalice, he would not have made him drink it, he would have made him *sip* it! And the Sweat of blood, whose vivid crimson inundated the Emperor of the Poor, how he would have diligently altered its color, by mixing his gall into it! . . .

This monster, whose only excuse is to have *come before his time* and to be, in this way, a monster's fetus, found, notwithstanding, the means of procreating children and of suffering, it appears, for being unable to make himself loved. He consoles himself, in his manner, by sponsoring children's balls where in obscure corners of the dancehall he takes pleasure in inculcating in them his paternal lessons. Woe betide the parents who are imbecilic enough or criminal enough to throw their progeny into this barathrum.

One day, he was coming back from burying one of his own children, a little girl happy enough to have been ravished by this father, before the horror of knowing the infamy of the act or the even greater horror of not being disgusted by it.

He had dabbed his eyes, weeped perhaps, it is not entirely clear. But all was over, and he went on his way. Suddenly, not yet having crossed the cemetery gate:

"But it's necessary that I should write some verses for this child!" he said in an aeolian voice, to the people nearest him.

The sacrilegious dog is completely contained in these words.

Now here is another, one of the most surprising atrocities, where he is profiled, from head to foot, the reproved Jew:

Properce is out on the streets, one very cold night, with a man he calls his friend. An old shivering woman is encountered, who murmurs supplications while holding out her hand. He stops under a gas lamp,—the divine Deutz's nursling,—he exhibits a satchel swollen with gold, and under the dazzled eye of the miserable woman, he digs through the bag of gold, he kneads it, turns it, makes it jingle, makes it flash, then he stuffs it back into his pocket and shrugs his shoulders with an annoyed air of powerlessness:

"My good woman," he exhales, "I'm very sorry, I thought I had *some money*, and I don't have any at all." The observer of this scene tells how he saw at the feet of the specter, in the bitumen of the walkway, a little luminous opening, by which one could see hell . . .

An obscure cloud of religious images floats perpetually around this poet, who feels deeply his reprobation, but who flatters himself, after all, for being capable of seducing his Judge and cheating Paradise, if this sojourn of delights veritably exists.

While waiting, he is unsuccessful in defending himself effectively against certain terrors that appear to have arisen with the express purpose of causing others to despise him. It is the revenge of the poor and of the massacred innocents who are, in this world, the lamentable ambassadors of a patient God.

His hour come, the ignominy of the Sullier of souls will be seen in full and this will be, like a moon ten times paler, at the level of the most fetid swamp on which the mortal Stymphalides of Lust and Sacrilege have ever hovered over!

LVI

Such was the powerful individual called to pronounce, after so many others, on Marchenoir's fate.

Editor-in-chief of the *Basile*, for three weeks now, without anyone being able to explain his elevation, which was the secret of several women and a small group of shady dealers and swindlers,—this Israelite, for a long time captive in subaltern roles, reigned finally over one of the most influential journals in our planetary system, in place of that heap of putrified flesh that was called Magnus Conrart, whose supreme exhalations had nearly asphyxiated the people who buried him.

That one, at least, had not hampered the minds of his contemporaries with any mystery. Everyone knew by what base maneuvers this ancient lackey capable of anything had, previously, suborned the senility of the *Basile*'s founder, who had appointed him his heir in order to degrade consciences, just as he had for such a long time degraded the sidewalks.

The hideous rascal's intellectual nullity had served him more efficaciously than even genius.

Having become the intendant of the quotidian pasturage of souls, his choice had naturally led him to literary bakers and pastry cooks, the most capable of contenting the ignoble appetite of a society whom the Republic instructed to search for their livelihood in the garbage.

Magnus had become, by consequence, a very great monarch, the monarch of open doors, offering the *Basile*'s Vespasian hospitality to any stinking advertisement, to any caseous announcement, to any ammoniacal launching of financial commitments, to any remunerative blackmail.

Insolent fortune, which ordinarily chooses such co-habitants, had fulfilled him to the point that the baseness even of his mind and the surprising adiposity of his soul separated him from personal enmities or aggressive rivals, that a pinch of merit would not have failed to attract to a servile courtier so scandalously arrived.

He was that friend of all the rabble that one calls a skeptic or a "good boy" and, joyously settled in at the trough to his bales of hay, he descended the river of life in a boat decked out with flowers and ballasted with the lard of universal camaraderie.

When he got it into his head to reprove Marchenoir from whom he had hoped to make money because of his rare rhinoceros' faculties,—too quickly forgetting that this pachyderm at liberty could get it into his head to trample all over him,—he had the extraordinary opportunity again of being silently contemned by him.

What a formidable caricature he would have made, in the style of Petronius, under such a quill, a simply exact portrait of this Trimalchio of journalism!

The satirist, dismissed almost shamefully from the *Basile*, would have had to triumph over terrible temptations and endured confounded assaults, for his vengeance was too easy!

But soon, Magnus took it upon himself to avenge everyone. Touched by a foot wound, that his blood's putridity promptly rendered incurable, devoured by gangrene and suffering from atrocious tortures, he took his life by ignobly hanging himself, the details of which have nauseated multiple virtuosos of suicide.

Properce Beauvivier did not bring, to tell the truth, a much superior morality. However, the two or three half-dozen artists whom his predecessor had not found the time to strangle caught their breath.

It is because Beauvivier had, doubtless owing to paradoxical deformities of his soul, an infernal predilection for talent! As long as his own interests would not be in play, one could count on him to a certain point. It was quite certain, for example, that the external pressure of a cohort of devils was needed to make him accept the prose of the hunchback Ohnet, to the prejudice of a *writer* of the tenth order, and even in the absence of any competition.

244

Rogue for rogue, it was quite something also to have to do with a man who was not exclusively a boor, who had not exclusively in mind, although Jewish, the accumulation of currency, and who was capable of understanding a little, when one honored him with the need to be heard out.

One began to dream of the chimerical godsend of a *Basile* turned literary again, as in the distant days of its foundation. One hoped that the single fact of knowing how to write would cease finally to be regarded as an irremissible infamy, and that the new prince was going to introduce some softening to the penal law published by the turgid Magnus, that condemned blasphemers of Mediocrity to the slow torture of inanition.

Whatever might be the probable cesspits of his ulterior motivation, one could not doubt that the sentiment of a real literary esteem had a lot to do with his desire to reintegrate Marchenoir.

That appeared all the more evident given that he had felt two or three times, first hand, the bite of this pamphleteer whom all his instincts as a voluptuary and a poisoner must have abhorred.

Two days after the dinner in Vaugirard, Marchenoir brought his article in person to the director of the *Basile*.

Beauvivier received him with the greatest cordiality, wearing something specially tailored for this interview from a haberdashery for archdukes.

The visitor at first expressed his surprise at having been considered a candidate by the *Basile* in its pursuit of a collaborator, after such a motivated banishment of his copy by the entire press. He added that he was intending to attribute the initiative of so honorable a move in his favor to the independent spirit of the new chief, lofty enough to quarrel openly with traditions deadly to letters . . .

"Your predecessor," he said, "did not spoil writers when he found them. He made them bitterly deplore having been put into apprenticeship with some diligent cobbler, from tender infancy. It is told that you have plans to lift the wall of China and dyke up the boorishness that menaces the celestial Empire of Journalism. If that is the case, I am all yours and I promise you an energetic lieutenancy. I am very persuaded that, even from the elevated point of view of speculation, a courageous and, frankly, scandalously literary press would not be anywise a fruitless endeavor. Contemporary society is hideously stunned stupid and degraded by the repetitive pollutions of a sidewalk chronicle that no longer has even the excuse of offering it a semblance of palpitation.

"Our journals, let us admit it, are killing us with boredom. The American delectations of reporting and advertising are not infinite. 'If you were an energetic and deep man,' I said one day to that brute Magnus Conrart, 'not only would you accept me just as I am, but you would group together men of my sort, absurdly distanced from your system, and, I swear to you, we would set a new standard. The world has always obeyed the will that is expressed, the riding crop or the cudgel in the air. We would form an intellectual obligarchy, all the more applauded by the crowd, whom we would be less capable of toadying to.' I do not know you personally, Monsieur Beauvivier. All I know about you is your books, which I have said a lot of bad things about. What does it matter? If you like talent, why not profit your quasi-royal *Basile* by attempting this magnificent adventure, which the previous director pushed back on as if it were madness?"

Properce, evidently prepared to hear him out, had taken an attitude of seduction. He had gotten up and leaned against the chimney, facing Marchenoir who was seated in front of him. With his arms supporting his desirable person, he took hold, with an expert hand, of the edge of the marble, made slender by the practice of stroking caresses, which ledge it was surprising to discover was not membranous like an albatross's foot. His other hand complimented his miter-shaped beard, whose silky fork had the air of bifurcating on some invisible croup. One of his fine Sardanapalus-like legs accustomed to frolicking about languishingly, was pulled back onto the other, the toe facing down, like a serpent that was winding about another serpent. His torso,

246

the flexible tabernacle of his corrupted heart, appeared through the freely flowing flannel, cream-colored and edged with nettle-green, of a morning mess jacket.

The light in the window, which fell directly on his face and on the faded blondness of his hair, did not make him look very handsome, however, that day. His pallor, habitually extraordinary, achieved an almost marbled lividness, like a slice of Roquefort cheese, menaced by the most imminent fecundity. Wan furrows, chalky lines ran there like sutures, and the blue of his eyes,—in the past considered cerulean,—began visibly to harden like crockery under the countless bakings of licentiousness.

No matter, he had made his most adolescent smile clear, and Marchenoir, the most easily fooled man, when one wanted to palm off on him the counterfeit money of a worthless sympathy, was taken in by it, as always, in spite of the cruel warnings of his experience.

"Monsieur Marchenoir," responded the Proxenete, dilating his smile enough to expose a row of syphilitic buboes on the inside of his inferior lip, "I have no trouble guessing that you have brought me a first article of rare vehemence. Give it to me, I will simply glance at it with my eyes and you can instantly judge me by my actions."

Marchenoir handed over the manuscript.

"*The Sedition of Excrement*! Superb title! . . . Léo Taxil . . . wall pornography . . . excellent!" He sat down and, taking his pen, wrote while syllabling in a loud voice:

> We are happy to offer the hospitality of our columns to the following article by our valiant colleague, Caïn Marchenoir, one of the most somber coryphées of contemporary literature, whom a recent mourning had withdrawn from the battlefield and whom a monstrous scandal has brought back today, more formidable than ever. Our readers will certainly applaud this energetic voice moving im-

mediately into the midst of a cowardly silence of opinion. They will accept the audacities of form by a genial satirist, whose generous indignations are expressed while shuddering, and who thinks any weapon is good for the repression of dirty manufacturers who have undertaken to sully our walls. The *Basile*, traditionally attentive to divert, as much as possible, the immoral effects of these attempts, voluntarily puts its columns at the service of the writer most capable of demonstrating the dangers. Caïn Marchenoir is above all a conscience. His numerous enemies have been able to accuse him of being passionate to the point of intolerance, but no one has ever thought to cast doubt on his perfect sincerity, even when his polemics appear excessive.

—P.B.

Properce slipped this nonsense into an envelope with the article and rang. A clerk, with a hypothetical ingenuousness, appeared.

"Take this to the printing office, without delay," he said to this servant. "Tell them, from me, that it should be typeset immediately."

Standing, then, and addressing himself to Marchenoir, who was surprised and already gratified:

"Are you content with me, terrible man? As you can see I'm docile and quick. Please do me, in return, a real favor. Tomorrow night I'm gathering some colleagues for dinner. Be among us. I'm quite aware that these reunions aren't to your taste as a loner. But I think that it's politic of you to show yourself a little to these good people, who detest you for the most part and who will suck up to you, in the most civil manner in the world, when they have learned that you have returned to the *Basile*. I'm managing a complete triumph for you. Come just as you are and do me the honor from now on of counting on my friendship," he added, while offering him one of those two hands that had done the most.

Marchenoir, almost touched, promised to return the following day and left, gently dreaming.

LVII

Marchenoir's illusions, as stupid as they were spontaneous, did not ordinarily last very long. He lived for a day on the demented hope of a literary justice procured by this procurer. He dreamed of extraordinary polemics, sublime flights of imprecations, a vengeful lyre full of reprobatory hurricanes! He would finally say everything that he had in his heart, to this dirty society, whose unacceptable ignominy made him roar! . . .

Leverdier tried in vain to make this desperate man see the palpable danger of hoping for too much. To temper his enthusiasm, he reminded him of all that they knew, each of them, about Beauvivier, his treacherous nature, the screws, the triple bars, the padlocks, the complicated locksmithery of that dangerous conscience, surrounded by traps and oubliettes designed to swallow elephants, penetrable only by rare guillotine trapdoors where the haughtiest temerarious men could not pass except by crawling . . .

"Doubtless," he responded, "but who knows? I am, perhaps, a bargain in this man's eyes. Besides, I need to hope. Even after putting aside all the considerations of an elevated order, imagine then, my friend, that this could be *bread* for my poor companion and myself."

"Alas!" said the other, accompanying him through the streets, "I desire it, but this dinner makes me a bit nervous. A funny idea that he had, this animal, to shove your muzzle, from the get-go, into the swines' trough! In short, be prudent, endure for Véronique all that will not be absolutely intolerable, and then excuse yourself early. You will find me at the café."

The two friends parted at Beauvivier's door.

From the moment he entered this vast hall, packed with numerous guests, Marchenoir was brought back down to earth, instantly. He felt, as if by a gust of disgust, the irremediable, infinite incompatibility of his whole being with these beings necessarily hostile to him, and some of whom were so low that he was surprised to see them admitted, even in this place of prostitution.

They represented, however, all the so-called *literary* press, and even a small portion of literature, and there was not one individual among them surely who would have made a gesture to aid him, if he had been in danger,—not a single gesture,—or who, even, would have hesitated to push him in deeper, while protesting the *impartiality* of the kick that was applied to his pericranium. Not a single woman was present, moreover, which gave the impression that one was going to be a little loutish here. He found himself dreadfully alone and detested.

Beauvivier rushed forward. "My dear Monsieur Marchenoir," he said, "we were expecting you with the most devouring impatience. Gentlemen, here he is, our new *chef*."

Nevertheless, he did not use his precious pharynx in superfluous presentations. The bigwigs of publicity bowed like grain stalks, the unfortunate man had to suffer the contact of many sordid hands that were offered to him. Suddenly, he found himself flanked by Dr. Des Bois and Dulaurier, in whom was reborn an unlimited esteem for this resuscitation from the dead. The lycanthrope, already enervated, barely heard the babbling of the first, whereas the second paid the price. Without even thinking, he shook his hand with such force that the courtly knight poet could not keep back this cry: "Ouch! you're hurting me!"—"I grip you as I love you! my dear," he responded, fixing him with those cold, clear eyes more disquieting than anger. Dulaurier got away under the wing of a Cherub, like a beaten dog, and Marchenoir, tranquil at last, took out a cigarette, and, sitting back in an armchair, began to consider silently this population of the quill, who moved their tongues while waiting for someone to announce the pigswill.

LVIII

He saw, to start with, not far from him, the king of kings, the literary Agamemnon, the arch-celebrity, the European novelist, Gaston Chaudesaigues, matchless and respected recruiter of money. Only, the gibbous Ohnet gets the better of him, like a queen to his pawn, and rakes in even more money. But the author of *The Owner of the Ironworks* is a successful barkeeper who waters down a semblance of old, cheap wine with dirty public bath water, for the refreshment of three or four million center-left bourgeois who get themselves drunk at his trough, and he does not enter the conversation otherwise. He is unanimously excluded from the world of letters, something he weeps about, sometimes, in solitude. Without his heroic friend Chérubin des Bois, who naturally has a taste for millionaires and who welcomes him with open arms when he is alone, this triumphant general would be completely inconsolable.

Chaudesaigues swims, truth be told, in a little less opulence. However, he surpasses even the most avaricious literary summits of all the Himalayan heights. One must imagine a kind of Jewish Auvergne, born in the south, and compatriot of the Mistral, a troubadour business man, a Toady in the *Thousand and One Nights*, who needs only to be rubbed to make his *genie* appear and GIVE LIGHT. One is reminded of the enormous success of his book on the Duke de Morny, who had served as patron of his debuts, to whom he owes everything, and whose old trousers he brushes down and returns to a presentable state for the avid public who covers the enlightener with gold.

He is what one calls, in a scarcly noble language, "a horrible carpet beater." In 1870, he attacked Gambetta, whose shameless dictatorship he railed against, as best he could. When Republican France decided to get back in bed with this large man, this candle-carrier nature of his began to cry out and he negotiated a reconciliation, engaging *provisionally* to no longer publish the volume where the persiflage was consigned to.

A little before May 16, he went to call on the director of the *Correspondent*, a totally aristocratic and religious review, as everyone knows. He offered a novel: *The King without a Country*. The theme was this: to display royalty so divine that, even in exile and in indigence, dispossessed kings did not succeed in becoming ordinary people, who they are still more august than ever and whom their crown repels all by itself, like the hair, on their sublime brows, above the diadem of their virtues. One imagines the joy of the *Correspondent*. But May 16 misfired,[1] Chaudesaigues changes his prospectus, realizes exactly the opposite of what he had announced, and transfers his copy to a Republican journal.

All the same, he is not a pure traitor, he is a traitor for pleasure, like Beauvivier. He needs money, that is all there is to it, infinite money, not only to satisfy his oriental tastes of a nocturnal rodent, but finally to raise, in an occidental innocence, his children with profiles of camels and Astrakhan fleeces, who betray, with the most complete return to character, the infamous origin of their father.

One has perhaps never seen, before him, a literature so strikingly venal. His recent book, *Sancho Panza of the Pyrenees*, conceived commercially, in the form of a comical guide, of universal delivery, with advertisements for inns and fictions of sympathetic strangers, is, from the point of view of art, an unspeakable disgrace.

His talent, moreover, which mediocre writers had made so much noise about, is, principally, the incontestable dexterity of a copyist and a canvasser. This plagiarist with long hair seemed to have been formed expressly for demonstrating experimentally our profound ignorance of foreign literature. Armed with an incredible and confounding cheek, he took fifteen years to copy Dickens, outrageously. He skins him, he dismembers him, he

---

1 May 16, presumably 1877, when the Royalists lost power to the Republicans.

sucks him, he scrapes him, he makes gravy and soup out of him, without anyone catching him, without anyone even noticing.

Virtuoso of conversation, in the fatiguing manner of Southerners whose accent he shares, he is easily bothered by the presence of Monsieur Cold, who looks at him while listening, without saying a word. This equivocal Don Juan lacks good manners in front of the Commander's statue.

Just now, he was perorating with two of his compatriots, Raoul Denisme and Léonidas Rieupeyroux, so little capable either of them of intimidating him. The first, a failed félibre and sticky journalist, is generally regarded as a lesser Chaudesaigues, which is a lucrative way of being nothing at all. But the master's credit is so strong that the vomitive Denisme succeeds, all the same, in making himself digested. Incapable of writing a book, he puts down, a little bit everywhere, the secretions of his thought. This bald and bearded yokel is feared like a spy, who must have paid, it seems, for his red ribbon with some superlative infamy, the perfidy of which passes for surprising.

As for Léonidas Rieupeyroux, he is a really divine character, that man, capable of restoring the taste for life in the most atra-bilious disciples of Schopenhauer. He is grotesque, like a poet who calls himself an Aeschylus. He has the madness of the Cross of the Grotesque. Meridional, as much as one can be in hell, endowed with an accent that would make the devil appear, he laughs, from morning to evening, in a vanity able to set the bottom of a well on fire.

He is the inventor of rustic epics. The old sow, known by the name of Georges Sand, made them idyllic and sentimental. Marchenoir, elevated in the midst of these cowards and covetous brutes, asked himself, while watching Léonidas gesticulating, who could be the stupider of these two authors. As far as this went, he decided that the man was superior.

The fecundity of this latter consists in publishing ever and again the same book under different titles. It is a Tarn-et-Garonne kind of finesse. At least if his fellow countrymen are content to be epic, they are civic, thank heavens! For a hundred pages, he gurgles and vomits the most worn-out, misshapen, discarded and unwanted hackneyed phrases on the Rights of man and the duties of citizens, without prejudice for the brotherhood of peoples.

One of the most distinguished contemporary poets, one day, called Rieupeyroux the *Tartuffe of the Danube*, an exact and spiritual epithet which many imbeciles sought to have themselves honored with. He is, in fact, a vehement hypocrite, a most common species in the Midi. Hypocrite in feelings, hypocrite in ideas and a fake poor person, he belongs to that category of odious cockroaches whose beggar bags are bulging with the bread of indigents, which he took from them by stealing the rich man's pity.

One day, this individual went to find Chaudesaigues and several other financiers of letters, whom he knew had influence on a first-rate publisher. A grandiloquent and sumptuous lamenter, he recounted how his mother had just passed away and that he was without money to bury her. At the same time, he had been hit with unpayable arrears. What was going to become of him and his wife and children? Of course, he was not asking for money from his colleagues, but in a word, one could act on his behalf such that the publisher would not refuse to rely on his genius. Up until now, the story is banal. But this is what happened: a little while later, Léonidas shows up, alone, and says to his creditor who was somewhat proud of being a benefactor:

"Sir, I'm an honest man. You advanced me money and I'm upset to be unable to pay you back. I can no longer sleep. Ah! well, what I have here is an astonishing manuscript. Pay yourself what I owe you by publishing it."

The publisher, already exhausted by his first sacrifice, and whom the mere idea of printing something of Rieupeyroux's, on top of it, filled him with terror, attempted in vain to protest and escape. He tried, without success, to flow through the cracks, to climb the wall, to hide under the doormat. It was absolutely necessary that he get away. This honest man, insolvable, was perhaps going to hang himself.

And this is how that astonishing volume was published, wherein this child of the Midi, informing all his people about his amicable relationship with Baudelaire, recounts with candor the personal mystification that his ostrich vanity was the prodigious substrate of and that he himself was, for twenty years, unable to understand.

Rieupeyroux's physical uncleanliness is well-known. He is an oily and verminous citizen. River waters and the virginal dew of heavens are not known to him. He wanders under the azure like a flower of grime, imperishable like the purity of angels. His hair, which he wears even longer than Chaudesaigues, and which floats on the winds' wing, fecundates space with the most imperceptible nutation of its chef. One does not approach him without trembling, and thieves, whom he should have much fear of, look at him many times before robbing him.

Another trio, curious and illustrious, was that composed of Hamilcar Lécuyer, Andoche Sylvain and Gilles de Vaudoré, three poet novelists.

Marchenoir knew his Lécuyer by heart, whom he had, once, cinched in the most memorable way. They had met, many years ago, at Dulaurier's, who was very humble at the time, whose little room was a cenacle.

This African, hard-working and boastful, but gnawed at by ambition, and who meditated on the classic roles of Cataline or Coriolanus, would have sold his mother at auction, on the floor of the Halles, to grab a bit of publicity. A sensual cymbal and only vibrating from the pulsations coming from below, he was admirably given access to all the interior stages, by which an elected acrobatic soul warms up, at first, in the deafening din of popularity.

The moment arrived, the tub had overflown. He exited, as from a monstrous abscess, with waves of scarlet sanies, overcooked and granular purulences, the bile of an unlucky and craven assassin, inexpressible runny molds and calcined excrement. At that time, they screamed at the marvel. The cliched redundancies and piqued frenzy of verses from his *Sacrilegious Chants* had appeared sufficiently Aeschylusian to a generation deprived of literature, which has not got enough tongues in its animal mouth to lick the feet of histrions.

Prostituted publicly to a cosmopolitan comedienne, become himself an actor and playing in his own pieces on the crowded theater of the boulevard, he had finished by placing, on his frizzy head of a Nubian slave, a closed crown of ideal debauchery and transcendent cynicism, which Marchenoir discerned, from the beginning, the fragility and base fraud of.

Miserable reality! This acrobat was not even a acrobat! He did not have in him the skill of a real jumper, sincerely smitten by his balancing pole. It was enough to scratch this smoking skull to immediately make a serialized novelist of the twentieth rank jump out. He is a masked bourgeois of art, very opinionated and very laborious, but aspiring to retire from business affairs. The vile prose on his marriage had well illuminated some obscure points, and the language of verse used by this Capaneous of praise,—pathetic and prudish language, to the point of blasphemous paroxysm,—betrays enough, for the connoisseur, of the professional, intimate *disinterestedness* of this blasphemer, who only chose the enhancement of impiety to attract a little more attention to himself than someone else and which causes desirable money to pour in a bit more than the pure bourgeois would receive, with his language, in the lively sludge of the charnel house!

However considerable it may have been, in reality, the literary situation of this merchant, the equitable glory had not however deprived Andoche Sylvain of his teat, this latter being the most read, perhaps, of all the virtuosos assembled here at the house of the *Basile*'s editor-in-chief.

This guy has the look of a congested train station messenger, with the thick and dirty beard, the complexion of raw and bluish meat, the bloodshot and idiotic eye, which one might fear to see any minute rolling dishonestly among packages that one had confided to him while trembling.

The well-known journal where he *vomits* his prose and even his verse, owes to him, it appears, its prosperity and doubles its circulation on those days when the coryphée's name gleams in the briefs. It owes to him, in effect, the creation of a bicephalous chronicle, which has an incredible power on ministerial employees and commercial travelers. Alternatively, it farts and coos. From one hour to the next, it is Pan's flute or the kazoo.

His lyrical side is highly appreciated among notary clerks and pharmacy students who copy, in secret, his verses, to pay homage to their laundresses. But his other face is universally kissed, like a paten, by the devotees of old Gallic tradition. Andoche Sylvain represents, as much to say, the *Gallic spirit*. He commends Rabelais, whose genius he believes he possesses, and whom he thinks he revives while rehearsing the Odysseys of rectal innards and the large intestine.

This scum skimmer of chamber pots has found, thereby, the means to package himself as a speciality of patriotism. From his castle in Asnières, where his digestive works are fulfilled to the satisfaction of a joyous public of antique prostitutes and retired comedians, he sounds, in his fashion, the *revenge* of old, lax French gaiety with sonorous defiances in the foreigner's face.

The intelligent Republican oligarchy has remunerated this champion with a lucrative sinecure in a ministry. It has even finished by decorating him, though clumsily, it is true. He was promoted to a knight, as a bureaucrat and not as a poet, which the journals unanimously proclaimed for one whole week,— offering in this way the unexpectedly ignoble spectacle of a government of pirates reprimanded by a press of purse-snatchers, for not having vilified literature enough, in the incongruously recompensed person of a salary grabber, whom both of them have the pretension of honoring.

As for Vaudoré and what he is like, he is the happiest of men. Whatever mediocrity of mind, perfect absence of heart and absolute skepticism can give to a man in terms of felicity, he was granted it.

He is called, willingly, one of the masters of the contemporary novel, in opposition to Ohnet, ever envisaged as the extreme opposite side of the most degrading comparisons. However, it would be difficult to specify precisely the difference in their levels. Their readers are different, doubtless. But they say the same things, in the same language, and are equitably paid with an equal success.

Only Vaudoré bests him infinitely by the inaccessible superiorities of his shamelessness. This mediocre man divined, from the first moment, his destiny. Without groping around in the dark one minute, he chose bastardization and standardization. Such are the two keys with which he has entered into his present paradise.

Loved by this great blindman Flaubert who believed, maybe, in the aurora of a nascent genius, not only did he worm out of him his famous *novella*, written entirely in the hand of the old artist and which, signed with the name Vaudoré, began the young plagiarist's reputation, but after Flaubert's death, he spread about everywhere that this defunct man had engendered it, not hesitating to dishonor his own mother, whom Flaubert never knew. By means of these industries, he came to be filled with a vivifying atom of the glory of the novelist, who had the most powerful influence on new generations, and he inherited all his credit.

Such a disproportionate triumph still not sufficient for this pedicle of a great man, he inaugurated the fruitful sport of standardization. Until this innovator, one was content to make love virtuously or lewdly, but in the obscurity suitable to obscenities preliminary of putrefaction. When he left this shadow, as did the Marquis de Sade, it was deliberately to violate some primordial law of equilibrium, risking his life or his liberty. The pseudo-bastard of Flaubert was ignorant of this kind of grandeur, just as he was of all others. He simply imagined fornicating, from time to time, in the presence of the expert, in order to obtain the renown of a virile writer and to subjugate the curiosity of women. Remarkably gifted, it appears, this ithyphallic novelist gathered the approval of the most rigid arbiters, and Russian princesses, with the most hitched up skirts, came running, surging and in a swoon, from the most distant steppes, to his feet, to bring him brine from all over the Orient.

His colleagues, although penetrated with respect for the enormity of his success, nominate him from among them, voluntarily, the *baggage train soldier* of literature. Such is, in verity, the precise physiognomy of his character and such his degree of distinction. He is a train sub-officer and even *sub-off*. Small, stocky, with a red taint and brown hair, he wears a mustache and a goatee and has diamonds on his shirt. He is the traditional decked-out dandy who throws café waitresses into a panic and can never get over his cheeky good luck. An endless desire to be believed every inch a Parisian is the hidden desire of this incorrigible provincial.

Surprisingly devoid of thought and of all comprehension of others' thoughts, it is impossible to encounter a person more incapable of expressing the semblance of an idea, or articulating a single traitorous word on whatsoever it might be, outside of his eternal preoccupation with bordellos. This player's perfect stupidity is principally manifested by his eyes of a dazed cow or of a dog pissing, half there under the superior eyelids and which look at you with such idiotic impertinence that a million slaps could not pay back.

He is not the person who will ever kill himself while attempting to write a good book, or to write even a good page! "I only care about money," he said, "without troubling myself, because money permits me to amuse myself. Conscientious artists are imbeciles."

In consequence, he is admired by the Parisian Jewry, who receive him with honor, which fills him with jubilation. When he is invited to the Rothschild's residence, the baggage train soldier tells us about it, for fifteen days, wherever he goes. It is from this school, without any doubt, that he has learned the science of business affairs. He was seen, at Étretat, selling plots to his colleagues whom he knew were in financial difficulties, only to buy them back again, dirt cheap.

His vanity, otherwise, is in his image. His mansion on the avenue de Villiers has, in terms of furnishings, the esthetics of a Swedish dentist or a racecourse doorkeeper. What to think, for example, of the sky-blue silk door curtains, enhanced with oriental gold embroidery, and a divan in the same style, a carved-wood Dutch sleigh serving as a chaise lounge and padded, in a clear blue color, and finally an immense white bear hide on the Carmanian rug, probably bought from the *Louvre*? "It is the apartment of a Caribbean procurer," said an exact observer. One loves to think that this is the place where he wrote that famous autobiography of such unconscious cynicism,—that Falstaff would not have dared to sign,—where he offers himself as an example for all the inexperienced pimps who could have need of a guide.

Dulaurier, apparently consoled by Marchenoir's handshake, had approached with these three glorious men. That made four glorious in total, of whom three are "young masters," for Sylvain has begun to become decrepit. The affinity of this flute ought to go naturally with these tambours.

Truly, Dulaurier has, in common with Gilles de Vaudoré, the inestimable favor of all the ghettos and all the Judengasses. He had just published, under the amorphous title of *Sin of Love*, a collection of moral and psychological fragments collected from all over the place, which he had dedicated to a Jewish vixen, whose buttocks Samson himself would have renounced putting a match to and whose bags he carried all over Europe,—doleful beggar of an indefatigable cruelty which made him expiate the atrocious *meconium* of his amorous deprecations by the most geographic of eternal corporal punishments!

LIX

Marchenoir really would have preferred to be able to leave. He saw too well the abominable hours he was going to pass. "What a bunch of hooligans!" he said to himself with dismay. "Nevertheless, I will need to mix with all that, speak with it, also eat with it, make a breach in the disgust that my mouth is filled with in order to stuff into it the aliment that they are going to offer me."

He was despairing that he had in front of him not a single being, with whom he could exchange three words without exploding with contempt.

A white blackbird he most certainly was not, that normal-school alumnus with the faded blond hair and beard, the man with dripping eyes, the augural viscount Nestor de Tinville, the epicurean doctrinarian of the great press, who was on display there. One would be hard-pressed to lay hands on a more intense pedant. He is, at the present moment, one of the most accomplished types among that intolerable bellyful of oracular journalists whom Prévost-Paradol was the prototype of.

Nothing can be accomplished in the world without God's will, but subject to the noble viscount's preliminary preambles. He is the true sage, strengthened by an experience of granite and, by consequence, dispensing with every invention, every style, and even every manner of writing. For this, he has wisdom, nothing but wisdom. He is the one person whom nobody fools. Wisdom is his great resort. If you refuse him his wisdom, you assassinate him. When the vulgar Fates had grown pale after a long time on the skein, he let out, serenely, a heavy observation and everything was untangled. The only thing that remains is to unwind the light.

He has,—like all sages, moreover,—an infinite respect for riches and for the rich, without exception. Riches are, in his eyes, a criterium of justice, of virtue, of aristocracy,—maybe even of *virginity*, because he speaks about virginity often, without anyone knowing why this vocable is so dear to his heart.

He utters the pronouncement that the first duty of the rich is "to love luxury," and that those dying of misery, instead of envying the people who are amusing themselves, they ought to *bless* them. "What does it matter to me?" he wrote, regarding a naturalist novel that recounted the anguish of a poor wretch dying of hunger, "I've such a fine cook!"

The sterile solemnity, the constipated arrogance, the low stiffness of this mule of the press, had the knack of irritating Marchenoir to the highest degree. He also knew the alarming ignominy of his private life and the shame of his marriage to the overworked widow of an ultra-debonair man of letters, who had admitted her as a *third person* into his conjugal bed.

"Could you not," he said to Beauvivier who came passing by, "have me dine at a small separate table, or simply send me into the kitchen? I assure you that I will wholeheartedly enjoy making the acquaintance of your domestics."

"Do my guests disgust you so terribly? You're quite a delicate animal! And yet, it's the cream of the crop that's offered to you! . . . But, let's see, you're making me think. Who do you want me to place you next to, or rather, who do you absolutely not want to be placed next to? You'll already have me at your left. My nearness disgusts you? No. Who'll I put then to your right? Tell me, there's still time."

With a sidelong glance, Marchenoir scanned the large room.

"Put me next to that squinting fellow there," he responded, designating Octave Loriot in the back of a group. "He at least is only an imbecile."

Octave Loriot is, in fact, nothing but an imbecile. The most attentive critical analyses have not been able to extract any other element of cerebral pulp from this novelist for women. He loyally cooks his little turnip of a third-rate novel with macaroni, according to Octave Feuillet, Jules Sandeau, Pontmartin or Charles de Bernard's time-tested formulas. Some claim abusively that he comes right out of *The Owner of the Ironworks*. He is really too anemic and frail, to be compared to that Crotonian, to that

Farnese Hercules, to that Colossus of Rhodes of French imbecility. He is barely the Narcissus of it and would not even have the energy to drown himself in his own image.

But there you go, that is precisely what makes him precious to sentimental folk whose passionate transports he encourages,— without compromising his own heart. Because he does not expose himself to any risks in the hazardous business of grand passions. He restricts his vows to the humble traffic of emollients and preservatives. He is a modest nurse aide for inguinal or scrotal hernias of love.

He continues then the series of novelists trusted by correct society, for whom Chaudesaigues has too much originality, Vaudoré too much feeling, and the rascal Ohnet too much profundity. Dulaurier alone could discomfit him. But the author of *Sin of Love* is a pony of too few merry-go-rounds, whom one is not yet sure enough of. Tomorrow, maybe, he will break everything, while everyone is quite contented with this honest nag, who has never snorted, and who a happily convergent strabismus permits them to manage without blinkers.

In consequence, virtuous people whom he has discreetly lubricated with his imagination, during their lifetimes, remember him at their hour of death and record him in their wills. The fortunate Loriot is the only novelist who sleeps in castles that were bequeathed to him by admiration.

The group, which the proprietor was a part of, assembled respectfully around Valérien Denizot, the monocled officer of the light cavalry of journalism. A man of letters consecrated by Dumas *fils*, the great archon, and probably born for some other thing, Denizot is the most universal failure of his century. Failed at poetry, failed at the novel, failed at the theater, failed at politics, failed even at love, having been cuckolded on Lesbos,—which is a hopeless cuckoldry.

In Paris, the only person known who could compare to him in the capacity of a churl of writing is Bergerat. Even then, Bergerat was varnished with literature by his father-in-law, Théophile

Gautier, whose voluptuous paunch had a soft spot for this son of a preacher.

Denizot himself goes quite well without literature. He is a pure churl, a complete boor,—at table principally, when he drinks Rhine wine to give himself the air of a burgrave. Women are obliged, at that time, to take flight. This old guttersnipe has never suspected that other things could exist besides girls and card players, because he is the prince of the dive, just as he is king of the dirty trick, having been paid for his services as a hired assassin of the quill and for his functions as private ass-wipe of Waldeck-Rousseau,—whose ministry he had the genius of dishonoring a little bit more,—by a diploma of knighthood and the adjutant octroi of a benefice.

The spirit of words so vaunted by Valérien Denizot is drawn from a source that it would be difficult to dry up. He possesses an Alexandrine library of tall tales, wisecracks, salacious collections, and burlesque compilations. There is no end to it. It is only up to him to be, for another one hundred years, "the most spiritual of journalists."

Unfortunately, he has some doubts about his non-being and that enrages him against the universe. Nobody is absolved from his impotence. If he had a sou's worth of talent to take advantage of in his desperate fury as a failure, nothing would escape the venom of his abominable fangs,—with the exception, perhaps, of some firm-handed racetrack goer, accustomed to thrashing more noble beasts, but highly capable, after Champagne, of demeaning himself as far as his slappable face.

Probably fatigued by holding himself up, he leans on his worthy colleague, Adolphe Busard, known in all the theaters under the significant sobriquet of *Old Dog Mimi*. This old dog has the allures and the physiognomy of a cavalry officer, superior in grade to Denizot, but with a weightier weapon.

He is an obsequious and harsh Bonapartist, a plagiarist full of impudence, very powerful at the *Basile* and a blackmailer. An old *regular*, if ever there was one, and from the best times! Napoleon

III paid his debts multiple times one is assured. Alas! the poor sire would have done better to come to the aid of several disdained noble artists, who would have effectively protected him by their ink and with their blood, against the hideous vermin that devoured him.

Busard's blood, if that flowing matter exists in him, is a treasure which he seems singularly avaricious of. As for his ink, he utilizes it exclusively, to make, in literature, expeditionary works. His zeal as a copyist is indefatigable. One of his most cherished pretensions is to pass for a literary historian, for a knowledgeable and documented bibliophile. Naturally, he is a *Moliereist*, as befits all mean minds. Jules Vallès is probably the only scoundrel who despised Moliere. Truth be told, Vallès was a talented scoundrel.

Busard is content to copy others' talent or, more simply, to rob them wholesale, without discernment and without selection, for he is incapable of even detecting talent. One recalls that important, that definitive work, so much announced, on Villon, on his life and his times, reinforced by unpublished pieces and all the means of erudition at his disposal. On investigation, one finds that the thing had been copied, integrally, from the *Journal of Chartres*. The real author who had been robbed, who still possessed his watch, by good fortune, felt that the time had come to come out and protest. So he displayed his notes and Busard, demolished, was submerged in an unfortunately very short silence.

Where he stands out, absolutely, is blackmail. The most exact statistics have established the enormous numerical superiority of his fleeced clientele. Wolff excepted, no other journalist can boast of as great a power of attraction over ecus. These two haruspices distribute justice, like Danae awarded love. They are virginal and incorruptible, for the same amount of time as Jupiter's golden showers. Truth be told, Albert Wolff ransomed the earth, and Busard, less equipped, operates principally on the theater, where he imposes even on its leading ladies. But as far as this market is concerned, he is without equal.

And God knows whether Germain Gâteau, ancestor of Denizot's group, is a novice in this fruitful art of fattening himself on others' labor. This smarmy and whitish Géronte,[1] with a blotchy putty-colored complexion, is an understudy of Wolff and proud of it. Weekly, at the *Basile,* he defecates the tapioca of a gelatinous and molecular bibliography, which serious subscribers lick up. He is the one who is charged with informing two hundred thousand readers about the contemporary French intellectual movement.

For this reason, he is one of the biggest influences in Paris today, and interminable theories of imploring debutants come to unload at his feet their printed fruits of the previous day. But a long practice of trade has blinded his heart against the tearful solicitations of Malfilâtres, and the silver tears are only allowed to roll on the funereal sheet of his impartiality. This thaumaturge has discovered threads of gold in the holes of the pockets of literature. He is the Peruvian of nice financial reports and the alchemical quarryman of the transmutations of Advertisement.

Marchenoir, doomed, by nature, to the observation of social hideousness, had never been able to get over the bewilderment that he felt at first sight of this individual, whom he could imagine disgusting, but not of that same type or degree of disgust. No matter how much he pinched himself, shouted into his own ears, treated himself as three times an idiot,—he could not get over the fact that a steward of renown, a being who keeps under lock and key, in order to distribute, as he sees fit, the bread of artists whose shoes he was unworthy to clean,—supposing even he possessed the beauty of a God,—would have precisely the ignoble physiognomy of Germain Gâteau!

It is the visible form that Vulgarity would necessarily take, if it were to become incarnate for the redemption of Poetry's captives; it is a Medusa of vulgarity! There was the usurious campaign notary and the old fellow of gambling dens, the merchant of twentieth-rate soup and the concierge of the Place Pigalle,

1 Géronte, a character is Moliere's play *Les Fourberies de Scapin.*

who sold his daughter to the retired captain of the mezzanine. There was, above all, the insolent lackey and thief, tolerated by his masters who are not much better, whose dirty secrets he would have discovered. The old worn-out shoe,—already removed,— falls down again immediately before this discouraging face where immoderate abjection is visibly amalgamated to an imbecility that one is forced to conjecture unfathomable.

To the right and left of these leaders, Marchenoir noticed several young thurifers in the throes of ecstasy: Hilaire Dupoignet, Jules Dutrou, Chlodomir Desneux, Félix Champignolle and Hippolyte Maubec,—journalist-pirate tadpoles and novelists without genius, flowers bloomed on the dung of the old, in the salivary sweepings of the boulevard, and who it must be feared will grow larger, by bothering to despise them.

Hilaire Dupoignet is a second-rate apothecary hero of the Tonkin War, where he gained distinction as a male nurse. The troops nicknamed him *Five against One*, because of a shameful habit that he was in a hurry to reveal to his contemporaries in an autobiographical novel of incredible fetidness. He wrote it on his return, with that same hand with which he had rendered such great services, and covered himself in a new glory, that his mind's qualities had not shown promise of, but that the villainy of his soul had obtained for him instantly.

This masturbator has a speciality of attacking people who cannot defend themselves. He displayed this prowess by sending to Brother Philippe the first copy of his stinking novel, wherein the public is informed that the brothers of Christian Doctrine were instituted for the unique purpose of corrupting children.

An obvious coward, probably a murderer, a poisoner by principle, but a frigid arsonist, he offers for observation the sebaceous lividity of a man on whose face one would have formed the habit of pissing . . .

Jules Dutrou, the least young among these tadpoles, gives the impression of a viper who would be a fox, expressly to succumb to the attacks of an inexorable alopecia. This cradle-cap became a journalist to have women, despite his hair loss and baldness. He chronicles in a boulevard sheet renowned for the exceptional emptiness of its virtuosos, and distributes, on the asphalt, spring-loaded smiles and dangerous pressures of his suspect hand.

His voice is that of a castrato from birth, who never had the need of any surgery to become a singer and who carries his scissors in his brain.

Dutrou considers himself to be a writer and speaks sometimes with an equitable disdain for the "scoundrels of letters."

One day, someone mentioned Chlodomir Desneux to a celebrated novelist. It had to do with obtaining from this head of a literary school, all-powerful at the time at the *Voltaire*, that he promote the debutant stricken by poverty, it was said, and interesting from all points of view.

The master let himself be persuaded and came to impose on the director of the *Voltaire* a novel by Chlodomir. The director immediately withdraws a sum, makes off with the manuscript, publishes it elsewhere, becomes the friend of Arthur Meyer who entrusts him with a magistrature, and, at the first opportunity, drags his patron through the gutter.

This Merovingian is a creature of Dulaurier, who has never mentioned giving him money, but who has guided him with his experience, and instructed him to become the semblance of something.

Chlodomir Desneux's strength is, perhaps, in his smile. A ghastly smile that totally exposes his gums and makes his wolf's teeth appear. But he is a good wolf, well-trained, who retracts his fangs at the most distant appearance of a possible club.

He is easily recognizable by his clergyman-style fitted coat, buttoned with licorice pastilles, and with his faux waistcoats laced up in the back, made of an old armchair's olive velour,—these last touches servilely copied from Lécuyer, whose high-class panderer's dandyism strongly influenced him.

He has this in common with Denizot, that he would make, in reigns of terror, a delightful proconsul of the guillotine. As much as they could, one and the other of these envious men would cut off heads to avenge themselves for having been fortunate impotents.

Marchenoir was not afraid that Félix Champignolle would approach him. This young bandit, with an equivocal flunkey's face, was too prudent to put himself within hands reach, knowing his strength. He was not ignorant that Marchenoir had been the friend of a poor devil of a man of letters whom he, Champignolle, had procured the tragic death of by letting him fall into the ambush of a duel, and, what is more, he had been on the verge of skipping out, under any pretext, when he saw the desperate man enter the room. But one would have known too well the true motive of his departure, and politics constrained him to stay. As for Marchenoir, he needed all his strength to remain calm, while waiting for a better occasion. What a dance then!

Champignolle is one of the most remarkable individuals, in this sense that he has the air of a complete miscreant who makes a band of cut-throats look like a bunch of inoffensive bourgeois. With the exception of a courageous or spiritual act, one could say that he is absolutely capable of anything. His effrontery is without example and without precedence. He is the only man of letters having dared to publish a book that plagiarized everybody, almost without exception, made up of cuttings stolen from the most common books, without other modification than the indispensable soldering to adapt them to his subject. It is surprising even that this audacity would have its limits and that he has not claimed, as his own, Lamartine's *Lake* or one of Barbey d'Aurevilly's *She Devils*. But it is easy to conceive the esthetic results of such a method.

The presence of a rascal of this quality would not be tolerated for a quarter of a minute in the society of highway robbers, where some revival of virile solidarity would subsist. The society of letters accepts him, however, with honor and embraces him willingly to put him at his ease. He is offered as an example for emulation to the *young*, who covet his dexterity and navigate as a group in his wake.

His power is, moreover, attested to by the precautions that one is obliged to take in order to receive him. Not only that, one is counseled to carefully hide any papers of importance, but it is still necessary to surveil the agile hands of the visitor, as long as he stands in a place where something can be taken.

Champfort recommended to ambitious people that they swallow a toad each morning, before leaving home, to make a face. Champignolle did even better. He passed the morning of his life soliciting kicks in the rear by every passerby, whose boot could usefully tintinabulate, and when he failed to obtain them, he invented a way to steal them.

Everything then can be predicted for an adventurer of such character. The journals recounted the touching ceremony of his marriage with a young friend of *Madam* Valesse . . . Where will he not go, from now on, this young conqueror, who began yesterday, barely by slipping, like a bug, through the cracks in the parquet and for whom soon no portal, no arc de triumph will rise sufficiently above the ground?

Finally, there is Hippolyte Maubec, *first reporter* of Paris, as he qualifies himself. He passes, at least, for one of the better intuiters and most tenacious trackers among all the dogs of journalism whose heroic employment consists in discovering, in the private life of contemporary illustrious men and women, the decried maneuvers that martial law rewards with a half-dozen balls in the presumed suburbs of the heart. This profession demands, before anything, effrontery and stomach. As for mind, what is needed is just enough of it to see, at the right time, when someone is about to lose their temper, or to welcome kicks to the seat of the pants by exasperated persons, with the smile of a gladiator of information.

However, this envied position not fulfilling his desires, Hippolyte Maubec improvises as a moralist consulting at the famous journal that is impregnated by *honest* republicans, where he happens,—despite the vicinity of Sarcey,—to be the ugliest caterpillar on this nasty fig tree leaf that makes the shameful parts of our contemporary history a bit more visible.

He is gifted with a type of syphilitic and pock-marked face, with perpetually-juicy cutaneous glands. It is precisely the contrary of his scabby and flaky colleague, Jules Dutrou, whose leprosy is dry. When the liquid humor threatens to harden, he presses delicately on the pustules that are refractory to oozing moisture and makes their filth squirt out. A misfortune to whoever happens to find himself at that moment in front of this abominable mug.

No matter. The shopkeepers and commercial travelers, who assiduously read his journal, write to him many an anxious epistle, to whom he responds, publicly, with a patriotic zeal barely surpassed by the extraordinary ridicule of his augural tone, for this venomous man is in favor of virtue and this haunter of shady dens a supporter of probity.

Feared like a pestilent fly and full of *coal-burning* notions on the conjectural morality of the these and those, he is left indisputably in possession of all the authority he wishes to take, and the strange, unclean man profits from it to organize, for his own purposes, a sort of royalty of espionage and intimidation. Thus, he gives orders to all the press, organizes scandal, makes rumors discreet, promulgates silence and, as savant an informer as he is redoubted an accomplice, makes everyone tremble for his omnipotent ignobility.

It is a just royalty, a thrice legitimate primacy, no one,—not even Albert Wolff and Valérien Denizot!—being more vile, more miry, more devoid of talent, more invulnerable to elevated feelings, more impossible to calumniate.

LX

"Is that all?" Marchenoir said to himself, after taking count. "The several stooges that I still see do not appear to me to belong to the house. They are here only to make the numbers swell and for the exultation of the newly made Beauvivier. And now that I think about it, are these really the nurturers of intelligence?

They are almost all decorated, God help me! We are going to the Round table! What will become of me in the midst of all these knights?"

With this reflection, an immense sadness and an unbounded discouragement came over him. He feared, more atrociously than ever, his powerlessness. Without access to wealth, enamored with all the decried grandeurs, and alone against the world! What a destiny!

Ah! if it had simply been a matter of physical combat, in a full cave, he would have felt a valiancy to defy and to massacre them all. At least he would have the consolation of making them pay terribly dear for their skin! This empty idea transported him. He would have presented himself as a knight errant, without banner and without shield, before these high barons licensed for feast and brigandage. He would have affronted them in the name of the Virgin and the Holy Angels, for the honor of Beauty which they have renounced and in vengeance of the feeble who they massacre. To expire under the multitude of scoundrels, he would definitely have to, but he would die in the crimson of a blood-soaked carpet!

Instead of this superb death, he had to count on the ignoble and interminable modern agony of the poor artist who does not wish to be dishonored. Poverty, Aristocracy of mind, and Independence of heart,—these three dreadful fairies that had kissed him in the cradle,—had manifested, for him, the predilection of their bronze entrails, by an unordinary luxury of all the natal gifts that they lavish on their favorites. Poor Marchenoir was one of those men whose entire policy was to offer his life, and whose raging hunger for the absolute, in a society devoid of heroes, condemns him, in advance, to being perpetually vanquished. The most divine courage can do nothing for them. The sublime Gautier Sans-Avoir[1] would be today promptly coffered, and it was already extremely fine that the incorruptible pamphleteer had not been, as of yet, incarcerated in a cell!

---

1 Gautier Sans-Avoir, an eleventh-century knight.

He saw, in a desolating light, the extraordinary insufficiency of his effort, and the terrifying pointlessness of his speech in a world so refractory to every truth. It seemed to him that he was on a defunct planet without atmosphere, similar to a silent moon, where the most thunderous clamors would not equal the sound of an atom and could not be divined but by the inaudible movement of lips . . .

His collaboration with the *Basile* was decidedly a chimera, an insane dream, that would not last three days, faced with the commercial prejudice of modifying nothing of the ordinary fare at the intellectual dive where the modern public is accustomed to stuffing their faces. Moreover, his untroubled solitude at the back of the room, where everyone left him perfectly alone, immediately after the sham effusion in the first instance, clearly demonstrated to him the separating chasms that no consideration could have convinced him to cross, to lower himself fraternally to the level of these maggots of intelligence.

He noticed, after an instant, the highly expressed impatience of some and the manifest disquietude of all. A last guest was expected before everyone sat down at the table, and whoever it was must have been important, to judge by the Amphytron-like host's anxious perplexity.

The door finally opened and Marchenoir saw appear the man before whom every journalist stepped aside, the infinite follicular, the most high Minos of literary hell, the sublime sultan of theatrical criticism, the indestructible Manitou of Common Sense, Mérovée Beauclerc!

"Will wonders never cease!" the overcome loner groaned to himself. "I had forgotten about him, that fellow. If I had been able to predict his arrival, Beauvivier would not have so easily invited me to his mess hall. Now, here I am trapped at this infernal dinner and I will need to use all my strength to remain patient. But, God help me if someone should bother me!"

Mérovée Beauclerc is a normal-school alumnus like Tinville, like Prévost-Paradol, like Taine, like About, who was a close

273

friend. He belongs to the illustrious batch of those university pedants to whom France is indebted for the only turpitude left to be desired by doctrinaires and republicans: the supreme optimism of the pawn of fortune. Only Mérovée Beauclerc surpasses them all. He is the serenest, unalterable, absolute pawn.

Ernest Renan is the only person who could be compared to him. He is the unique paragon that destiny created for him. The author of the *Life of Jesus* is, in effect, a goatskin bag of perfect felicity. Swollen with the gifts of fortune that never stop filling him up again, he offers for observation the exceptional case of a hydrops of happiness. Reputed as a writer, without having ever written in any other way than the first prig to come along, renowned as a philosopher for having rehashed doubts hundreds of years old and made criticism vaunted in all the councils of falsehood,—he is adored in salons and served on bent knee in antechambers. He is the God of cowardly spirits, the sovereign Lord of naturally enslaved souls, and the psychologist Dulaurier wilts before this sun of *dilettantism*, whose "sensibility" he recounts. If the history of the nineteenth century is ever written, this extraordinary word will be collected as a documentary gem of inestimable price. We will just have to be content to judge everything for ourselves, alas! But, what difference does that future make to the happy Buddha of the College of France whose belly full of delicacies is caressed by such Eliakims?

Mérovée Beauclerc is barely a little less fawned over than that idol. Immediately below him, he is the most outrageous of our pontiffs. It would be misunderstanding him, however, to inquire about any sort of book that he came out with. Beauclerc is not a poet, nor a novelist, nor even a critic. He is not even a historian or a philosopher, and has never written a book or anything close to it. He is the Pawn, without epithet, the Pawn of the century, the monitor and the repeater of conquering mediocrity.

Some have inexactly denominated him, "Good Sense in the Flesh," which would imply an altitude of reason, outrageous for his contemporaries and denied by the universal popularity where he has grazed, feeding for twenty years now on magic clover, in the lowest recesses of all the plains. He is Common Sense, one should say, if one remains firm in supposing an incarnation.

In the reserve collection of Albert Wolff,—who inexplicably was missing at this sinister congress,—he is the only example of a man having succeeded at confiscating a nearly unlimited influence, without having done *anything* that could serve as pretext for the usurpation of his tripod. The subaltern oracles, mentioned above, are much less astonishing. To begin with, their credit is less and almost null, in comparison with his. Then, they have the air of having drawn something from their intestines. The Dulauriers, the Sylains, the Chaudesaigues, the Vaudorés, the Tinvilles even, have at least the external look of probable individuals. They appear to have written, and the besotted public, which adores them, would be able to justify the slaver of its cult, by designating the phantom books signed with their names.

Beauclerc possesses absolutely nothing but common sense, in which he passes for never having had an equal, and he would be nothing at all, if he was not the first among pawns. But that is enough, it appears, for the dictatorship of intelligences. Nestor de Tinville, with all his wisdom, is crushed by him. The fact is that Mérovée has no need of any arrogance, nor any solemnity to accredit his word. It has gotten to the point that he needs only to make an appearance and announce no matter what, for jubilation to break out.

At public conferences, which have so inordinately enlarged his glory, it is a kind of miracle, never seen before, the emptiness of his rambling discourse that one applauds! This paradoxical and confounding fact for foreigners unaware of our frightening degradation is so extraordinary that one can mention it matter-of-factly without appearing a calumniator. Common sense, whose nature is to roll out the rug under the feet of the masses, has the mythological privilege of growing ever stronger as it lowers itself and gathers its victories from off the ground. During his time here on earth, Beauclerc has grown smaller and lowered himself, with a constancy of will that would have sufficed another man to soar above the stars, and he has come so *low*, that he has the appearance of losing himself at the bottom of the skies. He flies backwards, at the level of the abyss, and his attractive force is identical to the law of gravitation. His prey sweep down on him. He has merely but to show himself to receive heavy matter and dejections.

He has no more need to be familiar with the least part of the world about which he speaks, and no more need to read in any books that he has the pretension of judging in his harangues. Two or three bluestocking sacristans, devoted to their tabernacle, read in his stead, and their suggestive notations suffice for this intuitive man. At that time, what joy to dishonor a good work, when it is found, to roll it in the mud of his analysis, to lower it to the level of his audience's groins.

And the journalist is in the image of the lecturer. He appears, here as well as there, like a chastisement, an infinite withering, the lively tare of a society so out of shape as to no longer have consciousness of attitudes that it is forced to take and vomitings that it is made to eat. This Beauclerc, did he not have the impudence of boasting, in the most incredible of his regular columns, to be the Minotaur of theatrical criticisms and to exact bestowals of fornication from debutants, forced to pass through his hands under pain of fatal failure? . . . Such a declaration would have attracted to its author, in any other place in the world, a tempest of boos, a clamor of reprobation such as to turn off all the lights in the firmament. He was roundly applauded, on the contrary, and secretly envied. This rascal swims with serenity in liquid garbage, in which he has the power to transmute all that approaches him. He is the Midas of mud.

His hideous snout, which might be believed to have been fashioned to inspire disgust, adds probably to the vertigo of his fascinating debauchery. He has often been compared to a wild boar, by an unpardonable forgetfulness of the sculptural greatness of that savage animal pursued by the Gods. He is pork and not game. The bucolic denomination of piglet is already almost honorable for this tenant of Ignominy. But the bourgeoisie are complacent in this figure symbolizing all the bestialities that their souls are full of, and which they presume to be sufficiently episcopal in illustration that they legitimately absolve them of their trichinosis.

Evidently Beauvivier's dinner would have been ruined without this last guest, whom only Wolff could have replaced at the table. All categories of influences of the quill are now represented at the new satrap's trough, from mastodons to acarus. All that was left to do was to sit down at table.

LXI

The provender was copius and of sublime cuisine. For some time, all that could be heard was the sound of mandibles and the dishware, accompanied, from below, by old men's gurgling hiccups of commencing deglutition. A whispered chitchat undulated vaguely around the immense table, preliminary of a general conversation that sought precision. Brief interjections, suspended exclamations, timid interrogatives, prehistoric jokes and tertiary puns, basted little by little the joyous sound, while waiting for it to burst out like a fanfare, under the excitement of strong wines.

Beauvivier, flanked on his right by Marchenoir and pressed on his left by Chaudesaigues, struggled, ineffectually enough, to establish, through his own person, a cordial electrical current between his two immediate neighbors. Marchenoir, impassive as a window covered in frost, responded, while eating, with a boreal concision that made Chaudesaigues cough.

Nevertheless, Properce, as sagacious as he was patient, calculated that the anchorite would finish by flaring up, like a pyrophorus, in the ambient oxygen of the general stupidity and that then he would belch one of those vehement *paradoxes* that he is customarily known for, the promise of which, passed along deceitfully from ear to ear, would make up part of the menu of this surprising feast. He had even given Machiavellian instructions to be very attentive not to let him die of thirst . . .

After not a little buzzing and incoherency of phrases, the conversation finished by fixing, at the other end of the table, on the event of the previous day that all the journals had picked up on. It had to do with a duel, as unfortunate as it was ridiculous, between a Catholic colleague who was independent enough, by miracle, and courageous enough to write a book against Jewish society, but thoughtless enough to have accepted *crossing swords* with one of the most decried representatives of that vermin. Now, this duel had been one of the most fatal. The Jew had simply assassinated the Christian, to the unanimous applause of Semitic rogues, and criminal justice, permeated with respect for this potentate, had not filed a report against the assassin.

It goes without saying that no one, among the guests, groaned bitterly over the victim. The majority, subsidized by the Synagogue or servants at heart of high Jewish society, would have considered it in very bad taste to be moved by the just punishment of an energumen who had pushed insolence to the point of pissing on the golden Calf. Such domesticated novelists as Vaudoré and Dulaurier could not be expected, for example, to become indignant of something that gave their masters joy.

Only the *incorrectness* of this encounter was discussed then from a sporting point of view, without any thought or feeling having the least occasion whatsoever of entering into the conversation. Beauvivier hoped prematurely that his savage was going to flare up:

"What do you think of this matter?" he asked him.

The question, coming from this Jew, seemed singular to Marchenoir who understood that he wanted to put him on the spot, and who decided, immediately, to disconcert the malicious skepticism of his questioner with a most disquieting calmness.

"I think," he said, "that it is a fool's affair. What do you want me to say about an unfortunate man who demonstrates according to the evidence, in several hundred pages, that the Jews are robbers, traitors, and assassins, a race of illegitimate swine engendered by bastard dogs, and who hastens, soon afterwards, to accept a duel with the most vile among them. For this poor devil had chosen,—everyone will agree,—the adversary most capable of slitting his throat by ridicule, while supposing that the opposite would not have occurred. This absurd victim's courage is, besides, incontestable. His book, although poorly constructed and even more feebly written, gave him honor enough. He was poorly paid to desire anything more than that. As for the circumstances themselves of the duel, I am indifferent to them. The known character of the murderer authorizes the least informed Parisian to judge the assassin harshly. I only have to say that the man is fortunate that I am not the brother of the deceased . . ."

That was uttered with an exquisite tone that surprised Marchenoir himself. "They want to make me bellow," he thought to himself. "I will tell them all they want to know, with the same tone of voice I would use to order a portion of tripe in a restaurant."

"What would you do then?" interrogated, in turn, Denizot, who generally passes for an oracle in matters of honor.

"I would knock him out without saying anything and without anger . . . with nothing but a club," responded suavely Marchenoir, looking down at his plate, to avoid seeing the monocle of the most spiritual of our journalists.

The attention became widespread. The refractory man visibly excited their curiosity. He recalled, fortunately, the "complete triumph" that Beauvivier had assured him of, the day before, when he had dismissed him, and it was with an extraordinary vigor that he held himself in check.

"If I understand you well," then said the Viscount de Tinville, not without some haughtiness, "you absolutely reject the custom of a duel?"

"Absolutely. Would you care to inform me, sir, how I could not reject it? Without speaking of a certain religious instruction that would be little understood, and that I would probably not have the courage to explain to you, there is this that is too easily forgotten: The duel is a prowess of gentlemen and we are *churls*. Sublime churls, perhaps, but in the end, irremediable churls. With the exception of some rare individuals, like yourself,—whose ancestors in bygone days scaled the walls of Jerusalem or Antioch,—we do not seem to differ sensibly from these yokels, to whom one would give two enormous sticks and the combat area of a large pit, to be done with their quarrels. I confess to you that the ridicule of a sword in the hand of men of our sort has always seemed terrifying to me. It would be then perfectly useless to propose a duel to me. If that is your thought, it is admirably judicious and does the greatest honor to your penetration. I want also to tell you that in my eyes, the veritable outrage would start precisely at that instant then. I would consider that I am regarded as a Catholic clown or as an imbecile, and my wrath would explode, right that minute, in a completely surprising manner."

"But, however, Monsieur Reactionary," brayed Rieupeyroux immediately, in a hilarious tone of pure Gascon, which tore in two the velarium of general seriousness, "you're so violent, it seems to me, when you attack your colleagues, and it'd be perhaps right that you didn't refuse them the reparations they've a right to claim from you, when you drag them through the mud. It's too easy, really, to entrench oneself behind Catholicism in order to escape all consequences of your acts and of your words!"

Marchenoir who was sipping, while smiling, a glass of the most delicious of all Châteaux and who was interested in the strident comicalness of this marquis of the Apulian marches, responded to him with perfect mildness:

"If I was reactionary, as you say inexactly, my very gentle sir, you would see me as ardent as you yourself in every heated exchange and at every kind of tournament. It is, on the contrary, because I am the most surpassing of progressives, the pioneer of the extreme future, that I contemn these practices as outdated. You assert that I am violent. God knows, however, if I hold myself back, because I could be much more violent . . .

"As for the beautiful souls who my writings have afflicted, who prevents them from afflicting me, in their own turn, in the same way? I would be the most iniquitous critic if I got upset over a riposte, even imbecilic. I sharpen my projectiles with as much art as I can and I ruin myself to choose, for this purpose, the most expensive materials. One of my dreams is to be a jeweler of maledictions. But I do not demand that my victims be lapidarists themselves and that they set up shop. One does what one can and it would be disgraceful of me to contest the choice of defensive arm from any rogue that I would be the aggressor of. If I pursue a polecat, sword in hand, and he combats me with the juice of his behind, that is absolutely his right, and I have nothing to say. It is legal for anyone to publish that I am a bandit, a forger, a tramp, a proxenete, and even an idiot. You have not the faintest idea with what indifference I receive these vocables of yours. For example, you need not ask more from me, because I oppose assault with the most unusual temperament . . .

"I will die certainly without having understood what the word *reparation* means, in the sense that duelists want it to mean. I do not forbid, moreover, the disgruntled from bringing their snouts to me, if it appears expedient to make this transit. My domicile is known to everyone in the world and is in no way equipped with Catholic or other entrenchments. My door opens easily, as well as my window, but I do not advise any brave man to select his dearest friends and dispatch them to me as witnesses. I would accord them about three minutes of courtesy, at the expiration of which it could be that I send them back fairly deteriorated in order to get over, after some time healing, the need to bother recluses in their hermitage."

Léonidas, previously mistreated by this pamphleteer, and who several words from this serious persiflage had clearly stung, opened his mouth to speak again, when Beauvivier stopped him with a gesture.

"Pardon, my dear Rieupeyroux, the debate is over. You've forced Monsieur Marchenoir to renew already ancient declarations and which we've all known for a long time. You don't expect, doubtless, to lead him, in order to please you, to modify his views or his feelings. Our guest is an exotic man and from another century. He has other ideas than we do about honor, but this divergence is not important, as his personal intrepidness is off-topic.

"Also, from the point of view of this last comment, I believe that his columns will be of useful scandal on the cover of the *Basile*. If nobody finds it inconvenient, and if the author consents," he added, turning toward his neighbor, "I'd be of the opinion that he read to us, right now, the opening article that I'll be publishing the day after tomorrow, the proofs of which are in my office now. I believe, gentlemen, that your surprise won't be small. Have you any repugnance to giving us this intellectual pleasure, Monsieur Marchenoir?"

The latter hesitated a minute, then decided. He felt vaguely that, already, Beauvivier was looking for an occasion to compromise him and break his back, and that he was making things impossible for him, since he was pushing him to read this philippic, wherein two-thirds of the guests were scuppered. But the mere thought of such a risk settled it for him,—being one of those proud horses who eviscerate themselves on the bayonets while neighing from the voluptuousness of suffering!

LXII

Marchenoir had his scatological retribution. The tattletale prudishness of Ernest Renan's contemporaries had blamed him harshly for the stercoraceous energy of his anathemas. But, for him, it had to do with the need to take sides. He saw the modern world, with all its institutions and all its ideas, in an ocean of mud. It was, in his eyes, an Atlanta submerged in the garbage dump. It was impossible for him to see the world differently. On the other hand, his writer's poetics demanded that the expression of some reality be forever adequate to the mind's vision. In consequence, he found himself, habitually, in the most inevitable necessity of turning away from contemporary life, or expressing it in repulsive images, which the incandescence of his feeling could, alone, applaud. The article that he had given to Beauvivier on the scandal of pornographic publicity was, in this genre, an unprecedented *tour de force*. It was a Vesuvius of filth on fire.

When he was enjoined to execute the perilous leap of reading, the unhappy man, a bit overheated by the exorbitant food that had been imposed on him, began to lose the occasioned caution that had preserved him, thus far, from the messy familiarity of the herd that he endured being encircled by. He noticed, with a joy full of dread, that his armor of ice was melting visibly under the abnormal temperature of that excessive meal. What would come later, he knew too well. The wild animal would come out of him without him being able to stop it, and the exhibition that he had to perform,—in whatever manner he could,—appeared all the more like a defiance, that he would overheat even more by putting his voice and his gestures in diapason with his aggressive periods. He had, in spite of everything, come to desire it, this reading, like a release. The enormity of stupidities and infamies that he had heard, for an hour, called for an eruption.

He stood up then, as soon as Beauvivier had given him the packet of proofs, and there was a profound silence, the malevolent curiosity of his auditors being at its height.

"*The Sedition of Excrement*," slowly articulated the thunderbolt thrower.

At this enunciation, the pawn Mérovée, in the middle of dabbing, with his handkerchief, the impure viscosity of his diseased eyes, had a start.

"The title is promising," he said. "Monsieur Marchenoir has not changed. He holds on forever to fecal eloquence."

"Gentlemen, I implore you," Beauvivier immediately intervened, "no comments."

Marchenoir, nowise disconcerted, read then, without interruption, the three hundred lines of his article. He had the voice of a whelk, very like his mountainously oratorical style, and calculated, it seemed, for vociferation. He read *badly*, as befits any prophet. Turbulent and tumultuous, this unleashed vaticinator was full of sobs, catafalques, and hoots. He made Mardi-Gras chariots and thunder tumbrels roll over their heads. He had sarcastic emotions and gave them a solemn bawling-out. The abject word, whose usage he was reproached so often for, he had a manner of shouting, as if he had been, all by himself, a multitude, and this word became sublime, as much as the desperate imprecation of an entire people.

Then something happened that Marchenoir had noticed on other occasions. The silent immobility of those who were listening to him became a stupor. Not one complaint rose from this group of men who were ridiculed, scolded, trampled on, thrashed with an unprecedented ferocity and the executionary authority of slave traders. Except for two or three who had already heard it, those present had never imagined such a thing and did not consider getting upset about it. Beauvivier, himself, who had however read the article, but who did not recognize it any more, uttered in this fashion, had some difficulty recovering from his stupefaction.

"My faith, gentlemen," he said, perfectly sincere, "confess that what we have just heard is astounding. We owe it to ourselves to bring down the house here," and he clapped his hands. The others, brought back from their surprise and following the patron's example, applauded in a riotous manner.

"But,. . . Monsieur Marchenoir," continued the *Basile*'s colonel,—addressing himself to his guest who had just sat down again after an imperceptible inclination of the head,—"I didn't know you had this tragic force, which astonishes me even more, I assure you, than your talent as a writer, which I hold, however, as you already know, in the highest esteem. It begs the question of why you're not in the theater. You'd become master and God . . . What do you think, Beauclerc?"

The great Sentencer did not have a chance to draw up his judgment. These last words had procured for Marchenoir the sensation of a formidable slap in the face. Beauvivier's evident good faith, at this moment, effected in the end what his insidious malice was unable to do. The lycanthrope was really in a rage. He grew pale and his eyes blackened.

"Pardon," he said, while stretching out his hand, as if to impose silence on the pile of hairy meat that had just been consulted and who was preparing to respond, "Monsieur Beauclerc's opinion is of no interest to me. I am of a mind even to absolutely ignore it, and I am astonished, Monsieur Beauvivier, that you had the idea of making me sit at your table to put the dignity of my person under examination. I was far from supposing that the reading that you have just applauded and which I did in order to satisfy you, would be, so soon, an occasion for the mortifying praise that you heap on me, and the more outrageous arbitration that it pleases you to invoke."

Beauvivier, surprised, cried out:

"How is this possible, dear sir, that you misrepresent at this point my words and my intentions? In truth, I don't see what I've done to offend you . . ."

Many spoke at once.—"He was raised badly, this Catholic!" said Beauclerc.—"He was bitten by Veuillot," added Tinville. Other exclamations of the same kind ran from one end of the table to the other. The kennel, brought to heel for an instant, found its mouth again.

"If you need me to explain to you how your words have revolted me," replied Marchenoir, "it is doubtful that my explanations will enlighten and satisfy you. Nevertheless, here it is, in as few words as possible. I regard the state of a comedian as the shame of shames. I have the most old-fashioned and absolute ideas about it. The theatrical vocation is, in my eyes, the lowest of miseries in this abject world and passive sodomy is, I believe, a little less vile. The catamite, although venal, is, at least, forced to restrict, each time, his vileness, to the cohabitation with one person only and can still retain,—as the basis of his atrocious ignominy,—the freedom of a certain choice. The comedian abandons himself, without choice, before the multitude, and his industry is not less ignoble, as it is his *body* that is the instrument of pleasure provided by his art. The opprobrium of the scene is, for a woman, infinitely less, for it is, for her, in harmony with the mystery of Prostitution, which only lowers the poor wretch in the sense of her nature; it debases her without being able to disfigure her.

"The metaphysical destitution of the nineteenth century and the surprising energy of its derision was necessary to rehabilitate this art that sixteen hundred years of Christian reasoning had condemned. It appears quite simple today to receive with honor and to drape with decorations abominable curs, who the good people of yesteryear would have refused to bed down in the stable, lest their horses be infected with the glanders of their profession. But you have said it just now, I am not of this century, I have other ideas than it has, and among the repugnant things that it idolizes, the brothel of the footlights is above all blasphemed by me . . . It would have been easy for you to conclude, just as many others have done before you, from the intensity of my thrust, an assassin's vocation, for example,—something that would have in no way altered my humor. You could infer from my prose and from my diction, furious madness or, at the very least, some shameful scrofula, some vile ulcer whose hidden purulence would be discharged through my eyes . . . Without hesitating, you explain everything about me by the faculties of acrobats and you offer to me the future of a buffoon before the rabble. There you have it, I avow it, something that completely surpasses my capacities of resignation."

While the strange rebel spoke, a more than hostile murmur rose up around him and mounted to the point of growling. As soon as he had finished, the barking exploded. They must have been seething for a long time. An unknown person, spewing forth such impieties, would have only obtained interjections of a call to order or silence and compassionate smiles,—for the world of the quill is, in general, extremely attentive to exterior observances of the most urbane indulgence, above all in the presence of ferocious beasts.

But here it was a matter of a common enemy, a person who nobody could be friends with and who could not be a friend of anyone. Marchenoir was a heretical negator of the Holy Sacrament of riff-raff, in the midst of a reveling council of theologians and high prelates of proxenetism. The vomiting on comedians had splattered on nearly all the courtiers of lust or vanity, who prospered by exploiting the most vile passions of their time. And then, it was quite necessary that they took vengeance for the surprise that they had had and the applause they had given as a result of an inexplicable ascendancy.

There was then a concert of trepidations, a crackling of injuries, a squall of bad blasts, a clamor composed of all the formulas of excommunication and interdiction, customary at the most tempestuous sessions of rabble parliaments. Heads, heated from the spirits of the wine and fuming under the girandole, were no longer in a state to keep any restraint, and the truth of their churlishness transpired through their congestion. It was not until Dr. Des Bois, everyone's intimate acquaintance and, in particular, the glorious Paulus', who had something to say, and who expressed simply,—in a style verified by the author of *The Owner of the Ironworks*,—that Marchenoir had the misfortune of "not knowing how to handle himself in society."

Beauvivier, excessively disquieted, began to fear, for good reason, that his plot would have a regrettable denouement, and that the amusing exhibition of the monster that he had dreamed up would become,—by the bad luck of a considerable addition of blows,—a cheerless tragedy. Vainly, he tried, by gestures and by impotent conjurations of his frail voice, to re-establish order.

In fact, the demeanor of the monster was not exactly inspiring a sense of security. He had remained seated, it is true, and very calm in appearance, but his eyes, dilated internally, reverberated, in a profound blackness, his general rage. It was supposed that he was more at his ease, to see himself exposed to all eyes, and was enjoying the feeling of showing his courage. He waited for the first fury to quiet down on its own, naturally, by the pure and simple exhalation of injury or denial that each of his adversaries were able to bestow on him.

When the moment seemed to him to have come, he rose, and this devil of a man began to speak, beginning in a tone so particularly sonorous and serious that he obtained silence.

"It would be extremely easy for me, gentlemen, to pick up whatsoever object here,—if not Monsieur Champignolle,—and use it to thrash you all. Some among you who know me,"—he emphasized, while looking at Dulaurier whose dandyism was fixed on edge,—"know that I am capable of it, and I would not try to dissimulate from you that I am strongly tempted to do it. That exercise would relieve me and render my digestion more active. But . . . what is the point? I will simply leave and you can then intertwine your brotherly spirits in perfect peace. I am not one of you, and I felt it the minute I walked in. I am a sort of madman, dreaming of Beauty and impossible justices. You dream of enjoying yourselves, you others, and that is the reason why there is no means of our understanding each other.

"But, be careful. Reprehensible and debauched behavior is not an eternal refuge, and I see an enormous maw that rises on your horizon. People suffer a lot, I assure you, in the world that you have cultivated. They are on the point of having had a hell of enough of it, and you could reap some confounded surprises . . . God keep me from the temptation of explaining to you the sweat of prostitution that makes you fetid! The situation has filled you with a power that no monarch, before this century, has wielded, because you govern over intelligences and because you possess the secret of making hapless people swallow stones, who cried out for bread."

"You have prostituted the Word, while exalting the foulest egoism. Ah! well, it is the terrible modern boorishness, unleashed by you, that will strike you to the ground and replace your backsides marked with infamy, to reign over a society forever deposed. And then, by an unprecedented derision, capable of precipitating the end of days, you will be, in your turn, the famished representatives of the universally shouted down Word. I see in you the stale Malfilâtres and the seedy Gilberts in the nearest future. Never will one have seen so prodigious a dishonor to the human spirit. This will be the punishment reserved specially for you, at your expense, to learn, by this monstrous irony, the infernal sufferings of the lovers of Truth, that justice for you as reprobates condemns to despair completely naked, like Truth itself. My most cherished dream, from this moment forward, is that you *appear* manifestly abominable, because you cannot, with any conscience, be anything more than that. In the name of literature that you renounce with horror, you will live exclusively by deception, by pillage, by baseness and by cowardice. You will devour the innocence of the weak and you will refresh yourselves by licking the putrid feet of the strong. There is not in any of you the wherewithal to hire a slave generous enough to wish to endure merely his congruous part of the debasement, and disposed to balk at the too withering strap. I hope therefore to see you, in a bit, penniless and sheared right down to the living flesh, as there exists no other expiation for your swine souls.

"I hope also that this will be the end of ends,"—continued Marchenoir, becoming more and more exasperated,—"because it is not possible to suppose a proconsulate of human sewage that would surpass you in infection, save conjecturing, at the same time, the apoplexy of humanity. On this day, perhaps, the Lord God will repent,—as he did for Sodom,—and without doubt come back down,— finally!—from the highest heaven, into the suffocating mud of our planet, to set ablaze, once and for all, all our places of putrefaction. The exterminating angels will hightail it and bury themselves deep in the suns, to avoid being exterminated themselves by the disgust of seeing our termination, and the horses of the Apocalypse, at the appearance of our last filth, will rear and return into space, while neighing in the terror of contaminating their hooves! . . ."

Having vociferated these last words with a voice that seemed almost superhuman, the imprecator left, shaking, head high and eyes on fire. The auditors understood probably that it would do nobody any good to get in his way, while presenting to him a modicum of civility, because those standing where he had to pass got out of his way with visible eagerness.

A half hour later, while collapsing onto a café bench where Leverdier was waiting for him, he said:

"Dear friend, my days in journalism are over, but it does not matter, I did not pay too dearly for the voluptuousness of busting their chops!"

LXIII

From this day, the rebel locked himself up in the highest citadel of his spirit. He picked up again courageously his book on Symbolism. He represented to himself that it was the last resource left to him, and he calculated that with the money from the good father general of the Carthusians, he could go on for several months still, and could, without a doubt, finish it. Then, God only knew what would happen next, but, at least, this work, which he felt a vocation for and which cried out in him to be born, would have been accomplished.

No door, besides, seemed ready to open. His first article in the *Basile* had been his last. It had appeared, effectively, two days after the famous dinner, but so disfigured by innumerable attenuations and omissions, that he did not recognize it any more, and which the first journalist who came along could have signed his name to. He waited for a while and felt no anger at all. He only deplored that his name had also not been struck out like his epithets and, he felt, as a result of his weak-minded foolishness, a poignant bitterness that paralyzed him, intellectually, for an entire day. Then, it was over.

From the Catholics, he had experienced, for a long time, such aversions, that there was no need to think about them. The telltale hostility of this group was, perhaps, even more enraged than the declared hatred of the miscreants. He had seen it clearly with his *Life of St. Radegund*, an exclusively religious book, if ever there had been one, which the Catholics should have turned into a success, and which they had snuffed out, right off the press, under an implacable silence. For these hemeralopes, Marchenoir's brilliant wealth of talent was an optic scandal, capable of putting into danger the health of their weak eyes, and which they made it their duty to stifle like a temptation from the Devil. The new book that he was preparing would not make them any less indignant. Supposing he could find a publisher,—which looked scarcely probable,—what means would his work have to get before the public and obtain the half success in sales so necessary to the author's subsistence? Decidedly, the future was horrible.

Marchenoir worked wholeheartedly, keeping at bay, as best he could, that vision of despair. But it returned, all the same, imposing itself despotically on the unfortunate man. It was then that the quill fell from his hand and, no matter what he could do, he had to pass before his eyes again his entire life and redrink all his bitter memories. It was a melancholy of the damned. At these moments, Véronique drew near and, bending over the shoulder of this cross-bearer charged with such a heavy load, tried to re-animate him,—"Poor dear soul," she said, "if only I could take all your pain on me!" and, often, these two beings felt sorry for each other, and cried together.

Now, that itself was another danger and a source of new sorrows,—incomparable. Marchenoir felt more in love than ever. With an immense terror, he saw himself more and more a captive and bound in chains. However much he looked at the mutilated woman, in the hopes of taking in the horror that she had intended to mask her visage with, that salutary impression never came. He found in her only an object of pity that made him grow soft, which culminated in suggestive incitations. This dreamer, chaste as a monk, burned inside like tinder . . .

Such was the definitive result, the supreme outcome of so many efforts, of such complete victories over his flesh or over his spirit acquired previously. At forty years of age he returned to the troubles of adolescence. He needed to resist again, his resolve already broken so many times, that terrifying return of youth that uproots souls less cut into and more robust. And he saw no way of escape. Work, prayer even, did not calm him. All betrayed him. The eucharistic tendernesses of his faith only served to tilt his heart a bit more over that chasm of the woman's *body*, where human torrents, hurtling down from the highest peaks, come to lose themselves, rumbling. Christ bleeding on his cross, the Virgin with Seven Glaives, the Angels and the Saints tendered to him the identical trap of liquifying his soul in their furnaces . . .

Marchenoir's moral situation was appalling. No human being would know how to deal with the perpetual privation of all happiness. The most miserable humans refuse this unacceptable deprivation. One can always take up a vice, a mania, or hasten to suicide. But these three solutions equally revolted the amorous mystic, and he was no more able than the least of vagabonds to uncover a fourth. Happiness! He had been ravenous for it all his life, without hope of satisfaction. Nobody had ever searched for it with such a fury . . . and such a perfect incredulity. And yet, he had searched too high, in an ether too subtle, even for the illusion of it.

Now, by a satanic derision, this eternal desire to be happy,— that inappeasable thirst from the fountain that did not exist for superior beings,—became more precise, at two paces from him, in the form of a palpable object, the possession of which would have filled him with horror. He writhed with rage, he slapped himself, at the thought that this saint,—who was his glory and his ransom,—who he coveted carnally like a vulgar mistress! Ah! it was really the pain of forty martyrs to endure, to be extenuated by so many labors, to be consumed at the foot of altars and to wash the feet of Jesus with a million tears, to end up finally at the filthiness of this obsession! . . .

He escaped far from the house, forced to abandon his work, and walked outside of Paris, on the routes and along the deserted roads, crying to God in interminable solitary perambulations. But Temptation did not let go of him and often became even more active. It perched like an eagle on this marcher, claws planted into his neck, blinding him with its wings, tearing him apart with its beak, devouring his brain, and dominating with its cries of victory the Desperate Man's clamor of distress.

Sudden frenzies seized him, made him truly an energumen. He threw himself, bellowing like a pursued buffalo, in the copses, at risk of cutting his face and blinding his eyes, insensitive to the scrapes and to the bruises,—sometimes also he rolled in the grass foaming at the mouth like an epileptic, calling out for help, indistinctly, from the powers of all abysses. One evening, he woke up in a ditch in the Verrières woods, frozen to the marrow, having fallen asleep with the perfidious and deep sleep of those spent by sorrow, which comforts them so that they can suffer a little more.

In the nervous lull that followed these crises, his imagination, ever disquieted, represented to him, to vary his punishment, Véronique such as she had been, yesterday even, before having massacred herself, out of love for him. Then, he imagined the calculations of a slave trader, telling himself that after all, evil was not irreparable, that the hairs and the teeth could be *bought* and that it was up to him to recover his idol from her perdition. Then, the feeling returned, soon after, of his eternal indigence,— bringing this unfortunate soul back to the most desolate center of his infernal sufferings!

LXIV

One of the religious practices that he was most fond of was the parish high mass, which was named, in an abject style, the "work of the people," probably by antiphrasis, because the people are forbidden to attend.

To be sure, the *clergy* do not jest with the poor world and Jesus himself, followed by the Sacred College and the twelve Apostles, would be promptly swept away by the beadle,—if that company came, in rags, and not having the money to pay for their seats. The rich and notable devotees, who have their names engraved on their padded prie-Dieu, would not suffer the nearness of the Savior lamentably dressed, who wanted to assist in person at the sacrifice of his own Body. These ladies' bow-wows would certainly be expelled with more consideration than the divine Vagabond.

This simony inspired a boundless horror in Marchenoir. Also, one never saw him among the crowd of parishioners in their Sunday best. He left Véronique at the front row, in front of the altar which she loved to see before her, and went to install himself, safe from all eyes, in a lateral chapel and, almost alone, where his grievous soul had less risk of being elbowed by souls with money or makeup, who pollute with their toilettes the house of the Poor.

He tried also not to look at the architecture of that modern church,—second-rate, out-of-place imitation of a decadent art, executed by some mason devoid of geometric pulchritude.

All his attention was given to that profound Liturgy that has traversed the centuries, encountering the apostasies of the drawing pencil and the renunciations of the compass. The comprehension he had of that marvel of Christian Symbolism procured for him a supernatural appeasement. His religious soul, three quarters submerged by the diabolism of his passion, found a foothold for several instants on these sacred forms, beyond which he had a foreboding of the glory of divine compassion. He fell, immediately afterwards, in the crazed surges of his delirium. No matter! he had an hour of sublime reconciliation, run through with dazzlements. A hypertrophy of joy swelled his heart, until his breast burst.

The high mass is a holocaustal agony accompanied by nuptial chants. It epitomizes the incommensurability of sorrows and the infinity of joys. It renews, without lassitude, in ever-identical ceremonies, the enormous confabulation of the Lord with men:

"I created you, most dear vermin, in my thrice-holy resemblance, and you have repaid me by betraying me. So, in place of castigating you, I have punished myself. It no longer sufficed me that you should resemble me. I, the Impassive, felt a divine thirst to make myself similar to you, so that you could become my equals, and I made myself vermin in your image.

"You squat, as you please, in the mire reddened by my blood, at the foot of the cross where you have fixed me by all my members so that I could not get away. Here we are then, you and I, after nearly two thousand years. Now, this wood is terribly hard and you do not feel well, my dear children . . .

"I barely see my servant Elijah who could come and deliver me, because it would be possible for me, finally, to baptize you and to cleanse you in fire, as I have so often announced. But this prophet has been asleep, doubtless, in a deep sleep, for so long that I say he is in the anguish of *Sabachthani*! . . .

"He will come, though, I beg you to believe it, and you will learn then, imbecile ingrates, just what I am capable of accomplishing.

"On that day, the fear of God will battle against man, because one will see the unprecedented and perfectly unexpected thing, which will tear down, to the foundations, the human abode, that is to say that there will be the translation of figures into realities . . . I will blind you, because I am the author of Faith, I will drive you to despair, because I am the first born of Hope, I will burn you because I am Charity itself. I will be pitiless, in the name of Mercy and my Paternity will have no more guts, except to devour you.

"My despised Cross will shine out in splendor, like a conflagration in the black night, and an unknown terror will recruit, in this brightness, the trembling multitude of bad flocks and bad pastors. Ah! you told me to come down from there and that you would believe me. You shouted to me to save myself, as I saved others. Well! I will fulfill all your wishes. I will effectively come down from my Cross when this ignominious spouse will be completely covered in flames,—because of Elijah's arrival,—and when it is no longer possible to ignore what has been, under the appearance of abjection and cruelty, that instrument of torture for so many centuries! . . .

"All the earth will learn to agonize in terror of it, that this Sign was my Love itself, in other words, the HOLY GHOST, hidden under an unimaginable travesty.

"That Cross *that exceeds me on all sides*, to express, in its Madness, the adorable exaggerations of your Redemption will extend its torrefying Arms over all the earth. The mountains and the valleys will liquify like wax, and your God, unnailed from his bleeding bed, will set again, on Adam's soil, his two pierced feet, to know whether you will keep your word by believing in him.

"He will look at you with the Face of his Passion, but streaming, this time, with the light of all prefigurative symbols that this wonder will illuminate, in front of him, like flames, and,—for having made, in times of darkness, use of your freedom for putrefaction, as it will have pleased you—you will recognize, in your turn, what it means to be abandoned by my Father, you will be taught Thirst and all justice will be consummated in you, in the terrifying ardent Hands that you have blasphemed!"

Such was within Marchenoir the strange echo of the sacred liturgy. The fervor of this millenarian tended ceaselessly toward the accomplishments of the end of ends. All the desiderata of the most sublime souls rushed to this soul, like an invasion of rivers, and his interior prayer boomed like the impatience of cataracts.

This extraordinary Christian did not even think any more about his sad times. The immense rages that were roused in him by the promiscuity of ambient turpitudes, were forgotten. Involuntarily, he assumed, in superhuman transports, the dereliction of all ages.

"You promised to come back," he cried to God, "why then do you not come back? Hundreds of millions of men have counted on your Word, and are dead in the torments of incertitude. The earth is swollen with the cadavers of sixty generations of orphans who have waited for you. You who speak of others' sleep, what kind of sleep are you taking, given one can vociferate for nineteen centuries without waking you? . . . When your first disciples called to you in the storm, you rose to command silence of the wind. We do not perish any less than them, I suppose, and we are a billion times more unfortunate, we others, the disinherited of your presence, who do not even have the disappointing comfort of knowing in what part of your universe you sleep your interminable sleep!"

These objurgations, that doctors of law would have condemned, he could not prevent himself from renewing without respite. It was his soul's respiration, when he exhaled towards heaven, and,—since the death of the priest who previously had opened his understanding,—he had been unable to meet anyone but Véronique whose simple mind was not scandalized by this impetuous fashion of speaking to God.

The recollection of this dear creature was mixed, by consequence, with his prayer and traversed in flaming arrows his prophetic exaltations. He was wrapped up in his loftiest thoughts and participated in their enthusiasm. He found, analogically, his place in the liturgical peripeteias and phases of the vast drama of propitiation that was accomplished under his eyes of an obsessed contemplative.

When, after the curate or his vicar had given his Dominican *instruction,*—which Marchenoir, at the back of the chapel, had been very pleased not to hear,—the organ, coming to thunder with the words of the officiant, promulgated, once again, accompanied by the voices of the singers, this antique Nicene Creed that fifteen centuries have not yet exhausted the adolescence of, the solitary man was, in spite of everything, together with Véronique in the Gregorian swell of twelve incommutable articles of faith. His flesh quieted down, without doubt, and his beloved was transfigured into a light of extraterrestrial apperceptions. His obsession became divine for not being exorcised, but it did not go away for an instant.

Maybe it had to be like this. The canonical prayers of the Roman Church have such a universal character, so essential a virtue of bringing back to the absolute all reducible human sentiment, that Marchenoir, his tortures momentarily lightened, took to considering this violence exercised on him as a necessary test.

From this point of view, the oblation of the Host and the oblation of the Chalice suggested to this burning exegete immediate applications, that the rumblings of the organ, with the inciting versicles from the beginning of the Preface, had the air of paraphrasing. *Sursum corda!* "Alas! I really want it," responded the miserable man, "but my strength is drained and my sad heart is as heavy as the world . . ."

At the immense explosion of *Sanctus*, he sat back up, brandishing himself before heaven in the redemptive drunkenness of that oecumenical praise. It seemed to him, at that moment, to present before God's throne that saint of the earth who he had formed in the likeness of his saints in Paradise.

"Take her from me," he said, "hide her from me in your gulfs of light, preserve for me this wage of remission that I have worked so hard for."

A little while later, during the seraphic hymn of *O salutaris*, he melted with melancholic sweetness, and this was the exact minute when ordinarily he believed he had become completely powerful.

All the ceremonies, all the particular acts of this Sacrifice, that the theologians regard as the greatest act that could be accomplished on earth, penetrated Marchenoir to his intestines and to his marrow. He was saturated with the superior Dilection and only then became more accessible to the inferior solicitations of his animality . . .

It is a lamentable mystery of our nature, that the highest appetencies of free beings should be precisely what precipitates them to their damnation,—so that they fall hopelessly, like Lucifer. The unfortunate man knew it. That is why he would have preferred that this mass never ended, and that the amorous or comminatory chants continued as well, right up to the luke-warm faithful, who had come to make a semblance of listening to them, that they would have crumbled to dust with him and his Véronique! . . .

He left finally, his nerves shattered, his head ringing, exhaust-ed to the point of fainting.

LXV

Véronique would not have been a woman if Marchenoir's appall-ing state had been able to escape her. Besides, he fell short of be-ing able to dissimulate it. All he could do was to give the slip to Leverdier, by letting this person, ignorant about matters of love, believe that his work alone was drawing him away from his nor-mal life. Véronique, more clairvoyant, had discerned, from the first moment, the hopeless truth. She kept silent, having nothing else to do, but with an inexpressible desolation and trembling.

The apparent inutility of her martyrdom crushed her. She saw that all was lost, this time, and had the presentiment of a near catastrophe.

But, she desired with an all-powerful desire to be the only victim, so that her disappearance might deliver him who had delivered her. She began to covet the savorous fruit of her own death, like great Eve coveted the fruit of universal death.

Her continual orisons acquired an unprecedented intensity and transported her to delirium. She wrung her heart with both hands to squeeze the life out of it. By the example of St. Theresa, she built herself "a seven-floored castle," no longer, like the Carmelite reformer, to mount from the initial detachment from this world to the perfect consumption of divine peace, but to transfer her grieved soul into some definitive prison, luminous or gloomy, which was not, at any rate, this carnal tabernacle so pointlessly disfigured,—while passing through successive jails of supreme renunciation,—and such was the dungeon of her silent agony.

It was one of those dark and deep dramas, hidden beneath the *little blue mantle* of charity's smiles,—as the horrible ebony of space is masked with that azure that is the aliment of men's lives. These two singular victims of the Ideal prorogued beyond time, carefully avoided any word that could have shed light on the one or the other, and this prudence was only vain with regard to Véronique,—for Marchenoir, well assured that his friend did not share his turmoil, was far, however, from conjecturing the sublime turmoil that the unperturbed physiognomy of this women kept secret. They almost never spoke anymore, terrified of the despotism by this silence that was sitting over their house.

Soon they saw each other only at mealtimes, rapidly expedited and sadder still than the other quotidian events of their common life,—except on the days when Leverdier came to interrupt the unsuspected suffocations of this tête-à-tête with his presence. The good man, a hundred leagues away from divining the infinite tortures that were secreted from him with the greatest of care, spoke of Symbolism to Marchenoir, who was happy to bury himself under this intellectual blanket that he used to arbitrate everything. For, from both sides of the table, they judged the difficulty to be without remedy, why sadden in advance such a tender soul? He would suffer forever soon enough, the poor devil, when the necessarily disastrous denouement should come, which the two unfortunate souls apperceived more or less distinct, but inevitable.

One night, the damned, alone in his room, having passed several hours at consulting the historic *similitudes* in the abominable epic of the Late Empire, realized all of a sudden that he was toiling in vain. The smoky torch of his mind, uselessly agitated, gave no more light. He put down his quill and began to think.

It was the month of June and day was breaking. Through his open window, which looked out over the sleeping neighborhood, a mild breeze blew over him, refreshing and heady with the scent of fruits . . . It is the hour of dangerous enervations and languid instigations of the carnal spirit. A man, habitually chaste and fatigued by a long period of wakefulness, is, at that time, without energy to resist. In Marchenoir's case, this very simple phenomenon was complicated by passionate predispositions that would sink forty wills of the highest rank. All of a sudden, a violent frenzy of concupiscence pounced on him, like a tiger.

Knocked down, rolled over, lacerated, devoured in the same instant, his free will, attenuated for so many days, disappeared finally. Strangled by the spasm of hysteria, agitated by shudders, his teeth chattering, he got up, put his head out the window, exhaled, in the morning air, the dreadful whinnying of eroto-maniacs and,—silently,—with the miraculous circumspection of a lunatic, opened the door of his room without making the faintest sound, slid like a ghost through the dining room, and arrived at Véronique's door.

A line of yellow light passed beneath it and a more luminous ray streamed through the keyhole. The penitent was still awake. He stopped and put both hands on his head, which was on fire, asking himself what he wanted, what he had come to do . . . when he heard a moan within and did not hesitate.

Abandoning all precaution, he entered and saw what he coveted with such a flagellating desire, the very "harsh scourge of his soul," on her knees, her eyes fixed on the crucifix, her arms crossed on her chest, her face swollen, streaming with tears and, distressing thing, the parquet, before her, wet with her tears. She must have cried like this all night.

The effect of this vision was such as to transform immediately Marchenoir's inspired frenzy into a heartrending compassion. "I am her executioner!" he thought. He was going to rush towards her and help her up, when the poor saint, who had not noticed his intrusion, began to speak.

"My beloved," she said, with a broken voice, "how hard you are for those who love you! They aren't too many, however! What hasn't he done for you, this unfortunate man who only breathes for your glory? . . . He isn't pure before you, it's quite possible . . . Ha! who then is pure? But he's always given all he had, he's wept with all those who are in sorrow's travail and he's had pity on you yourself in the person of those your Church calls the suffering members of your sacred Majesty . . . Is it just, tell me, that he be thrown into the fire for having wanted to save Madeleine? . . ."

Then, in a sort of transport, and her reasoning becoming unsettled, she began to inveigh against her God. Marchenoir, stricken with terror, saw his most stormy passions as a blasphemer for love surpassed by this ingenuous woman whom he had pulled out of extreme filth, like a diamond from alluvium, and whose paradoxical innocences he had hoarded for two years.

"All you want," the delirious woman almost shouted, "except this iniquity that dishonors you. Plunge me back, if you must, into that horrible ditch that he pulled me out of, and then, throw me, like a disgusting rag, into your eternal hell. If you damn me, I'm very sure, at least, *I'll not grate my teeth!*"

Suddenly, as if the presence of her panting friend, immobile and standing at the extremity of her oratory, had disturbed her, she turned around and coming towards him, slowly, her magnificent eyes dilated by all the stupefactions of her dementia, she pronounced distinctly, but with a voice henceforth soft and plaintive, these inconceivable words:

"*Quid feci tibi, aut in quo contristavi te?*"

This interrogation of a victim, that is sung on Good Friday, in the churches with stripped altars, in the antiphon of the adoration of the Cross, and which Véronique, in her distraction, applied, with poignant confusion, to the very person whose distress she had just laid out before God, succeeded in breaking the desperate Marchenoir. Tears gushed from his eyes and sparkled in the two lamps' red glow.

Upon seeing this, the crazed woman came to herself, performing the unconscious gesture common to all beings who suffer at the upper reaches of their soul, and which consists in wiping their forehead with the ends of their fingers, from eyebrows to temples, in order to be rid of care. Then, she let out a cry and, with a movement of irresistible femininity, threw her arms about the neck of her companion in exile.

"O my Joseph!" she said to him, while pressing her head against his chest, "dear miserable man because of me, don't cry, I beg you, your suffering will be over soon . . . Maybe you were here, just now, when I insulted my very sweet Master, and you must have thought I was crazy or extremely ungrateful. I regret them now, as if I had said them to you, my cruel words! . . . It's true, however, that I lost my head! When I saw you so sad, at the back of my room, I thought, for a moment, I was seeing Jesus himself who'd come to accuse me of nastiness and injustice, it's rare I succeed in separating you two, even in my prayers, my two Saviors, both agonizing for love of me and both so poor! . . . Those Latin words, you explained them to me at the Adoration of the Cross and you must've been surprised to hear them,—right?—it seemed to me it was Jesus himself who put them in my mouth, by way of reproach, under your painful appearance, and my mouth repeated them like an echo . . . Don't try to explain it, my dear scholar. You've enough on your mind, without bothering yourself with my craziness . . . You're a prisoner, like the first Joseph, in a very harsh prison, and I can't stop begging God to deliver you from it. Do you think he can resist so persistent a girl for long? . . .

"Ah! that, but,"—she added, straightening up suddenly, and putting her hands on Marchenoir's shoulders, "you don't know then *who you are*, my friend, you don't see anything, you guess nothing. This job of saving others, in spite of your misery, this thirst for justice that eats you alive, this hatred of everyone that inspires you and makes an exile of you,—all that doesn't say anything to you, you who read in the dreams of history and in the faces of life? . . ."

This unusual question,—it was not the first time that Véronique had addressed it to her lamentable friend. It was not any more incredible to him than so many other insoluble or heteroclitic things that had made a paradox of his life. This inhabitant "of the other shore,"—Herzen might have said,—which no other devotee resembled, appeared to have received, at the same time as the gift of perpetual prayer, the superhuman faculty of bringing everything back to so perfectly simple an objective vision that the synthetical Marchenoir was confounded by it. Often, she suggested it, without knowing it herself, and shed light on it, without doubting the wonder of her unconscious pedagogy.

One day, as the scriptural symbolist read in her presence, interpreting the first chapters of Genesis, she interrupted him at the place of the famous justification of Eve's fall: "The serpent deceived me." She said to him: "Turn that around, my friend, and you'll have the consummation of all justice. One way or the other, it must be that the Serpent answers, in turn: '*It's the Woman who deceived me*'..."

Marchenoir had been on the verge of prostrating himself with admiration before this divine ingenuity that obliterated the wisdom of more or less forty subtle doctors of the Church, by forcing, by means of a single naïve phrase, all the energies of Intelligence to be absorbed into the rudimentary concept of Retaliation.

The marvel had been repeated such a large number of times that he regarded this girl much like a prophetess,—all the more incontestable since she was ignorant of it herself, considering herself too honored to receive the lessons of certain apostles who would have trembled while listening to her.

All the same, insofar as what concerned him personally, the awe-struck confidant kept an austere reserve, which rendered him deaf-mute to the amphibological overtures similar to those just made to him, under the specious form of an interrogation full of innocence, but being able, after all, to emanate indifferently from any abyss whatsoever . . .

That this astonishing girl had the intuition of such absolute *solidarity*, that all the attingent ideas of space, time and number, were dissipated like the mist of dreams, and that she grouped, together with the unhappy man who had redeemed her, all the scattered identities of immolated Saviors and defunct, heroic Nourishers, whose story she had recounted to him; that by virtue of a woman's exorbitantly sublime love, he appeared to her, in a substantial fashion, like her Adam, her Joseph of Egypt, her Christ and her King; he did not find it expedient to contravene,—his own thoughts often taking their growth and their definitive being from extra-logical formulas, which the illiterate seer struggled to algebraize, for him, her indeterminable apperceptions of.

But, on that day, vibrating still with the carnal turmoil that had preceded this formal notice, by her, for him to come forward as a God, he felt crushed with humiliation and repentance. Véronique's extraordinary exaltation also frightened him, and he reproached himself bitterly for having, doubtless, encouraged, by his silence, an illusion full of dangers and resolved to protest, in the future, with a sovereign authority.

"Alas," he responded, "to begin with, I see nothing. I know, my sweet visionary, that you believe me called to great things, but how could I believe you? I would need another *sign* than this perpetual agony . . . What I see more clearly is that you are killing yourself. Look, the day has already begun, and you have been without rest for such a long time. You must go to sleep immediately, I demand it, and because I am an important person, you will obey me without discussion. I will throw myself on my bed as well, because I am worn out. *Au revoir*, dear sacrificial victim, sleep in peace and Our Lord will place at your door a half dozen of his greatest angels."

LXVI

Several days later, Marchenoir received from Périgueux the following letter from his family's notary, in response to a hopeless complaint sent several weeks before:

> Sir, I have the honor of responding to your letter of May 25, relative to the definitive settlement of the departed gentleman your father, a settlement that I was unable to conclude any earlier, notwith-

standing my desire to be agreeable to you, because of formalities that needed to be completed and difficulties that we have had in effecting the sale of the property.

All being finally terminated under the best possible conditions, I remit to you, herewith, the detailed accounting of the succession, which results in an amount of *Two thousand five hundred (2500) francs.* As you have given me full authorization and quittance, I send this sum to you by registered letter.

Please accept, sir and dear client, my respectful salutations.

CHARLEMAGNE VOBIDON.

This unexpected message produced on Marchenoir the admirable effect of immediately restoring all his energy. There was in this Périgordian such a spring, that one could always expect some surprising manifestation of its force, at the very moment when he appeared the most knocked down and the most irremediably discomfited. Within the hour, he had pulled himself up by the bootstraps, dusted himself off and made a formidable resolution, that he began, immediately, to act on.

As all the journals were closed off to him and his future book was a distant financial operation, of almost certain failure, he was going to risk this sum that had fallen from heaven, in one of the most hazardous enterprises, but able, all the same,—supposing Fortune smiled on him,—to remunerate the temerarious man. For he was going to be short of resources sooner than later, and this too familiar anguish was added to all the others that he had.

He decided to publish, at his own expense, a periodical pamphlet which he would be the sole editor of, which he would fill with all the indignations he could think of, and which he would hurl, each week, on Paris, like a firebrand. Who knows? Maybe Paris would catch on fire somewhere.

He roughly calculated that with his money alone, without the addition of any fruitful receipt, he could hold out for about two months. All the demons would really need to be mixed up in it though to make it so that the unprecedented vociferation that he was meditating to assail his contemporaries with, had no effect. A favorable circumstance, assuredly, would leap out of the shadows, until then implacable, of his destiny. A partnership, some efficacious adhesion, would allow him to push further ahead and to make himself as redoubtable by the duration as by the savage vigor of his claims and his anathemas.

And also, above all he needed to change his moral hygiene, if he did not want to perish, and the furious activity of so terrible a fight would infallibly discourage the mortal obsession that was killing him.

He considered himself saved and ran to Leverdier's who trembled with fear, seeing a semblance of joy on the habitually desolate visage of his friend. It was something else altogether when he knew his intention.

"But, madman," he said to him, "you want to tempt God then? Your pamphlet will be stifled by the entire press. You will lose, with no profit at all, the money you have just received, which would enable you to live for one entire year, Véronique and you, while permitting you to finish your book. You would need fifty thousand francs of advertisements and the complicity of all the journals, to launch such a machine. The most capable and best-commissioned salesman will not be able to sell ten copies out of one hundred."

His honest henchman, who did not know the desperate man's distress of soul, exhausted in vain the treasures of his wisdom. Marchenoir had made his decision. It was necessary, while groaning, to prepare again for this shipwreck.

Both of them expended so feverish an activity that at the end of eight days, in the middle of the week of the national holiday, the first edition of the weekly *PILLORY* appeared, in the format of the ancient *Lantern*, with a cover the color of fire, offering this strange drawing, dictated by the author to Félicien Rops, who Leverdier had introduced him to: A satyr laughing with tears, fixed by the neck to an immense black post, going from the earth to the sky, and his dirty sabots on a pile of dead bodies.

This pamphlet, which had the fate predicted by Leverdier, and which the journals' silence snuffed out without difficulty, was, nevertheless, noticed by all the artists, and his counterfeit failure is still regarded, by some independent minds, as one of the most deplorable iniquities of this accursed time.

It will suffice to cite two articles to give an idea of this work of high justice and magnificent fury, which tended to have no effect on derailing the train of contemporary opinions,—as if any effect of the simply human Word could accomplish this desirable marvel!

Here then is the first article, with which Marchenoir opened his too short campaign:

THE IRREMISSABLE SIN

This evening, July 14, is over finally, in the muggy lunar brightness of the most delicious of nights, the great national holiday of the Republic of the Vanquished. Ah! it is a little thing, now, this calendrical jubilation, and look at us terribly distant from the anachronous frenzies of the first of the year! This beginning,—already legendary!—of the most villainous of republican solemnities, I have, today, too easily brought it back to mind, faced with the universal constipated effort of patriotism, evidently indefecatable, and possessing an enthusiasm that declares itself from now on incombustible.

No matter what the night did to make itself desirable like a prostitute, and no matter what the Parisian municipality procuress did to multiply her mural incitements with perfect joy, people got manifestly bored. The pissed-on flags of the precedent commemorations floated lamentably over the rare and sooty lanterns, the afflictive glow of which offended the clichéd plaster mask of Republicans, that the boorish piety of some of its faithful had scattered under fake foliage. As always, noble trees had been mutilated or destroyed, to shelter with their expiring leafage drunkenness without conviction or the out-of-doors parties well provisioned by ambient prostitution. No invention, no fantasy, no attempt at novelty, no infusion of unpublished simpletonry, in this imbecilic apotheosis of the Rabble.

We had been too sublime, the first time! Each acephalous person was anxious, then, to make himself a head, to honor the dreadful whore from whom modern France was engendered. The entire nation had rushed to pillage the common treasure of universal stupidity. But, at present, it is quite over, all that. We continue to celebrate the anniversary of the victory of three hundred thousand men over eighty invalids, because we have some honor and because we are faithful to great memories, and also because it is an occasion to sell wine mixed with litharge and donkey piss. One is anxious, above all, to affirm the royalty of the Lout who can at least, on this day, wallow with his croup on the lawn, contaminate the City with his excrement and terrify women with insolent firecrackers. But the faith is gone, as well as the hope of not dying of hunger under a republic whose starving ignominy discourages even the austere supporters who handed the most beautiful empire of the world over to it.

✳

309

This deception of an idiot holiday, this stinking backwash of national shame in the wake of bankruptcy, makes me think, once again, of the not so jolly idea that this miserable French nation is quite decidedly vanquished in all manners imaginable, as it is vanquished even like that, in the opprobrium of its infertile rejoicings.

This Vomit of God does not even have the strength any more to amuse itself ignobly. Of all the ancient superiorities that made it the regulator of peoples, one alone, in truth, has remained,—but so unrecognized, so despised, decried, dishonored, thrown down the drain, that it turns out to have discovered precisely another way of being vanquished, having found the way to convert into its irreparable discomfiture the unique wealth that could still pay its ransom!

France is vanquished militarily and politically, in the East as in the West; it is vanquished in its finances, in its industry and in its commerce; vanquished even scientifically, by a heap of foreigners whose discoveries it does not even know how to use; it is vanquished everywhere and forever, to the point of not being able ever, it seems, to rise up again.

It did not even know how to conserve its superiority over Vice. The most irrefragable documents attest that Protestant cities, like London, Berlin, Lausanne, have the right to consider the juvenile debauchery of Paris as nonexistent, where the sensualist filled with a subtle hypocrisy is barely noticed.

Ah! we are extremely vanquished, arch-vanquished in heart and in mind! We enjoy ourselves like the vanquished and we work like the vanquished. We laugh, we weep, we love, we speculate, we write and we sing like the vanquished. All our intellectual and moral life is explained by this one fact, that we are the cowardly and dishonored vanquished. We have become tributaries of all that has some moving energy in this world in decline, terrified by our inexpressible degradation.

We are like a city of shame sitting on a great river of depravity, come down for us from the decried mountains of the ancient history of nations, which humankind has cursed.

But finally, we have a superiority, one only, incontestable, to tell the truth, and absolute: literary superiority. Ascending so victorious, that no one in the world bothers to affirm it anymore, and that anything capable of an intellectual vibration, in any place wheresoever, humbly solicits a dog house under the fat kitchen sink where French literature is seasoned.

One could believe that France, overcome with gratitude, no longer knows with what renascent Phoenix down to pad the bed of its half-dozen marvelous children who make up its supreme glory. One ought to suppose, at least, that it rewards them with riches and honors and that afterwards it declares itself completely unworthy to lick their footprints . . . It makes them simply die of misery in obscurity.

It does not have enormous enough contempt and snubs to saturate them. From Baudelaire to Verlaine, all the abominations and all the filth have been poured into waterfalls of drenching rain on all their shining faces. Journals, full of terror, have barricaded themselves in with fury against these ideal victims of the plague, contact with whom terrifies contemporary boorishness. This horror is so great and the repression that it demands is so attentive, that one was able to see ill-fated imbeciles condemned to perish for despair as a result of deceptive inculpation of talent and originality.

But this war would be poorly waged if it were content to be defensive. Literary harlots have consequently been aroused to supplant their genius. Three hundred journals go forward to brush them off the pavement, with a diligent hand, and universal suffrage is their dispensary. Old and young, suffering from cradle-cap or baldness, liquid or dusty, it sufficed that their stupidity or their ignobility be irreproachable. One would go even so far as to hand them a semblance of freshness, if it is one more stew for senile concupiscences whose erethism is sought after.

To Baudelaire agonizing in indigence and quasi-mad, one opposes, for example, a Jean Richepin gleaming with glory and stuffed with gold. This latter, moreover, perfectly assured of being first among the woman's children, judges his share insufficient and vociferates under his cap against the robbed patron. The delectable Paul Bourget, cherished *preface writer* for barons, stands up on his little tail, whistling against the immense artist Barbey d'Aurevilly, who lies down, formidable, at the far end of heaven, and . . . he effaces him. Flaubert, in turn, is cut into pieces and nibbled on by the acarid Maupassant, engendered by his magnanimous testicles, the which, having become his protégé, promulgates literarily procurement and standardization.

No one, among these greats, is excepted. The garbage collector passes through the street and calls for men of talent. The world's queen wants no more of it. She is sick at heart on account of these tubercles. What she needs, at the present hour, exclusively, is the oil of stupidity and the triple extract of putrescence, which are offered to her by the shady hands of dealers of juice that her own deliquescence is in the process of saturating.

It would be long, the procession of mediocre and abject people, that the cheese of our decadence has spontaneously given birth to for the inexorable devouring of esthetic sense!

And to begin with, the most glorious of all these elect,—the thundering Jupiter of French imbecility,—Georges Ohnet, the squalid millionaire hunchback whose submissive prose effects a suction of one hundred thousand ecus a year on the obscene pulp of the bourgeois who are contemptuous of art. Immediately after him, his illustrious son, Albert Delpit, virtuoso of the correct hearth and the vaunted assessor of psychological starch, the eunuch Lovelace with an innocently predatory squint.

Then, the dirty plebs: Bonnetain, the Paganini of solitudes, whose frenetic hand knew how to work the bow;—Armand Sylvestre, the eternal rhapsodist of the fart, who was adored by multitudes for his latrine idylls;—the virginal Fouquier, haughty moralist, heir to the bedstead of the late Feydeau, his four feet shod with all the conjugal disciplines and a rigid judge in the matter of literary dignity;—the aquatic Mendès, with azure squamae, Judas' friend through charity and lapidarist of adultery by a spirit of justice, a type of two-faced Semite with double sex, the one to empoison, the other to betray;—Dumas *fils*, legislator of divorce and of *setting things right*, who invented replacing the Cross with the speculum, for the redemption of societies; Alphonse Daudet, the Tartarin on the Alps of success, for having bothered to be born a copyist of Dickens, a too fecund eunuch whom he has found the means of cutting into sections for fifteen years;—the two oracular Bactrians, Wolff and Sarcey, from whom rise all human judgments and whose calamitous disappearance, supposing it conjectural, would produce immediately universal blindness;—and finally, so as not to name fifty others, Ernest Renan, the pot-bellied sage, the fine scientific chamber pot, whence is exhaled towards heaven, in redoubted volutes of eagles, the unctuous odor of an exiled soul of commodities that witnessed his birth, and regretting his fatherland among the papers that he carries away with him, like ever-precious relics, for the critical education of future centuries! . . .

After that, what do you want them to do, the little flock of true artists, who know nothing at all except how to shiver in the light and who were never able to prepare great potboilers for the populace? They are not numerous, today, five or six, at that, and the dirty avalanche has little merit in swallowing them up.

That would be enough, however, if France had any heart left in it, to claw back, intellectually, first place. Europe has no living writer, among the young, to balance out the two or three novelists of genius, who are dying of famine this very minute, in the voluntary dungeon of their probity as artists. The death of Dostoevsky was greeted with universal silence around Paris, and Paris, on its knees before the comedians that dishonor it, has not even one morsel of bread to give them who still keep its old symbolic boat from capsizing in the dung! . . .

If that is not the irremissible Sin that is spoken about in the Gospel, I ask what it might be, this great sin, this blasphemy against the Spirit, that nothing, it is said, can pardon . . .

It is incredible that Providence would have made men of genius expressly to be vomited. The adventure, I well know, happened to a famous prophet. But this Vomiting has picked itself up again and gone off to speak with the most terrible city of all the East, which listened to it respectfully. Paris would not have listened to Jonas in any way, shape or form and that unfortunate servant of God would have perhaps been forced to supplicate his shark to swallow him.

Men unfortunate enough, today, to be great writers, must wait for death and be diligent and sure to desire it, for their life is from that moment forward without savor as without object. All that they can do, supposing them saints, is to supplicate a terrible God—too tolerant!—to consider them, in turn, as less than nothing and not to open, for their vengeance, the stercoraceous riparian locks that evidently menace Paris with the only deluge it might merit, and that one is surprised to see so obstinately closed!

The other article that appeared in the sixth and last number of the *Pillory*, was, for Marchenoir, the most scandalous of all derisions of his enraged destiny. This article had a resounding success, enormous, and this success was useless to him. The receipts from this number, the only one that sold, barely covered his last expenses, without giving him any means to continue. The printer, full of defiance, and perhaps threatened, obstinately refused to extend any credit.

The pamphleteer thus saw luck slip away laughing at the very moment when it appeared to present itself, and he definitively had to renounce all hope, with the aggravation of the growing certainty that his triumph would have been assured if he had only thought of starting his first issue with this great shot.

THE PRUSSIAN HERMAPHRODITE
ALBERT WOLFF

Last Wednesday, I apologized for speaking about a subaltern rascal by the name of Maubec, alleging that no one, in the world of journals, surpassed him in ignominy. I called him, for this reason: *The King of the Press*.

Some readers found that excessive. I was reproached for having let myself be carried away by my subject, for having given too much importance to that strange runt, at the expense of Albert Wolff and some others, with his much more blinding splendor of moral depravity.

I confess that this reproach can seem founded. It is incontestable that from this point of view, the columnist of the *Figaro*,—not today, but at that period of time—has more credit and more scope.

He soars over the earth, this condor of abomination! He makes off with, so powerfully, by himself, universal contemporary putrefaction, that he becomes positively *volatile* and has the air of taking off into the clouds.

But, without claiming to equal him, one can still be devilishly prodigious, and that is the case with the little Maubec.

Moreover, all these monsters engendered from the same greenish oozing of our carrion society, in immediate copulation with nothingness, are so identical in origin, that one always believes he is contemplating the most horrible among them, when he regards them successively.

Albert Wolff had his Plutarch in Monsieur Toudouze, the cynocephalous novelist who could have been content with being an impotent of letters, but who chose to keep close watch on the "great journalist," as if his pestilence did not suffice.

The book about this dog is, in effect, an attempt at Albert Wolff's apotheosis.

Certainly, I can flatter myself with having read a tremendous amount in my existence of forty years! But, never, have I read anything like it.

Here the baseness of the flattery has something of the supernatural to it, as one has found the secret of *admiring* a so-called human being, whose name alone is an evocative formula of all there is that is most dishonoring and hideous in humanity.

It seems that Monsieur Toudouze is a wealthy man who has no need to work at this dirty profession, which the most agonizing poverty would not excuse. But the vanity of a louse of letters is as inscrutable and deep as a night in space, it is a dreadful counterpart to the miraculous power of God . . . and this man, who goes looking for his fodder at the missing testicles of Albert Wolff,—in the inexpressible hope of a familiarity to appall lepers,—is one hundred times more confounding than a thaumaturge who would reanimate old bones.

The late Bastien Lepage, whom distant physical and moral resemblances rendered sympathetic to Albert Wolff, portrayed him, one day, in the ignoble slovenliness of his interior.

This portrait, resembling as much as possible a gorilla, had a terrifying success in the Salon of 1880.

The brutal as well as precious mediocrity of the painter, had found there his formula.

It was demonstrated that Bastien Lepage had been engendered to paint Wolff, and Wolff himself engendered to be surprised by Bastien Lepage's genius, whose destiny was, from then on, fulfilled and who, promptly, went to tuck the former back in bed, in the stinking gloom of their common esthetic.

This portrait should be acquired by the State and conserved with great care in our national Museum. It would recount most eloquently our history as a Tacitus could not, supposing that a French Tacitus were possible, and that the despairing platitude of our republican rabble would not discourage him.

He is well enough known by the people on the boulevard, this large hunchback with his head sunk between his shoulders, like a tumor between two excrescences; with the lopsided gait of a German dolt, that no Parisian frequentation could knock the rough edges off of after twenty years,—a boorish gawky gait that seems to encourage kicks, more imperiously than the abyss should invoke the abyss.

When he deigns to speak with someone nearby, the dextral oscillation of his horrible head opens at a painful angle of forty-five degrees to the vertebrae and forces his shoulder to rise a bit more, which gives the almost fantastic impression of the face of a fish emerging from behind a reef.

At that moment, one would think that that carcass was about to fall apart like a bad piece of furniture sold on credit at Crépin's, and the mild fear becomes a hope when the monster is shaken by this hysterical combination of neighing and chuckling, which substitutes with him for the virility of frank laughter.

Planted on immense legs that one might think had belonged to another individual, and that have the appearance of wanting to be rid of, with each pace, the disgusting pail of filth that they hold up regretfully, kept in equilibrium by the simian-like lateral appendages that seem to implore the Lord's good earth,—one wonders about his passage and comes to realize the foolish self-respect that still prevents him, at his age, from frankly getting down on all fours on the macadam.

✳

As for the visage, or, at least, what passes for it, I do not know what epithets could express the paradoxical, ravaging disgust of it.

I have said, a bit inconsiderately, that Maubec acted as a foil for Wolff and rendered him, thereby, almost handsome.

I had only, at that time, the stinking Maubec before my eyes, and I did not sort out my feelings very well.

In reality, this vomitive rogue is above all leprous. He carries on his face,—where so many slaps ring out,—the infinite purulence of a soul picked up for him in the gutter, and it has the appearance more of rotting flesh than of the monster to it.

Wolff is a pure monster, the *essential* monster, and he has no need of any pus to inspire horror. He could grow blue mushrooms on his visage, but it would not make him any more frightening. Maybe it would even help . . .

His general appearance recalls immediately, but in an invincible way, the famous *calf-headed man*, that was exhibited last year, and whose frightful image sullied our city walls for so long.

I know a poet who had heard: *the Wolff-headed man* and he will not budge an inch from it. He found, maybe, a bit less spiritual vivacity in the journalist's eye. Close up, he would have thought them to be twins.

✳

The entire hairless face, like that of an Annamite or a papion baboon, is the color of an enormous white cheese, in which a traveler's solid excrement was churned for a long time.

The nose, passably bony, as befits gibbosiacs, without finesse nor aquiline curvature, a little hideous at the extremity, solidly planted moreover, but without plastic precision, evokes confusedly the idea of a drawing of a religious monument, that the discouraged savages would have abandoned in an infertile plain.

On high, the eyebrows in the form of a cirrus cloud fly into the Tartar's face, above a pair of cupid eyes, slanting and pocketed like an old wench who has become a go-between and well-patronized patroness of a vile dive.

The mouth is of hilarious bestiality, populous cheekiness, monstrous supposable perversity.

It is a rictus, it is a vagina, it is a maw, it is a sucker, it is a dirty hiatus. It is impossible to say what it is . . .

The most despicable images present themselves on their own to the mind.

One cannot stop believing that this mouth of a bad slave, or of a discredited spy, was purposely made to gulp down filth and to lick the soles of the first master to come along who does not fear cleaning his shoe on that living mascaron.

And that is everything. There is no chin. The thick, hanging lower lip of this dotard of tomorrow, recovers nothing but the receding funnel bottom of his fish snout, which disappears just like that, to our sudden consternation, in the most ridiculous accoutrement of a sordid valet that one ever encountered on our boulevards.

✳

The sire's morals are in perfect harmony with his physique. His life, devoid of all petticoat peripeteia,—for the excellent reason of one of the most frigid cases of hermaphroditism,—is as dull as that of the first poseur who comes along, whose career would have been without tumult.

Albert Wolff was born Jewish and Prussian, in Cologne, in the arms of Béranger's grandmother.

Having arrived at the *virile* age,—in his case, derisory,—one finds him a copyist of proceedings at a notary public in Bonn, mixed up with University students, where he studies psychology.

He amuses himself even, says his biographer, by decapitating frogs,—while waiting for those that on one of his better days he will need to eat.

Then, the literary vocation catching on fire all of a sudden in him, like a torch, he writes *William the Weaver*, a moral story that makes families cry, one is assured.

Only, these things happened in Prussia and his ambition could not be satisfied with such small expenses.

He needed Paris and the Café Mulhouse, where the editors of the hebdomadal Figaro gathered then, around 1857, that completely healthy fetus of the powerful journal that reigns today over five parts of the world.

It had nothing at all to do with having genius to be allowed to share in the fortune of the periwig maker.

It had most of all to do with making Villemessant laugh and the oaf had arrived.

From that day forward, he was judged worthy of joining the group of clowns, by whom France has become, intellectually, what you know, and he never again stopped rising, slowly, doubtless, because of the weight of his large mind, but with the infallible security of a woodlouse.

The heroic Toudouze relates, without any charm, the story of that dull journalistic Odyssey, judged by him to be one hundred times more epic than the Odyssey of old Ulysses.

He stops here and there,—like an itchy donkey,—to exhale admirable idiotic reflections, treating of Aurélien Scholl, Jules Noriac, Alexandre Dumas, *père* and *fils*, or all the other lucky bastards of Parisian *arrival*.

Fundamentally, all this history is nothing more than a savings account book, where the accountant inscribes exactly the receipts and expenditures of its hero.

One can see quite clearly that that there is the essential thing for narrator and narrated.

Also, what exultation for the former, when he relates the monetary success of this honorable brochure: the *Mémoirs of Theresa, written by herself*, memoirs written by Wolff, in collaboration with Blum and Peragallo, and what desolate lyrical accents, when her implacable conscience forces her to mention a gambling loss of *one hundred ninety-five thousand francs*.

This catastrophe, which happened in 1877, was, without a doubt, for many, in the profession of the Salon, that of the *Figaro's* hermaphrodite.

He had, one minute, thought about suicide, but he kept his reasoning lucid, that after all it would be quite imbecilic to make oneself perish, like a vulgar loser, when he had in hand the rich breast of the milk cow of a sincere Salon.

Fortune resumed then to roll in his favor, dating from this salutary reflection.

He became very powerful, his Prussian *sincerity* having no longer any limits, and, at the same time, misfortune having caused the scales to drop that darkened his genius, the simple clown that he had been until then was replaced by a great moralist, whom the most severe magistrates consult, with respect, and who holds contemporary humanity under his arbitration.

✳

Such is his last, and probably, final incarnation. Albert Wolff died in the skin of a revered moralist.

We have come to this point.

This semblance of a man, failed as a eunuch, this *Germanic blue-stocking*,—following Glatigny's expression,—has at his disposal so great an authority, that the most sublime artist in the world would become popular at his good pleasure, and that he has the power to have heads fall or to determine the verdicts of their acquittal.

This verminous Jew of Prussia is the king whom we have elected in our inexpressible debasement, the king respected for his opinion, as Louis XIV was not, and who all the crawling villains of journals slaver before in fear.

Bismark can sleep tranquilly.

His good lieutenant is the master of France.

He is responsible for emasculating us, just as he emasculated himself, and for bringing us so back down to earth, that there is nothing left but to trample us under like people's dung, good for enriching the soil of the universal Germany of the future.

✳

When the war of 1870 broke out, the horrible rogue's situation, not stable as it is today, was no longer tenable.

He saw himself forced to disappear, like the majority of his compatriots. He wandered, he said, through all of Europe, like an unsated jackal, waiting for the Prussian Gladiator to have finished the job and for the old French lion, exhausted by old age, to be utterly cut down, before he came back to finish him off with his despicable gob.

He did not dare to return immediately after the Commune. There was still, for him, too much seething and too much aggression in the Parisian air.

He made himself imperceptible, he flattened himself under the furniture like a bug, melting into the woodwork.

With the woodlice tenacity of his double race, he held on to the bitumen, wiped off the spittle and filth that he was inundated with by passersby stupefied by his impudence, wishing, all the same, to impose himself on Paris, that an iota of pride counseled him to escape.

Humble, but inextractable to begin with, victorious and arrogant at the very end.

✳

It was not enough for him to have settled among us. He had to reign by means of the *Figaro*, and Villemessant was vile enough to abandon it to him.

One knows, besides, the legatee's gratitude, and the words, revelatory of the beauty of his soul, that he let escape, in the manner of a funeral orison, on the mountainous carcass of his benefactor.

He had just paid fourteen hundred fifty francs back into the journal's coffers, for a gaming debt contracted with the patron.

Almost immediately, the telegraph brings the news of Villemessant's death.

After the first *emotion*, Wolff says to his comrades: "I never had much luck with our editor-in-chief. If the news had arrived a few hours earlier, I would not have paid the fourteen hundred fifty francs and the family would never have reclaimed them."

The only thing that remains to be added to this anecdote is the German journals' hymn of joy, upon learning about the sinister farce of the journalist's naturalization, and congratulating Germany on having gotten rid of a proud *scoundrel* at the expense of that imbecile of France who was quick to receive him.

I spoke about gaming losses. A study on Albert Wolff would not be complete if one forgot to mention this essential trait.

Extremely tranquil as respects women, he made up for it at the gaming den.

Paris never knew a more fanatical player.

This passion was such that he instinctively avoided all honorable circles,—if they even existed,—and frequented only the infamous gaming dens where he was more at ease to satisfy it.

Detested by other players, feared by directors and loaners, because of his formidable situation at the *Figaro*, he reigned like a despot, there as elsewhere, abhorred but inexpellable.

Profiting from the terror he inspired, he was able to have enormous sums of credit extended to him. When he had lost his *pants*, as he expressed it, the lender was obliged, nine times out of ten, to wait for him to win his poor money back again, without any hope of return for the service even,— Wolff having displayed his principle of borrowing always and of never loaning.

The money he won, moreover, was promptly moved offshore.

The good Prussian faithfully sent his cash to a Berlin banker, and was quick to burn the receipts,— or to make believe he had burned them,—to avoid having to withdraw sums or to dispute entitlements, before settlement dates, complicated turpitude that I leave for competent meditations.

Nothing equals the insolent arrogance of this Disgusting person, in view of the miserable wretches that he can flatter himself to have terrified by his quill and nothing either could be compared to his humble reserve, when he is in the presence of a veritable man whom his vile rumors cannot touch.

It is said that he had some duels. I was not there, alas! but I strongly doubt that he accepts them going forward.

The time is passed when he has need of asking for them.

Then, age descends on this monster, as it would descend on the august face of a patriarch, sure thing that he knows will, perhaps, get worse from day to day, and, more than anyone, the VIRGINAL Albert Wolff must fear to be run through.

※

One knows that my soul is not open to such heady hopes, and that I do not expect any sort of thing in an even distant future.

However, if we should come upon a single minute of energy and generous revolt against the appalling vermin who devours us, it seems to me that we ought to employ it, that blessed minute, to immediately expel this wretched Prussian, who empoisons us, who sullies us, who defecates on us at his pleasure; who dares to permit himself to moralize to us and to judge us;—as if there was not enough rage over having been vanquished and trampled on by a million *men*, and it was necessary for us still to swallow the supreme humiliation of being oppressed, by this old BITCH without a soul, or heart, or sex, or conscience,—more pestilential, in his person, than the stagnant detritus of all a people in putrefaction!

If it finally arrives, the thrice desired hiccough of liberating disgust, it will be necessary to jump on the brooms, on the shovels, on the andirons, on the whips and the scourges, on any object suited to the extirpation of a poisonous malefactor, and to throw him back over the frontier,—with irremediable maledictions,—this German vomit, this enemy filth, this ineffable psychological and moral monstrosity, that a century of glory will not absolve us for having put up with!

LXVII

A misery darker than ever descended, at that time, on the rue des Fourneaux, and, so that nothing was wanting in the throes of mortal agony that were about to begin, Leverdier disappeared brusquely from Marchenoir's life.

This sublime being, seeing the imminence and enormity of peril, was determined, without warning, to sell the not considerable furniture and collection of books that he possessed and, after having given the money to his friend,—departed to live in the country, in Burgundy, with an old aunt who had been entreating him for many years.

This relative was keeping a small fortune for him that he was the sole heir to, and Leverdier would be living easy one day. But she did not intend to send him money to let him subsist in Paris, declaring to him that she was anxious to have him close to her when she *closed her eyes*, and that in Burgundy, he would live amply, in the house that would belong to him after her death, as if he were already the absolute master of it.

Leverdier calculated that in this way it would be more useful for Marchenoir and that he could easily send to him, each month, some money that would always prevent him at least from dying of hunger.

By the time Marchenoir had learned of his Mameluke's heroic decision, it was irrevocable. Leverdier had sold everything and deposited on the unfortunate man's table the several hundred francs that he had collected.

There was no explosion. Marchenoir lowered his head at the sight of this money and two slow tears,—issued from the most intimate wells of his grief,—ran down his pallid and already furrowed cheeks.

Leverdier, moved, drew near and hugged him tenderly.

"My dear poor man," he said, "do not be afflicted, if you know that I am going in peace. It is alright if I have the strength to separate from Véronique and you . . . I have not gotten rid of anything that was really precious to me, and even if I had, what would it matter? Do you not know that your life is more dear to me than any trinket that there might be in the world? Besides, have we not had, for a long time now, a common destiny? I want to save you, in order to save myself, you understand? You must live and this was the only way . . . We will be separated for some time. Again, what difference does it make? . . . I wish from the bottom of my heart all imaginable prosperities for my dear old aunt, who is certainly going to overwhelm me with chores, but it is impossible for me, with the best intentions in the world, to forget that I am her heir and that her fortune, one day or another, will belong to *us* . . . Then, Marchenoir, what an existence with Véronique, in that delicious countryside where we will have our own home! What peace! What perfect security! . . . But still, one must live until that unknown epoch. Lift up your heart! Deliverance is near, maybe, and when the universe rejects you, you have a proud friend, I guarantee it!"

Marchenoir, somber throughout, from the bottom of his emotions, responded to the consoler:

"It would be better for you, my devoted Georges, if you had never known a man so fatal to all those who loved him. The misfortune of certain individuals is contagious as well as incurable, and I have little faith in this peaceable existence that you show me in the future . . . However, I do not want to make you sad by my dark presentiments which can, after all, lead me astray. It would be a despicable and insensitive cruelty to pay you back like that for the extraordinary service you have rendered me . . . Véronique will return in a few moments. We will make a goodbye breakfast and accompany you to the train station . . . Ah! my old comrade, I had dreamed of something better than all this! . . . I have often been accused of ingratitude, because I refused to let my conscience wallow in certain hands that had welcomed me, but it was fortunate, all the same, that I was born a yokel, for I would not have been ungrateful enough as a good prince.—*Beatius est dare quam accipere.*[1] Such would have been, I believe, my motto, and this text would have made my majesty contemptible and my feet clay . . .

"You are, if nothing else, the king of impertinence, a hopeless beggar," responded the other, "and you could have spared me your motto which has nothing to do with this. One never knows who gives nor who receives," he added profoundly. "There, that is what I could teach you if you did not know it already better than I do. You have saved my skin in the past, I am endeavoring today to save your spirit, for your spirit is necessary to me so that I do not break my neck on the dark roads where we wade *per multam merdam,*[2] as Luther said. What do you have to say to that?"

The two friends continued a conversation that was much better than worse and agreed to let Véronique believe that Leverdier was going to be absent because of some family business and would doubtless return soon,—the real truth could quite possibly occasion a crisis of desolation that neither the one nor the other of them felt able to support.

Leverdier parted then that very evening, leaving his companion from then on alone, with the overwhelming impression that they had embraced for the last time and that they would never see each other again!

LXVIII

Salic law was never written down, because it was the vital, essential law of the French monarchy, and any attempt at redaction would have delimited it. The absolute is intranscribable.

For this reason, the Crime of being poor in not mentioned clearly in any code, nor in any compilation of penal jurispru-

---

1 Latin for "It is more blessed to give than to receive."
2 Latin for "through much shit."

dence. What is more, it is classified among the minor offenses within the jurisdiction of correctional tribunals and likened to vagabondage, which is, itself, a consequence of poverty.

But this silence is a peremptory sanction of the universal terror that refuses to specify its object.

Indisputably, Poverty is the most enormous of crimes, and the only one that no circumstance could attenuate in the eyes of an equitable judge. It is such a crime, that treason, incest, parricide, or sacrilege, appear small, in comparison, and solicit social sympathy.

Also, humankind has never been mistaken about it, and the infallible instinct of all people, in any place whatsoever on earth, has always struck with an identical reprobation the titularly holders of rags or an empty stomach.

Since one could enact any specific punishment for a type of violation that the terrifying legislatures did not consent to define, all infamous or afflictive forms of unanimous condemnation accumulate on the Poor. To be assured of coming out right, one piled on their head the multitude of expiations, amongst which it was impossible to make a choice, without danger of characterizing the forfeiture.

The indigent were not condemned formally either by fire, or by quartering, or by the strappado, or by flaying, or by impalement, or even by the guillotine. No legal disposition ever made it precise that one had to hang them, emasculate them, pull out their nails, blind them, put them in a barrel of molten lead, expose them, covered in molasses, to the scorching heat of the sun, or simply drag them, after having removed their skin, in a field of freshly mown lucerne . . . None of these charming punishments were literally applied to them, by virtue of any explicit law.

Only the tormentor genius, which was called societal Force, knew how to assemble for them, in a single spray of sovereign tribulation, all this scattered flora of criminal penalties. They were serenely, tacitly, excommunicated from life and made into outcasts. Every *man of the world*,—whether he knows it or not,—carries within himself an absolute contempt of Poverty, and such is HONOR's profound secret, that is the cornerstone of oligarchies.

To receive a thief at one's table, a murderer or a comedian, is a plausible and recommended thing,—if their industries prosper. The mucous membranes of the most delicate consideration could not suffer from it. It is even demonstrated that a certain virginity is recuperated by contact with poisoners of children,—as soon as they have gorged on gold.

The most lily-like innocences offer, in secret, the dew of their young vows to the gleaming Minotaur, and the most virtuous mothers weep sweet tears at the thought that one day, maybe, that millionnaire monopolizer, who has ruined a hundred families, will have the kindness of busying himself with the conjugal disembowelment of their "dear child."

But the opprobrium of poverty is absolutely inexpressible, because it is, fundamentally, the one stain and the only sin. It is such an enormous culpa, that the Lord God chose it for his own, when he made himself man to assume everything.

He wanted to be called, *par excellence*, the Poor One and God of the Poor. This gluttonous Savior,— *homo devorator et potator*, as the Jews designated him,—who came only to get drunk and to stuff his face with tortures, had judiciously selected Poverty to be the innkeeper. Also, honorable people have reproved, with a common voice, the scandal of such an orgy, and prohibited, at all times, frequentation of this divinely provisioned hostess.

And thus, soon, it will be two thousand years already since the Church has advocated poverty. Innumerable saints have embraced it, in order to resemble Jesus Christ, and the verminous proscript has not risen a millionth of a notch up in decent and well-raised people's esteem.

The fact is, that in effect, *voluntary* poverty is still a luxury, and, by consequence, it is not true poverty, which all men abhor. One can, assuredly, *become* poor, but on condition that the will is in it. St. Francis of Assisi was a lover, not a poor man. He was not *indigent* in anything, because he possessed his God and lived, by ecstasy, outside the sensible world. He bathed in the gold of his luminous tatters . . .

True poverty is involuntary, and its essence is that it can never be desired. Christianity realized the greatest miracle possible by aiding men to support it, by promising ulterior compensations. If there were no compensations, to hell with it all! It is insane to hope for anything better from our nature.

A plantigrade, endowed with reason and deprived of religious hope, is strictly incapable of accepting this jail of filth and consenting to a harsher treatment than what a parricide is given, for having lost his fortune or for being born without money. If he resigns himself to life without the Decalogue and without the eucharist, nothing can be said about him, other than that he is either a coward or an imbecile. From this point of view, the nihilists are one hundred times more correct. Let them all fall, let them all perish, let them all disappear in God's thunder, if one must endure indefinitely this abominable farce of suffering *for nothing*!

Yesterday evening, a millionaire cretin, who never assisted anybody, lost a thousand louis in a gambling circle, at the same time that forty poor girls whom this money would have saved fell, due to hunger, into the irremediable vortex of prostitution; and the charming viscount, whom all Paris knew so well, exposed the most authentic tits, in a robe the color of the fourth moon of Jupiter, the price of which would have nourished, for one month, eighty old men and one hundred twenty children!

So long as these things are seen under the cupola of impassible constellations, and recounted with tenderness by the ragtag bunch of journals, there will be—despite all the hackneyed claptrap and all the damned exhortations,—an absolute slap in the face of Justice, and,—for the souls dispossessed of the hope of a future life,—an ever growing need to crush humankind.

"Ah! you teach us that we are on earth to amuse ourselves. Well! let us go amuse ourselves, we others, dying of hunger and dressed in rags. You never see those who weep and you think of nothing but diverting yourself. But those who have wept while watching you, for thousands of years, will one day divert themselves when it's their turn and,—given Justice is decidedly absent,—they will come, at any rate, to inaugurate the simulacrum, using you for their entertainment.

"Given that we are criminals and the damned, we will promote ourselves to the dignity of perfect demons, in order to exterminate you ineffably.

"From now on, no more prayers muttered at the street corners, by shivering, hungry beggars, while you pass. There will be no more claims or harsh recriminations. It is finished, all that. We will become silent . . .

"You keep the money, the bread, the wine, the trees and the flowers. You keep all the joys of life and the inalterable serenity of your consciences. We will no longer make claims for anything, we will no longer desire all these things that we have desired and asked for in vain, for so many centuries. Our complete despair will promulgate, from this moment, *against ourselves*, the definitive prescription that adjudges them to you.

"Only, be on your guard! . . . We keep the fire, while supplicating you to not be too surprised by the next fricassee. Your palaces and your hotels will burn very well, when it pleases us, for we have attentively listened to the lessons given by your chemistry professors and we have invented small devices that you will marvel at.

"As for your persons, they will be made to acclimatize their last breath under the heelless sole of our threadbare slippers, at several hundred paces from your fuming intestines; and we will find, maybe, a large enough number of swine or errant dogs to console your chaste companions and the very innocent virgins that you have impregnated with your precious loins, with a bit of love . . .

"After that, if God's existence is not a perfect joke, which the example of your *virtues* predisposes us to believe, let him exterminate us when it is his turn, let him damn us without remedy, and let all be finished! Hell will not be, probably, more atrocious than the life that you have made for us.

"But in this case, we will be forced to confess before all his angels, that we were his instruments for consuming you, for he must have had enough of your visages! He must be, at least, as disgusted as we are, this hypothetical Lord; he has, doubtless, vomited you out one hundred times, and, if you subsist, it is because, apparently, he has the habit of returning to his vomit!?"

Such is the canticle of the modern poor, from whom the fortunate on earth,—not satisfied to possess all,—have imprudently snatched belief in God. It is the *Stabat* of desperate men.

They have remained standing, at the foot of the Cross, since the bloody Mass of Good Friday,—in the middle of darkness, stenches, derelictions, thorns, nails, tears, and agonies. Throughout the generations they have whispered impassioned prayers into the ear of the divine Host, and, all of a sudden,—it is revealed to them, with a spurt of electrical science, this dusty gibbet where the teeth of beasts have devoured their Redeemer . . . Damn! and then, they will go amuse themselves!

Consuming wealth. So who has noticed the symbolic enormity of this familiar locution? Does not money represent the life of the poor who die for want of it? The human phrase is deeper than one imagines. This phrase is strangely suggestive of the idea of anthropophagy, and it is not completely impossible, following this contingent idea, to represent to oneself a place of pleasure, like a butcher's stall or a simple bouillon restaurant where the succulent flesh of beggars is sold in portions. Gourmets, for example, would choose the rump, and those on a budget would use the giblets, all the while pleasure-seekers recovering from a recent night out would be content with a modest consommé made of their disadvantaged brothers. One is shocked by the tangible form such a dream takes, when the banal meaning of this phrase is interrogated.

All rich people who do not consider themselves the INTENDANTS *and the* DOMESTICS *of the Poor, are more loathsome than thieves and more despicable than fratricides.* Such is the spirit of Christianity and even the letter of the Gospel. Natural evidence that can, at a pinch, do without the supernatural Christian's sanction.

It is fortunate for robbers and assassins that the so-called thinking animal is so refractory to the perfect syllogism. A devilishly long time ago he would have come to an end by disembowelment and grilling, because pestilence, well perceived, by the wicked rich, is not humanly supportable. But the conclusion will come, all the same, and probably soon,—having been announced from all sides by undeniable prodomes . . .

The rich will understand too late, that the money that they were the fully proud usufructuaries of ABSOLUTELY *does not belong to them*, that it is a horror to have shouted from the mountains, to see a hard-working dog of a woman, with an infecund vulva, carrying on her head the bread of two hundred families of workers, stoked by journalists and shady-dealers into the ambush of a strike; or to dream that there is somewhere a noble artist who dies of starvation, at the same hour that a person who declares bankruptcy dies of indigestion! . . .

They writhe in terror, the pig-hearted Rich and their pitiless females, they bellow while opening their mouths, where the blood of the miserable wretches will appear in putrefied clots! They will forget, an inexpressible forgetfulness, the decent behavior and charming attitudes found in salons when their flesh is removed and their heads are burned with ardent coals,—and the shadow of a nauseous journalist will no longer be there, to inform a bourgeois public going to the dogs. Because it is indispensably necessary that it ends, all this filth of avarice and human egotism!

The German or Russian dynamiters are merely precursors or, if you like, sub-accessories to the unparalleled Tragedy, when the Poorest and, by consequence, the most Criminal among men that the ferocity of cowards has ever punished,—will end up judging everyone on earth in the Fire of Heaven!

LXIX

About eight months after his departure from Paris, where he had never laid foot again, Leverdier received in Burgundy this letter from Marchenoir:

> My dearest Georges,
> I am dying, and I have perhaps two days to live. I begin with that, so that you have less to suffer. As for Véronique, she has been at Sainte-Anne's[1] for two weeks now. It was after I conducted her there that a wagon ran over me and crushed my chest. They found on me, by good fortune, a letter from you that revealed my address and they brought me back, dying, to the rue des Forneaux.
> I moaned for several days. At this moment, I write to you from my bed, in a lot of pain, but, with a becalmed mind from now on, as it behooves recipients of eternity. I am not troubled, not even by the thought that this *necessary* letter will kill you with grief. I am already in the serenity of the dead . . .
> God wanted my life to end like this, so it is quite alright and nothing better could have happened to me. I am no longer the *Desperate Man* . . . I have asked, just now, the old concierge to go fetch me a priest.
> However, my friend, I do not want to go without saying goodbye to you one last time. Hurry, I beg you, if you can, without losing one second. These last days, when one thought that I was going to die at any moment, my worst suffering was a fearful thirst, the thirst of Jesus in his agony. I saw

---

1 Sainte-Anne's: a mental hospital in the sixteenth arrondissement of Paris.

rivers and waterfalls everywhere, that my dried lips could not reach, and,—I do not know how,—your memory was mixed in with these visions of my delirium. Your face appeared to me smiling, at the bottom of springs, and my thirst for you got mixed up confusedly with my thirst for water from the fountains . . .

You will pray for me, right, my only friend, poor joyous heart that I have made so sad? You are not a man of great faith! It does not matter, pray for me all the same . . . I will be near you. The souls of the dead, you see, surround us invisibly. They cannot go far, as they no longer have bodies and the notion of distance is inapplicable to pure spirits. I remember having explained that to you . . . In several hours, I will be the silent soul of a dead man, a defunct, a deceased. Maybe I will suffer a lot in this new state and I will have need of your prayers. I beg you, do not refuse me, because I will not have a voice any more to ask this of you! . . .

In as few words as possible, I will get you up to speed with what has happened since you left. I was enraged with passion for Véronique, to the point of believing that I was possessed by some demon. You did not notice it and I did not want to burden you with this confidence. But the unfortunate girl perceived it too well. She saw the evil without remedy, and the exorbitant suffering that she felt simply affected her reason.

As a moribund, I am unable to tell you the whole story. Day by day, hour by hour, I saw dissolve and come undone, in a horrible manner, that beautiful faculty of reason, that extra-luminous pearl from the robe of Christ, that Eastern spark of most divine simplicity!

She did not recognize me anymore . . . Her sustainer Joseph, her Savior,—as she used to call me,—was a captive in a faraway land, and I appeared an executioner come in his place to torment her.

I had to endure, in inexpressible torments, the nameless punishment of hearing her curse me, while looking at me with her sublime lost eyes, in which were painted I do not know what unknown images. I had to see this unfortunate girl on her knees, for hours on end, writhing at the foot of the cross, and crying to God to deliver me from my prison, to give her back the poor man who had given her bread and who was languishing in a place of darkness, as a reward for having loved her . . .

At this moment, I do not suffer from these things any more. All that a soul compressed and twisted by the most mortal anguish can exude of sorrow, has left me. It is over. I am wedded now to the nuptial anguishes of my final agony.

You must pardon me, my brother Georges, for having kept you in ignorance of all this. You had written to me about the unexpected difficulties of your new existence, which you had accepted out of love for me, and the narrow servitude that your miserly aunt had reduced you to. I have received regularly the sixty francs that you send me each month, and may God bless you for this charity, but you could not do more, when it had to do with saving me from death. Why would I bother you? . . . Besides, I was vaguely hoping that Véronique would come back to her senses and I could not persuade myself that she had really gone insane.

Your money not sufficing, I arranged to earn more, doing whatever it took. I became a manual laborer. I worked for grain merchants and movers.

I left my shirt at the shops where I was employed so that nobody would know my distress, on the rue des Fourneaux . . . When it became too imprudent to leave Véronique alone at the house, for the entire day, I obtained a writing job, working from home. I copied court documents and made meals, while watching over the sick person, under the triple menace of fire, strangulation and the knife.

Finally, that resource dried up. Then, bracing myself for the maniac's delirium, I fabricated some pretext to go out, and ran desperately through Paris, throwing myself at the feet of this person or that, to obtain some immediate help.

What humiliations I had to eat, disgusting things I had to gulp down, the pale Angels of Misery were my witnesses! I delivered myself, head in hand, to my enemies. I asked for alms from abject beings, who were happy to trample on me as cheaply as possible. I held out the hand of a mendicant to these queer people who I had decried justly, and whom the most appalling necessity should have constrained me to implore in preference to others, because I understood that the need of these ignoble men to triumph would encourage them to satisfy me. Some refused me, and, then, my friend, what wells of shame!

I was unable to draw anything, for example, from that repugnant industrialist, whom I had naïvely called previously, the *gentleman innkeeper*, who had made his fortune at the expense of poor artists who frequented his house, and to whom I dedicated,—submerging myself in opprobrium, —one of my books, in a flight of imbecilic grati-tude for that providential publisher, whose hideous exploitation I did not see. It cost me dearly, you know it too well, to let myself be caught up with this Mascarille[1], by this base lackey, who I saw, one day, spit, in a rage, into a *bock* that in the absence of his boy he was forced to serve himself,—without my having been enlightened by this incident. He owed me something, however, that guy, for having worked, for free, for eighteen months, at the journal annexed to his beer pump!

Dulaurier, before whom I humiliated myself as much as a man could be humiliated, turned me away declaring, with tears in his eyes, that in truth, he had on him several thousands of francs, but that the sum being, by great misfortune, in bank securities with a far-off due date, he could not turn any of it into cash without incurring an onerous penalty, which he had no doubt that the mere thought of ought to appear insupportable to me.

Dr. Des Bois found the means to be more atrocious still. For four or five hours I ran through the snow-filled streets in vain, in a moral state to make one weep,—having left Véronique broken by recent crisis, without fire and without food, myself extenuated by hunger, with the night about to fall, and not knowing anymore what I was going to do. I ran into Des Bois on the stairs of his house, accompanying a woman who was about to leave and whose car was stationed precisely in front of the door. I beseeched the doctor to accord me a single minute and I slipped into his ear some of those words that ought to reach a soul, wherever it may be, be it under a Himalaya of filth! He had begun to stammer perplexedly, when the woman, who had taken several steps under the vestibule,

1 Mascarille is a character in a play by Molière, *Les Précieuses ridicules.*

turned around, saying: "Well? Well, doctor?" she said to him, in a musical injunction that did away with me, "Pardon!" he responded immediately, "My dear friend, you will excuse me, yes?" and he disappeared.

That night, I marched on foot in the snow, from the place de l'Europe to Fontenay-aux-Roses, where I knew, by good fortune, an excellent man who assisted me.

The only person, among those so-called *worldly* people who could have effectively aided me was the Baronness de Poissy, the famous *Patron* who declared, for some time, for my books and my articles, so ardent an enthusiasm. This woman, in response to a card of despair that I had carried with me, had had a twenty-franc piece delivered to me on the doorsill by her domestic.

Georges, this existence lasted FIVE months. It is said that madness is contagious. We must believe that it is not true, because I was able to conserve my reason around her, in that frightening torment. Will you believe it? No longer having the means to sleep, I finished my work on *Symbolism*! . . .

Ah! The happy people in life, who enjoy the peace of a good book, not dreaming enough of the sufferings, sometimes nameless and measureless, that a poor artist without salary has had to endure to serve them this intoxication. Rich Christians, who admire my *St. Radegund*, have no idea that this book was written at the bedside of a moribund, in a room without fire, by a famished and desolate mendicant who did not earn a sou of author's rights! . . . Lord Jesus, have pity on the miserable lamps that are consumed in front of your sorrowful FACE!

But the horror that surpassed all others, that was the last scene of the drama. The removal of our Véronique, the voyage in fiacre and her internment at Sainte-Anne. The miserable girl, whom all my strength was not enough to contain, let out screams which my bones will remember, I believe, in the grave.

Let us leave that behind. My strength, besides, is leaving me . . .

I spent my life asking for two things. The Glory of God or Death. It is death that comes. Blessed be it. It could be that glory follows and that my dilemma had been senseless . . . I will be *judged* now, and not by men. My violent writings, that I was so reproached for, will be weighed, in an equitable balance, with my natural faculties and the profound desires of my heart. I have this at least, that I desperately coveted Justice and I hope to obtain the *satisfaction* that is assured us by the Holy Word.

You, my dear friend, watch over poor Véronique after you have me put in the ground . . . Poor girl! . . . Dear devoted beings, so compassionate and so gentle to my sad soul! I have cherished you both, above all other creatures, and I would have desired to have had something better to offer you than the sacrifice of a life saturated by anguish, that the miracle of your two affections have alone prevented from being insupportable.

Hurry up, my Georges, hurry up, I fear that you will arrive too late.

MARIE-JOSEPH CAÏN MARCHENOIR.

LXX

"As I only have a few instants left to live, my very dear friend, come sit down on my bed, rest my head, that head that is so dear to you, on your knees, and put your hands over my eyes. I imagine to myself that this position will spare me part of the suffering that my soul will experience, when it leaves its residence. Although mine must suffer a double torment, one by leaving this body that it inhabits and another by separating me from you, be persuaded that it will never forget you, if some memory still remains with those who descend to the abode of the dead."

Thus spoke to his faithful Cantacuzene, the dying emperor Andronicus.

Marchenoir on his deathbed was obsessed with this memory, while waiting for his friend, whose imminent arrival was announced to him by telegram.

Because it was necessary to consider Véronique as no longer alive, Marchenoir placed in Leverdier, from then onwards, all the love on earth. He would have wanted actually, like that emperor of extreme decadence, to put his head, like that of a child, on the knees of the man who had valued him nearly like a father, and to feel on his face that faithful hand, which would have protected him against possible visions of the last hour . . .

He was also waiting for the priest. He had waited for him in vain the day before. Of course! he could wait for him, his doorkeeper whom he had charged to go find him, having considered it something she need not bother herself to do.

She was not, for all that, a spiteful woman. She had even taken care of him with an evident solicitude, and had passed a part of each night in the room of this sick man whom the doctor had condemned, from the first day,—counting a little, it is true, on the arrival of Leverdier whom she knew would pay her for her trouble, but capable, all the same, of a certain affectionate disinterestedness.

She belonged to that class of people of Paris whom bourgeois stupidity has more deeply penetrated than any other, and that reproduces it in relief, like the imprint of the seal reproduces the incisions of the intaglio. It was not necessary to make her chat for long to see march past all the common places and all the hackneyed expressions that have constituted, for one hundred years or less, the public treasury of French intelligence: "God doesn't ask much," "Religion shouldn't hurt anyone," "When you're *honest*, you don't need to confess," "When you're dead, you've no need of anything," etc. She went very regularly to the Day of the Dead Cemetery,[1] as did one hundred thousand others, who knew no other pious practice and who go, once a year, to bring wreaths to their deceased, for whom they would never have thought to recite a prayer, in the unshakeable conviction that the *dearly departed* are all "in heaven."

"But why," she had asked, when leaving, "should I go look for a *priest*? To give the death blow to this poor sir!"

In consequence, she had not budged from the house, responding from hour to hour to Marchenoir that the gents of the parish were very busy, but that she had delivered the message, and that someone was sure to turn up any minute . . .

The morning had been a formidable tragedy. Unable to swallow anything the day before and tormented by a strange fever, he had asked for something to drink.

The old woman who was sleeping in the corner where the fire was, handed him a cup of tisane while slipping a cushion under his head and, moaning for unaccustomed pain that was biting into his throat, he tried to drink.

It did not take long. From the first mouthful, he rejected the liquid, the cup was thrown to the other side of the room, and the moribund, letting out a type of roar, sat up, terrible. He held his head in his two hands, as if he had wanted to pull it off, by a gesture of distress so frightening that the doorkeeper, already petrified, fell to her knees.

---

1 Père Lachaise Cemetery.

Then he got out from under his sheets completely and, pre-cipitating himself from one side of the bed to the other, rolled, twisted, struggled, groaning like a demoniac, causing his ban-dages to burst, tearing himself anew, crushing himself again, in omnipotent convulsions that no arm of man would have been able to repress.

This agitation having lasted nearly a half-hour, he finally fell back down, like a mass of suffering, crushed flesh and the old servant heard nothing any more but a wheezing.

She re-lit, trembling, the candle that had gone out when it rolled onto the floor next to her, and trembled even more, when she saw, in her queenly horror, the dreadful symptoms of *Trismus* of tetanus.

Rapidly, she threw the covers back onto the broken body of the dying man and ran to the doctor's. This individual, an old friend of Leverdier's, and who, for this reason treated Marchenoir on credit, with his science and his dressings, found his client in the state in which the guardian had left him. On sight, he shrugged his shoulders and smiled, precariously readjusted the bandages, appeared to give an order, made several pointless comments or observations, tending to demonstrate to the dying man that he considered the manifest signs of his near demise as unimportant symptoms, and, withdrawing, told the gossip who accompanied him:

"My dear woman, there's nothing more I can do. Our patient won't make it to tomorrow. He's already lost. Half his ribs are frac-tured, a shredded lung and, now, traumatic tetanus, it's over. He should've gone cold yesterday or the day before yesterday . . ."

It was true. The patient had remained almost without fire, as was normal for a person in the agony of death and deprived of money.

But something dreadful happened during the visit. Marchenoir had looked at the healer with crazy eyes which the latter would later remember. The desperate man whose teeth, swimming in foam and locked so tightly shut that the enamel broke, by the *capstan's contracture*, made a desperate effort to speak. His rolled up and violet lips tried in vain to configure the two syllables that he had wanted to be able to make heard. Understanding that his doorkeeper had been unfaithful, he desired,—with a supreme desire,—for the doctor to take it upon himself to send for a priest. In his powerlessness, he pointed at the crucifix, referred to a sheet of paper, made a half attempt at writing. It was all useless. He had to drink this last bitterness, which he could never have foreseen. Slowly, he sank into the deepest chasm of grief. All the old punishments of his life rose up again . . .

"To die like this," he cried at the bottom of his soul, "me a Christian! Is it possible, after so many troubles, that I should be deprived of this consolation?"

He could not, he did not want to believe it, and he waited, all the same, for a priest, telling himself that, in absence of a human message, heaven's pity would, doubtless, arouse some other means . . . Any priest whatsoever to absolve him, and the beloved visage of his Leverdier to fortify him!

At eight o'clock, the old woman put before his eyes a dispatch announcing the arrival of his friend in several hours.

"He will arrive too late!" he thought. "My God! will you demand even that from my poor soul! . . ." The hours sounded,—all the hours of this day of passing . . . No priest, no friend, nobody came.

Marchenoir, relaxed a bit by the visible approach of That which was decidedly going to release him, could finally articulate some words. The first usage he made of his recovered voice was to positively order this imbecilic creature who was knitting while watching him die to go and search for the recalcitrant ecclesiastic who persisted in not visiting him.

"If you do not obey," he said, "I will tell Leverdier who will make you pay dearly for this."

She obeyed then, but in vain. The parish beadle responded majestically to her that Monsieur the on-duty vicar, the only one present, would go, probably, see the dying man when he had finished the confessions that were occupying him at that moment, but that she must not dream of bothering him. The ambassadress could do no more and returned with that response.

Marchenoir looked with infinite desolation at the image of his Christ, and two tears, the last, emerged from his eyes and rolled slowly down his already cold cheeks, as if they were afraid of turning to ice.

What was going on in this abandoned soul? Did it hear, as has been told by so many others, the cruel Voices of Agony, that speak to the dying of the evil they have done and the good they could have done? Did it have to submit to the spectacle, illustrated in old woodcuts, of the combat of good and evil spirits relentless in deplorable conquest? The dead, who had preceded him on this crossing, did they appear to him more sensibly than in the dreams during his strong life, to distress him with their announcements of a dreadfully uncertain sentence? Or panicked images, launched, previously, by the pamphleteer, on a detested world, did they come back, to darken him, on this deathbed where their source remained silent? . . . Finally, Jesus Christ, resplendent with light and surrounded by his celestial multitude, would he want to descend instead of one of his priests, towards this exceptional being who had so desired his glory and who had sought Him, his entire life, among the poor and lamentable?

"Fancy that! he died, that poor man," said the concierge on entering the room, a bucket of coal in hand. "It is not too soon, all the same, when one has suffered so much! . . ."

The neighboring church sounded the angelus at the end of the day.

Leverdier arrived at eleven o'clock in the evening.

APPENDIX

CHARACTER KEY

In addition to its being highly autobiographical in nature, *The Desperate Man* is also, unsurprisingly perhaps, a *roman á clef*—a novel in which characters are based on a real-life people. Here below is a list in alphabetical order by last name, of the characters in the novel, followed by the name of the purported person in real life:

Athanase, Father: A composite character based on Fathers Roger (a Trappist monk) and Cyprien Marie Boutrais (a Carthusian monk)

Beauclerc, Mérovée: Fracisque Sarcey

Beauvivier, Properce: Catulle Mendès

Busard, Adolphe: Auguste Vitu

Champignolle, Félix: Félicien Champsaur

Chaudesaigues, Gaston: Alphonse Daudet

Cheminot, Véronique: Anne-Marie Roulé

Conrart, Magnus: Francis Magnard

Denisme, Raoul: Paule Arène

Denizot, Valérien: Aurélien Scholl

Des Bois, Chérubin: Albert Robin

Desneux, Chlodomir: Élémir Bourges

Dulaurier, Alexis: Paul Bourget

Dupoignet, Hilaire: Paul Bonnetain

Dutrou, Jules: Edmond Deschaumes

Gâteau, Germain: Philippe Gille

Lécuyer, Hamilcar: Jean Richepin

Lerat, Alcide: Louis Nicolardot

Levedier, Georges: A composite character based on Georges
    Landry and Louis Montchal
Loriot, Octave: Albert Delpit
Marchenoir, Marie Joseph Cäin: Léon Bloy
Maubec, Hippolyte: Gabriel Terrail (nom du plume: "Mermeix")
Nathan, Judas: Arthur Meyer
Ohnet, Georges: Georges Ohnet
Poissy, Baronne de: Baronness de Poilly, Agathe Éléonore Anne
    Élisabeth du Hallay-Coëtquen
Rieupeyroux, Léonidas: Léon Cladel
Sylvain, Andoche: Armand Silvestre
Tinville, Nestor de: Henri Fouquier
Vaudoré, Gilles de: Guy de Maupassant
Wolff, Albert: Albert Wolff

9 781645 250031